Vincent van Bever Donker

Recognition and Ethics in World Literature

Religion, Violence, and the Human

STUDIES IN WORLD LITERATURE

Editors:	Advisory Board:
Prof Janet Wilson, University of Northampton, UK	Dr Gerd Bayer, University of Erlangen, Germany
Dr Chris Ringrose, Monash University, Australia	Dr Fiona Tolan, Liverpool John Moores University, UK

The book series STUDIES IN WORLD LITERATURE is devoted to the analysis of global literature, and the multiple, sometimes contradictory, tendencies it accommodates. Its field of enquiry is the 'new' world literature, a category currently emerging through multiple changes from the old Romantic concept of *Weltliteratur*, attuned to the challenges posed by postcolonialism and multiculturalism, the increasing globalisation of literature (but also its reverse trend, regionalisation), and the diversification of the market place. STUDIES IN WORLD LITERATURE encourages research which celebrates and critically assesses a phenomenon that can be understood, as Pheng Cheah points out, as the 'literature of the world—imaginings and stories [...] that track and account for contemporary globalization as well as older historical narratives of worldhood'.

World literature can be brought into dialogue with postcolonial writing through scrutiny of how it is written, read, circulated, and received transnationally within the contemporary circuit of global cultural capital. The series also responds to the need to examine the inherent contradictions in the concept of a world literature and dependence on a hegemonic (often English-centred) literary and critical discourse.

The series seeks to address these tensions, and consequently welcomes:
1) volumes which debate such matters theoretically (including definitions of what counts as 'world literature' and the place of postcolonial literary production within this larger category);
2) comparative studies of texts and genres from different countries and cultures under common headings or concepts such as memory, ethics, and human rights.

Volumes on national literatures, when these are set in a world/comparative or generic context, will also be considered, and the series will include discussions of other complementary aspects of discourse, narratology, and media. While writing by 'canonical' authors will be covered, the series will additionally propose wider cultural and intellectual genealogies for 'minor' or occluded writers. A key aim of this series is to redeploy the familiar rhetoric of postcolonial theory and discourse in relation to concepts relevant to world literature by introducing arguments that will be integrated with the evidence of individual literary practice. This emphasis on contesting definitions of 'diasporic' or 'postcolonial' writing, 'transnational' or 'transcultural' literatures and 'world' literature as used by writers, critics and thinkers may lead to a reconsideration of the boundaries that divide and intersections that link these related fields.

Recent volumes:

1 *Nadia Anwar*
Dynamics of Distancing in Nigerian Drama
A Functional Approach to Metatheatre
ISBN 978-3-8382-0842-8

2 *Vincent van Bever Donker*
Recognition and Ethics in World Literature
Religion, Violence, and the Human
ISBN 978-3-8382-0847-3

3 *Bruce King*
From New Literatures to World Literatures
Essays and Reviews
ISBN 978-3-8382-0856-5

Vincent van Bever Donker

RECOGNITION AND ETHICS IN WORLD LITERATURE

Religion, Violence, and the Human

ibidem-Verlag
Stuttgart

Bibliografische Information der Deutschen Nationalbibliothek
Die Deutsche Nationalbibliothek verzeichnet diese Publikation in der
Deutschen Nationalbibliografie; detaillierte bibliografische Daten sind im
Internet über http://dnb.d-nb.de abrufbar.

Bibliographic information published by the Deutsche Nationalbibliothek
Die Deutsche Nationalbibliothek lists this publication in the Deutsche Nationalbibliografie;
detailed bibliographic data are available in the Internet at http://dnb.d-nb.de.

Cover picture: A sandy window photographed from inside a dark building at Kolmanskop.
© copyright 2013 by Martin Bailey. Reprint with kind permission.

∞

Gedruckt auf alterungsbeständigem, säurefreien Papier
Printed on acid-free paper

ISBN-13: 978-3-8382-0847-3

© *ibidem*-Verlag

Stuttgart 2016

Alle Rechte vorbehalten

Das Werk einschließlich aller seiner Teile ist urheberrechtlich geschützt. Jede Verwertung
außerhalb der engen Grenzen des Urheberrechtsgesetzes ist ohne Zustimmung des Verlages
unzulässig und strafbar. Dies gilt insbesondere für Vervielfältigungen,
Übersetzungen, Mikroverfilmungen und elektronische Speicherformen sowie die
Einspeicherung und Verarbeitung in elektronischen Systemen.

All rights reserved. No part of this publication may be reproduced, stored in or introduced into a retrieval
system, or transmitted, in any form, or by any means (electronical, mechanical, photocopying, recording or
otherwise) without the prior written permission of the publisher. Any person who does any unauthorized act
in relation to this publication may be liable to criminal prosecution and civil claims for damages.

Printed in the EU

Contents

Acknowledgments VII

Introduction
Ethics, the World, and the Postcolonial:
The Case of Kazuo Ishiguro 1

Chapter One
Anagnorisis and the Clash of Values 49

Chapter Two
Religion and the Ethics of Remembrance 85

Chapter Three
The Failure of Recognition 133

Chapter Four
The Beauty of the Mortal Human 203

Conclusion
Elizabeth Costello 241

Bibliography 253

Index 267

Acknowledgments

There are a number of people without whom this work would not have materialised, and whom I would like thank.

This book is the culmination of my graduate research at the University of Oxford (DPhil) and the University of the Western Cape (MA). As such, I remain grateful for the critical input of my research supervisors into those original projects, namely Elleke Boehmer and Cheryl-Ann Michael. I would also like to thank the editors of the Studies in World Literature series, Janet Wilson and Chris Ringrose, for their patience with me in preparing this manuscript and for their valuable comments and insight.

There have been numerous colleagues, friends and family members who have supported me along the way and who have contributed through discussion, debate, and commenting on various drafts. In particular, I would like to thank the academic communities of the University of Oxford, the University of the Western Cape (UWC), and the Centre for Humanities Research, UWC. More specifically, I would like to name Steve Whitla, Scott Teal, Nisha Manocha, Charlotta Salmi, Stephanie Yorke, Ankhi Mukherjee, Deborah Rosario, Neal McEwan, and Maurits van Bever Donker. I am ever grateful to my wife, Machilu, for her continual encouragement and unswerving support. Needless to say, any errors remain my own.

This project draws on the research that was enabled by funding from the Commonwealth Scholarship Commission and the Mandela Rhodes Foundation, without whose generosity it would not have been possible.

Introduction
Ethics, the World, and the Postcolonial: The Case of Kazuo Ishiguro

> Nobody would deny (though some of course do) that some works for some readers on some occasions do provide a precious melting of categories that would otherwise freeze the reader's soul. But are we to believe that every reader in every epoch most needs one kind of shock, or even a shock at all, and that there are no other ethical effects that for some readers in some circumstances might be more valuable?
>
> (Booth 1988, 68)

I

The question of ethics in literature is not new. Wayne Booth, in his work *The Company We Keep: An Ethics of Fiction* (1988), comments that ethical criticism is a "human practice" that "refuses to die, in spite of centuries of assault from theory" (6). Indeed, ethical concerns in and about literature (in its various forms) have run from Plato's banishment of poets from his ideal republic, through Sir Phillip Sidney's 16th-century *An Apology for Poetry*, to today's postcolonial, feminist and queer critics, to name only a few. The current prominence of ethics in literary criticism is, then, a return to a concern that has, in the past, been absent from world literature. Focused as world literature tends to be on universalizable aesthetic appreciations, more localised ethical commitments have generally failed to register. It is in postcolonial studies—many of whose texts could also be considered world literature—that contemporary concerns with the ethics of literature have been most robustly investigated. To approach the ethics of world literature is simultaneously to invoke the general (and ancient) question of ethics in literature, and the postcolonial insistence on the influence of the legacy of colonialism on the ethical commitments of texts.

Anne Morgan's recent book, *Reading the World: Confessions of a Literary Explorer* (2015), is illustrative. In it, Morgan relates the reflections and challenges that framed her year of reading a book from every country in the world. Translating her experience into the imagery of travel and exploration, she outlines several difficulties, from ideas of authenticity that result from framing her enterprise in nationalistic terms (what she dubs, in her chapter titles, "Identifying Landmarks") to the need for and limitations of the publishing industry (two features that she likens to following "trade winds" and departing from "the beaten track", respectively). In discussing the more specific challenges confronted in beginning her project—namely the immense quantity of literature in the world and the opacity of other cultures and unfamiliar languages—Morgan criticises the advice of David Damrosch, a leading theorist of world literature, to embed individual readings of texts in cultural knowledge through preliminary research. She comments,

> Damrosch overlooks somewhat [...] that, for many people, one of the major incentives for reading books from other cultures is discovery itself. Rightly or wrongly, we tend to regard literary works as windows on other worlds. [....] All this earnestness [of first researching the book's culture] takes the fun out of the idea of reading such works. (17-18)

Eschewing contextualizing research, on the grounds that it stamps out the desire with which one picked up the book in the first place, she, ironically, argues for Damrosch's understanding of world literature as "multiple windows on the world" or "worlds beyond our own place and time"—one part of Damrosch's definition of world literature (Damrosch 2003, 15, 281). Morgan's book is interesting, though, not only because a popular text on the challenges of reading works from around the world is indicative of the increasing popularity of world literature, both academically and in mainstream culture, but also because her chosen metaphor of travel and exploration raises the spectre of colonialism and thus evokes the tension between world and postcolonial literature within which this book is positioned.

There is first, somewhat obliquely, the ghost of empire past in the well-documented connections between exploration and travel (writing) and the colonial project (Hulme 1990; Pratt 2008; Boehmer 2005). A more pertinent problem, however, is the way in which the exploration of foreign cultures and lands, particularly its proximity to discourses of tourism, feeds into present imperial structures, namely through the figure of the exotic. Graham Huggan (2001) has explored in detail the tensions inherent in the field of postcolonial studies between

> contending regimes of value: one regime—postcolonialism—that posits itself as anti-colonial, and that works towards the dissolution of imperial epistemologies and institutional structures; and another—postcoloniality—that is more closely tied to the global market, and that capitalises both on the widespread circulation of ideas about cultural otherness and on the worldwide trafficking of culturally 'othered' artefacts and goods. (68)

The contemporary circulation of literature from other cultures runs the risk of exoticization: "the domesticating process through which commodities are taken from the margins and reabsorbed into mainstream culture" (Huggan 2001, 59). While Huggan's focus here is on postcolonial literature, this challenge is faced more sharply by world literature. A crucial part of Huggan's analysis focuses on the use by postcolonial writers of "strategic exoticism" in order to critique (continuing) imperial structures and discourses (75). Thus, Chinua Achebe's *Things Fall Apart*, despite containing anthropological elements—and frequently being read as ethnography—destabilises such readings through its use of irony and "postcolonial parody-reversal" in its closing movements (92). This is a form of critique that, as Robert Young (2014) remarks, is concerned with the impact of the text, through its various modes of resistance, on "realities beyond itself" (217), but it is this critical aspect of postcolonialism (in both writing and criticism) that risks being elided under the designation of world literature. As Elleke Boehmer (2014) has remarked, world literature is often taken as synonymous with, or as a replacement for, the postcolonial (299), a move that could, she suggests, be in part due to a contemporary discomfort with the latter's perpetually critical stance (306); world literature is considered to be more neutral. It is seen as focused on the literary rather than the political or ethical (Albrecht 2013; Young 2014), with the result that the critical concerns of postcolonialism, which are maintained in tension with the commercial appropriation of the exotic, can be passed over (Boehmer 2014, 306). It is for this reason, in part, that Huggan has more recently described world literature as "too much a *symptom* of the often profoundly anti-democratic and neo-imperialist tendencies within globalization" (2011, 491, emphasis in original).

The tension between the "world" and the "postcolonial" that Morgan's imagery of exploration evokes is salient for the study of ethics in world literature since postcolonialism is particularly distinctive in its ethical commitments. Robert Young comments that while world literature makes a claim to universality through its conception of literature "of such quality and insight that it transcends its local context to establish itself as universal, shared by all cultures" (2014, 213–214), postcolonial literature, with its focus on the local and particular, nevertheless "achieves a certain universality through its relation to the ethical" (218).[1] The ethical (or what could be termed the ethico-political, since its concerns are also political "in its broadest sense" [218]) constitutes one of the main focal points of debates between world and postcolonial literature. We have already seen something of the disquiet of postcolonialism at its gradual supplantation by world literature due to the erasure of the ethical. It is important to note, however, that this ethical concern in postcolonial studies has generally been dominated by singularity, or the relation with alterity (or otherness).

We can observe this in a dialogue between David Damrosch and Gayatri Spivak on world literature (Damrosch and Spivak 2011). Damrosch's argument pivots around concerns about translation and reading works in their original languages, the necessity for collaborative work in the study of world literature, and the importance of theoretical pluralism, all seen as attempts to move beyond the situation of "American specialists presuming to put together world anthologies, and [...] the publishing conglomerates trying to Americanize the world". Damrosch, however, relativises this situation by arguing that such anthologies were never meant for the "global market", since, in publishing, the "global rights [cost] twice as much as the North American rights". Consequently, "capitalism itself" has safeguarded the rest of the world "from the invasion of American world literature anthologies" (457). He is thus able to relocate this apparent global inequality onto the relationships between ivy league and other universities within the United States, which he describes as "neocolonial" (460), and diagnoses these problems, not as global, but as symptomatic of

---

[1] See also Burns (2015)

both comparative and world literature courses in the United States, when "either is done badly" (464).

Spivak, by contrast, is not concerned with "how to situate the peaks of the literary production of the world on a level playing field", which is Damrosch's focus, but instead "to ask what makes literary cases singular. The singular is always universalizable, never the universal. The site of readings is to make the singular visible in its ability" (Damrosch and Spivak 2011, 466). What Spivak resists here in her discussion with Damrosch is incorporating works of literature into a universal or world system where the text's singularity is consequently lost. As Lorna Burns (2015) glosses it: "what is at stake in Spivak's intervention in world literature and what marks her difference is alterity and ethics. Hers is a reframing of world literature that retains the critical gains made by postcolonial theory" (243). Spivak thus, in concurrence with her more general commitment to ethical singularity,[2] goes on to comment that "the ethical reflex is to go toward the other, and literature doesn't teach you that, but literature allows you to train for that" (Damrosch and Spivak 2011, 482).

This dialogue between Damrosch and Spivak is illustrative of the tension between world literature and postcolonial literature centred on an ethics of singularity. Such a privileging of alterity has itself been a focus of criticism of postcolonialism, both internally and externally. Monika Albrecht (2013), for instance, argues that some postcolonialism neglects the more literary aspects of texts, producing "predictable criticism" that is "remarkably superficial in its literary analyses" (52), as well as, in the words of Neil Lazarus, "a fetishizing [of] difference under the rubric of incommensurability" (quoted in Albrecht 2013, 53). I will consider the question of an ethics of singularity in literary criticism in more detail below but the approach to ethical criticism that I develop in this book is put to work within this tension between world and postcolonial literature. Insisting on the ethical in world literature, and the importance of the debates that surround it within postcolonialism, I agree, to an extent, with arguments such as Albrecht's. I therefore contend for a widening of the scope of the ethical that maintains the concerns of postcolonialism, but which simultaneously focuses on narrative form—specifically the functioning of recognition. To fill in the details of what exactly I mean by this will take us on a detour

---

[2] For a more general discussion of Spivak's engagement with an ethics of singularity see, in particular, Morton (2003, 43–69).

through the details of postcolonial ethics and the particular problems I see with an ethics of singularity (beyond simply claiming, as Albrecht does, a repetitiveness of conclusions), as well as a subsequent discussion of the approach I will develop over the course of this book. Finally, I will consider Kazuo Ishiguro's *The Remains of the Day*. A prominent text in both world and postcolonial literature, which has also been the focus of analysis from divergent perspectives on ethical criticism, it is primed to illustrate more concretely the ethical approach to world literature that I develop.

II

Since what is meant by the term "postcolonial" has been the focus of much debate, it is worth stating that its use in this book follows Stuart Hall (1996), who argues that the concept of the postcolonial—deployed at "a high level of abstraction"—helps to mark the (uneven) historical and epistemological "transition from the age of Empires to the post-independence or post-decolonisation moment" (246); or, in Peter Hulme's words, the "process of disengagement from the whole colonial syndrome" (quoted in Hall 1996, 246). Postcolonial literature is, therefore, understood as writing "which critically or subversively scrutinizes the colonial relationship. It is writing that sets out in some way or another to resist colonialist perspectives [and] to undercut thematically and formally the discourses which supported colonization" (Boehmer 2005, 3). While such a definition has some difficulty accounting for works which might be considered postcolonial—since coming from a former colony—but are not necessarily critical of the legacies of empire (such as the work of V.S. Naipaul), what this indicates is the fact that "postcolonial literature as a field is never neutral" (Young 2014, 219). The ethical concerns of postcolonial literatures are those predominantly aimed at a critique of imperialism and its legacies.

While postcolonialism can be understood to be distinctive in its ethical commitment, the presence of ethical concerns within postcolonial (or, indeed, world) literature should not be surprising. As already noted, postcolonial literature, as literature, participates in a long tradition in which the assertion of ethical positions is prominent. In one respect this is due to the fact that novels are inescapably ethically committed—particularly realist novels, which in presenting descriptions of reality represent the ethical side of life, even if these representations are sometimes reductively simple or crass (Phelan 1996). As Abraham Yehoshua (2005) observes, "whether we like it or not, every artistic work that deals with human relations has in it a moral aspect because all human relationships may be evaluated according to moral categories" (18). However even the most abstract, nonconventional or "unrealistic" work of literature implies an ethics: at the very least it implies that it is *worth* taking the time to engage with it rather than doing something else. As Wayne Booth (1988) argues,

> Each work of art or artifice, even the simplest wordless melody, determines to some degree *how at least this one moment will be lived*. The quality of life in the moment of our "listening" is not what it would have been if we had not listened. We can even say that the proffered work shows us how our moments *should* be lived. If the maker of the art work did not believe that simply experiencing it constitutes a superior form of life, why was the work created and presented to us in the first place? (17)

This ethical stance of all literature, at once implicit and explicit, is as it were the baseline of ethical criticism and is developed in different ways by various critics.

Within the form of narrative prose that is the purview of this study, however, postcolonial literature finds itself in a double bind: the criticism of colonialism is undertaken through the use of European and Enlightenment ideals and forms. Indeed, the spread of the novel form around the globe, disseminated as part of educational syllabi, was in large part due to its use in the cause of imperialism. As Appiah (1992) notes,

> When the colonialists attempted to tame the threatening cultural otherness of the African [...] the instrument of pedagogy was their most formidable weapon. [....] Colonial education, in short, produced a generation immersed in the literature of the colonisers, a literature which often reflected and transmitted the imperialist vision. (87)

The literature of Europe was used by colonialists to exercise control over the colonised.[3] And this legacy is still strong, as can be seen by the continued use of the novel form—often written in the languages of Europe—a connection that is strengthened through this tradition forming an object of critique. Yet, during the anti-colonial struggles and after the end of direct colonial rule, "European languages and European disciplines have been 'turned', like double agents, from projects of the metropole to the intellectual work of postcolonial cultural life" (Appiah 1992, 88). As Boehmer puts it, since literature "contributed to the making, definition and clarification" of colonialist ideas (2005, 5), there has been a corresponding "intervention by colonized people in the fiction and myths that presumed to describe them" (6). It is thus through its deployment in the service of what we might call postcolonial ends that postcolonial literature is marked as such; and it is for this reason, despite this double bind, that what can be described as distinctive about the postcolonial novel's ethics is its concern with critiquing and undermining the legacies and epistemologies of colonialism.

This gesture of using colonial forms to critique colonialism is an aporia that is poignantly felt in philosophy, particularly in ethics. In considering the ethical impetus of postcolonial criticism and literature, it becomes clear that universal Enlightenment ideals are at work. As Chakrabarty (2000) observes,

> Modern social critiques of caste, oppressions of women, the lack of rights for labouring and subaltern castes in India, and so on—and, in fact, the very critique of colonialism itself—are unthinkable except as a legacy, partially, of how Enlightenment Europe was appropriated in the subcontinent. (4)

The use of Enlightenment concepts in the criticism of colonialism and its legacies is ubiquitous in postcolonial criticism. Part of the difficulty with these concepts is their pretence to universalism: the problem is not that Europe has these ideals, but that they were, and are, taken as applicable to all different cultures. As such, the need is for true universals, not Eu-

---

[3] See also Viswanathan (1989), Said (1993) and (illustrating the colonial position) Macaulay and Young (1935).

ropean values masquerading as universal (Appiah 1992). Nevertheless, the need for universals remains, and there have been important arguments made by theorists, such as Peter Hallward (2001, 177-178), that if we abandon them, it is only a matter of time before right becomes equated with might. Together with the need to work towards universals, however, there is also a simultaneous obligation to focus upon, and do justice to, the particular and idiosyncratic, a demand that is inseparable from postcolonialism (Hallward 2001; Shohat 1992). As will become clear, these two central tensions—the interplay between the universal and the particular, and the simultaneous use and critique of Enlightenment concepts, what David Scott (2004) calls "the paradox of colonial Enlightenment" (131)— are integral to an ethics that addresses postcolonial concerns without over emphasizing singularity.[4]

In the Levinasian/Derridean understanding of ethics, from where the ethics of singularity is often sourced, the ethical is distinct from the political and the moral: the latter two have to do with general questions of conduct in the political and the social realm, what Levinas calls the realm of the third; the former has to do with an unregulated, undetermined openness and address to the singular other. As Derrida phrases it in an interview, "when I try to think the most rigorous relation with the other I must be ready to give up the hope for a return to salvation, the hope for resurrection, or even reconciliation" (Kearney 2004, 3). Any expectation of what the other should be like (just, kind, generous, etc.) or what the relation to the other should result in (reconciliation, salvation, etc.) begins to determine the relation, which is to slip out of the ethical, characterised by a radically open and undetermined hospitality, and into the political and juridical. For Levinas and Derrida, this unspecified relation to the other has the character of infinite responsibility and is the source of (though not the recipe for) law and morality/ethics as these are commonly understood.

One of the most systematic developments of such an ethics of singularity within literary criticism is perhaps that by Adam Newton (1995) in his *Narrative Ethics*. For Newton, "narrative ethics implies simply narrative *as* ethics: the ethical consequences of narrating story and fictionalizing person, and the reciprocal claims binding teller, listener, witness, and reader in that process" (11). For Levinas (1998), the ethical and the

---

[4] See also Slaughter (2007).

realm of the third can be respectively designated by the "saying" and the "said", both of which are simultaneously present in our relation to the other in language. "Saying" is the pure relation between the self and other, the moment of encounter that is the relation to the revelation of the face, that is, the revelation of the other as resisting and exceeding any determinations we might wish to impose on it. It is "the proximity of one to the other, the commitment of an approach, the one for the other, *the very signifyingness of signification*" (5, my emphasis). The "said" is the thematic content of the saying, the usual focus of our interactions with others which subordinates to itself the "saying" even in its very moment of revelation (7). Applying this distinction to literature, Newton locates his narrative ethics in its "saying"—that is, the moment of encounter or contact when one reads a text. He explains, "One faces a text as one might face a person, having to confront the claims raised by that very immediacy, an immediacy of contact, not of meaning" (Newton 1995, 11).

There are three aspects that Newton specifies in his narrative ethics, giving it a "triadic structure": "narrational ethics", "representational ethics", and "hermeneutic ethics" (1995, 17–18). All three are closely intertwined. The first, narrational ethics, is the "relational" aspect of reading, the encounter with the "saying" of the text "and the intersubjective responsibilities and claims which follow from acts of storytelling". Representational ethics designates "the costs incurred in fictionalizing oneself or others by exchanging 'person' for 'character'" (18), while hermeneutic ethics is closely connected to this, and designates the "responsibilities incurred in each singular act of reading", responsibilities that accrue around the risk of representing other people. Integrating them, we might say that for Newton, as soon as we pick up a book we are forced to respond to it regardless of its content, in the same way that we must respond to a person, regardless of what they say: responsibility—the obligation to respond—comes before we are aware exactly what it is we are responsible for. This responsibility is, however, primarily to do with the risks of representing others, giving us the hermeneutical responsibility of navigating the tension between both trying to "get" the other's story, and the "lesson that 'getting' someone else's story is also a way of losing them as 'real,' as 'what he is'" (19), that is to say, of replacing a relation to the face, in Levinas's sense, which always exceeds our comprehension, with a relation to its image which is comprehensible. We will see what this means for the ethical reading of a novel when we delve deeper into Ishiguro's *The Remains of the Day* in a moment. The question of the ethics of representation, the ethics of the image, is a central concern for Levinas, though, and one to which I will return.

It should be clear that Newton's approach is not overtly concerned with the thematic engagements of novels, which is to say that his concern with content has to do with the way in which these ethical responses in reading are dramatised (Newton 1995, 67-68). Derek Attridge's (2004a) approach to ethics in his *J.M. Coetzee and the Ethics of Reading: Literature in the Event* has certain similarities to Newton's. Attridge does not consider contact with the text itself as a necessarily ethical moment. Nevertheless, he similarly deploys a Levinasian/Derridean conception of the other as exceeding our comprehension, arguing that an experience of alterity can occur in the reading of narrative. For Attridge, to speak about the ethics of literature is to speak about having an experience of otherness in the event of reading. This alterity is located in the originality or singularity of the piece of literature: "The experience of singularity involves an apprehension of *otherness*, registered in the event of its apprehension, that is to say, in the mental and emotional opening that it produces" (Attridge 2004b, 67). The degree to which a work is original and singular is thus closely tied to the experience of alterity that it evokes, and so also to its ethics. Some works are more exemplary in this regard than others: the text that "most estranges itself from the reader, makes the strongest ethical demand" (Attridge 2004a, 11). Coetzee's late modernist texts are for Attridge of this exemplary sort.

There is an intriguing section in the opening moves of Attridge's argument which indicates some of the distance between Attridge and Newton's approaches, and begins to show why I consider Attridge's too restrictive. It occurs in his discussion of the ethical and political benefit arising from the formal innovation of modernist texts.

> To make this claim [about the ethics of formal singularity] is not to deny what has often been powerfully demonstrated: that a large part of modernist writing was insensitive to the otherness produced by patriarchal and imperialist policies and assumptions. [....] It is true that, with some notable exceptions, only in later developments of modernism have these [technical] resources

been exploited in conjunction with a thematic interest in gender, race, and colonialism. (2004a, 6)

A distinction is drawn here between the technical resources of form and an alignment of those resources with the meanings of the text. This is a concern with thematic content that is distinct from Newton's. However, it needs to be asked, how does this approach deal with the question of meanings and their impact on readers? Is a singular, innovative novel that is in its content insensitive to otherness ethical? Wayne Booth puts it well when he comments, "It is not the degree of otherness that distinguishes fiction of the highest ethical kind but the depth of education it yields in *dealing with* the 'other'" (1988: 195). Is ethics in a novel, then, reducible to the text's formal singularity?

Attridge wants to disrupt the opposition between form and meaning. He argues that "the literary use of language involves the *performing* of meanings and feelings, and that what has traditionally been called form is central to this performance" (2004a, 9). Although it is accurate to connect the meanings of a text to its form, this does not answer the question of their significance. To note the inextricability of form and meaning does not eliminate the fact that the same formal resources and innovations can be (and have been) an inextricable part of texts that are insensitive to alterity. Interestingly, this recognition does not prevent Attridge from emphasizing the formal inventiveness of a text. The importance of formal singularity for Attridge, irrespective of the ethics of the text's meanings, can be seen as he shifts his focus from literature in general to Coetzee's work in particular.

> Otherness, then, is at stake in every literary work, and in a particularly conspicuous way in the work that disrupts the illusions of linguistic immediacy and instrumentality. Among these works are some in which otherness is thematized as a central moral and political issue, and in these works modernist techniques may play a peculiarly important role. Coetzee's novels are cases in point. (12)

Despite the reiteration in this passage of the distance from Newton in the importance of content, it also illustrates their proximity. Otherness, for Attridge, can be seen as present in "every literary work" (keeping in mind that for Attridge "literature" refers to works that are singular), irrespective of either the work being a modernist text, or, importantly, of the work's meanings. The issue is formal singularity or originality, and works that have thematised otherness as a concern are a specific type within this broad categorization—a distinction that implicitly includes within it those texts which are insensitive to otherness. Attridge appears, then, to call texts ethical that in his own terms of sensitivity to alterity are arguably also (thematically) not so. To locate the ethics of a work primarily in its inventiveness, in its singularity, can therefore be seen to overlook key ethical aspects present within its meanings.

It is not, it must be emphasised, that Attridge is unaware of other ethically salient aspects in the novel. This becomes explicit when he comments on the "critique of colonialism and its avatars" in *Dusklands* and *In the Heart of the Country*:

> All this brutality and exploitation is certainly there in the novels to be felt and condemned, but it is not what makes them singular, and singularly powerful. It is what they do, how they happen, that matters: how otherness is engaged, staged, distanced, how it is manifested [...]. (30)

While this approach is perhaps effective for Coetzee's work (though not exclusively so, as will be seen), it is too restrictive for literature in general precisely due to this subordination of other ethical concerns to the manifestation of otherness, a subordination which, as the above has shown, results from the idea that "Modernism's foregrounding of language and other discursive and generic codes through its formal strategies" embodies the insight that "literature's distinctive power and potential ethical force" rests in precisely this opening "a space for the apprehension of otherness" (30).

What I find unsatisfactory about these two approaches, then, is the restriction of what is pertinent in reflecting upon the ethics of a novel. The exploration of environmental ethics and its tension with other ethical concerns in Amitav Ghosh's *The Hungry Tide*, which I will consider in the next chapter, cannot be reduced to a question of formal alterity, of evoking an experience of otherness, nor to the ethics of transforming people into characters. This is not to say that these are entirely absent, or that Attridge and Newton's approaches are unproductive. Indeed, the relation to others is often a significant feature, as is indeed the case in *The Hungry Tide*. It is to suggest, instead, that this concern is present alongside other, equally important, ones. At the same time, it is important to acknowledge that my understanding of intersubjective relations is heavily indebted to the work of both Levinas and Derrida. Rather than rejecting their work, I am concerned with broadening their applicability; I am in search of a pragmatic, strategic and context-based approach which will be productive in considering the multiplicity of specific ethical concerns present across world/postcolonial novels.

An approach that recognises the variety of ethical concerns, and which will clarify an additional difficulty that I have with Newton's and Attridge's approaches, is presented by James Phelan (2005) in his book *Living to Tell About it*. For Phelan, narrative is an act of communication: "somebody telling somebody else on some occasion and for some purpose(s) that something happened" (18). Narratives are therefore understood to be "designed by authors in order to affect readers in particular ways", and reading consequently involves the reader in a "feedback loop" between the "authorial agency, textual phenomena, and reader response" (18–19). The navigation of this "feedback loop" and the correlating "communication from author to audience" entails a full engagement from the readers, requiring their "intellect, emotions, psyche, and values"—an engagement that unfolds in tandem with the "narrative progression" (19). It is within these layered interactions with narrative that Phelan locates its ethics. In first person or character narration, which his study focuses on, the ethical situation is particularly complex, calling for a response from the reader to the characters themselves, to the narrator's stance towards the characters and the reader, and to the implied author's stance towards the narrator, the characters and the reader (20). What this suggests, and which will be seen in *The Remains of the Day*, is that the ethical emphasis is on how readers navigate the textual situation and all its attendant connections. Which is to say that while the narrative's representation of ethical situations is important, the main ethical question is how the reader negotiates this in terms of his or her own values (22, n.16).

Although Phelan's approach is suitable for engaging with a diverse range of ethical concerns—and indeed he distances himself from

Newton because of his narrow focus (22)—Phelan's focus on narrative as an act of communication results in too much of an emphasis on the author (implied or real) and the reader. I am in agreement with him about the importance of narrative sequence and textual phenomenon to a novel's ethical sense. My interest, however, is in the understanding of ethics that is explored as an argument within the bounds of the text, rather than primarily the ethical impact of a text upon a reader. The reader is of necessity fundamental to both ethics in literature and my own analyses: an analysis of character progression within a narrative, of narrative structure and technique all assume the point of view of a reader. However, when the reader's response does feature in my analyses it is in order to sharpen the understanding of ethics that is at work within the narrative, primarily through considering the possible emotional impact of it upon them—and my interest in such cases is with the textual aspects that evoke the response. As such, it is accurate to say that I am invested in an understanding of narrative as a means of thinking through ethics, an understanding that is particularly productive in upholding the concerns of postcolonialism, and that takes its bearings from the work of Martha Nussbaum.

For Nussbaum (1990), novels can make a definite contribution to ethics due to the presence of four features, the combination of which correlates to an Aristotelian understanding of ethics: the contingent and particular, the importance of the emotions, the incommensurability of goods, and the vulnerability of goodness. The first two features arise from the novel form itself, which emphasises the emotions, and the particular and contingent: novels "offer a distinctive patterning of desire and thought, in virtue of the ways in which they ask readers to care about particulars, and to feel for those particulars a distinctive combination of sympathy and excitement" (236). The last two features are not co-extensive with the novel, yet their presence results in a novel presenting, in its most complimentary form, the Aristotelian conception of ethics.[5]

The last two aspects—the incommensurability of goods and vulnerability of goodness—can best be illustrated from Greek tragedy, particularly Aeschylus' *Agamemnon*. The contingencies of life (in this case the

---

[5] That the novel can most precisely present the Aristotelian view of ethics is highly significant for Nussbaum's argument here, since it is this match between form and content that gives literature some of its ethical importance (Nussbaum 1990, 3–53).

conflicting wills of the gods) result in a situation where Agamemnon is under an equal demand from incommensurable goods: the life of his daughter and a divine command from Zeus. Having gathered his army to fulfil Zeus' command to conquer Troy, the expedition is becalmed by the goddess Artemis. As a result, starvation sets in and the only way to bring the needed wind is, by Artemis' command, for Agamemnon to sacrifice his daughter Iphigenia. Agamemnon must either refuse to sacrifice his daughter, and in addition to defying the will of Zeus everyone will die of starvation; or he performs a horrific act and the lives of his men are spared and he is able to fulfil Zeus's command. Either way, he is guilty: the contingencies of life have brought two incommensurable goods into conflict, with the result that the goodness of Agamemnon is impacted by that which is outside of his control. Nussbaum comments,

> We can see that one choice, the choice to sacrifice Iphigenia, seems clearly preferable, both because of consequences and because of the impiety involved in the other choice. Indeed, it is hard to imagine that Agamemnon could rationally have chosen any other way. But both courses involve him in guilt. (34)

This is, as Charles Taylor (1988) notes, an understanding of ethics quite contrary to Utilitarianism in that the moral goods in question are not commensurable:[6] "There is a good here of a particular kind, unsubstitutable by military success or divine favour, which remains forever destroyed and defiled" (807). It is therefore particularly significant that while Agamemnon is not held responsible for the sacrificing of his daughter—it is the gods who are primarily to blame—he is held responsible for the "inference from the necessity of the act to its rightness, and the rightness of supportive feelings" (Nussbaum 1986, 36). Agamemnon thinks that because this is the correct action to take there can be nothing abominable about it, and thus concludes that sacrificing his daughter ceases to be wrong and does the deed with joy. It is for this, Nussbaum shows, that Agamemnon is held responsible and criticised (35–37).

This conception of ethics is further expanded with the importance of the particular or contingent and the emotions. Nussbaum argues that

---

[6] And, for Nussbaum, contrary to the Kantian understanding (1986, 48–49).

for Aristotle, "Principles [...] fail to capture the fine detail of the concrete particular, which is the subject matter of ethical choice" (300–301). Principles, or general moral rules, are insufficient for navigating the contingencies of practical life. This is primarily because "practical matters", where ethical decisions are made, "are in their very nature indeterminate or indefinite" (302), but is also due to the possibility of encountering "particular and non-repeatable events" (304). The result is that there is always something of a distance between the general rule and the practical, contingent scenario in which a choice must be made. Ethical choices must therefore of necessity be guided by *phronêsis*, or practical wisdom, for which general rules are useful "only as summaries and guides; [practical wisdom] must itself be flexible, ready for surprise, prepared to see, resourceful at improvisation" (305). As Taylor summarises, "Moral understanding cannot be conceived simply as a grasp of truths or principles. To know what to do is to know this in a particular situation, and the relevance of no particular situation can be exhaustively captured in a set of rules" (1988, 810).

It is for navigating these particular, practical situations that the emotions become crucial. Nussbaum writes, "The experienced person confronting a new situation does not attempt to face it with the intellect 'itself by itself'. He or she faces it, instead, with desires informed by deliberation and deliberations informed by desire, and responds to it appropriately in both passion and act". Situations are marked for us by our desires; the "very way things present themselves to our desires" enables us to discern contours of pleasure and pain, the "to-be-pursued and the to-be-avoided" (1986, 308). Without our feelings fulfilling this role, the skill of *phronêsis* fails. This does, however, require a specific understanding of our desires or emotions, one that acknowledges what Nussbaum in a later study calls their intelligence.[7] For Aristotle, "emotions are individuated not simply by the way they feel, but, more importantly, by the kinds of judgements or beliefs that are internal to each". Thus anger can be understood as a "composite of painful feeling with the belief that one has been wronged". If it later becomes clear that the offense was imagined, then the feeling of

---

[7] See Nussbaum's *Upheavals of Thought: The Intelligence of Emotions* (2001) for an extensive study which, although arguing for what she terms a neo-Stoic understanding of emotions, is an extension and confirmation of the view that I use here under the designation Aristotelian.

anger would subside. If it did not, we would consider the lingering emotion as "irrational *irritation* or excitation, not as *anger*". In fact, it is this understanding of emotions that allows one to assess them as rational or irrational, "depending upon the nature of their grounding beliefs" (383). In this light, Aristotle's famous comments on the catharsis of pity and fear experienced by an audience while viewing tragedy gains added significance: understanding catharsis as "clearing up" (389), the presence of pity and fear indicates an increase in self-understanding. For Nussbaum, therefore, our emotions are able to reveal to us insights about values that cannot be grasped by the intellect alone:

> clarification, for [Aristotle], can certainly take place *through* emotional responses [...]. Just as, inside *Antigone*, Creon's learning came by way of the grief he felt for his son's death, so, as we watch a tragic character, it is frequently not thought but the emotional response itself that leads us to understand what our values are. (390)

This understanding of the intelligence of the emotions will be indispensable for my analyses over the course of this book. What can be concluded at this point is that the novel as a form is able to engage with ethical questions in an Aristotelian way, creating detailed descriptions of specific, unrepeatable scenarios which require an emotional response, and which can often (but do not necessarily always) represent a conflict of incommensurable goods. The usefulness of this conception of ethics for the concerns of postcolonialism is in part due to it paying heed to the particular, without neglecting the universal, which is what I endeavour to accomplish by relating the specific explorations of ethics in each novel to three general ethical themes. Before turning to them, there are two additional ways in which this understanding of ethics will prove productive.

First, the conception of the ethical subject and the good which is presented here is quite distinct from that expounded by Kant and other thinkers of the Enlightenment—a fact which David Scott notes. For Scott (2004), Greek tragedy—and Nussbaum reads Aristotle as a "re-articulation" of the understanding of ethics presented in tragedy (Charles Taylor 1988, 809)—can be used "as an interpretive framework for reconceiving conventional (largely Kantian) assumptions about moral agency and its implications for our understanding of justice, community, identity, history, and so on" (Scott 2004, 175). It is primarily the incommensurability of the good and the fragility of goodness that enable this. What these two features reveal is that "we are not entirely in control of our lives. Rather, tragedy presents us with a picture of ourselves as simultaneously authors of our ends and authored by forces and circumstances over which we have no—or little—rational control" (182). Human beings are both passive and active, shaped and shapers, able to subject our environment to control and vulnerable to contingency and that which exceeds our control. This is a crucial displacement of a fully autonomous (humanistic) Enlightenment subject. This displacement is emphasised by the possibility of conflicting goods: "We may be essentially good people, have good characters, but acting in the world necessarily presents us with situations that are anomalous or that make conflicting and incommensurable demands on us" (185). Scott, then, is interested in how tragedy works to display the degree to which autonomy is delimited; he is also, however, interested in the structure of these tragic moments, as a model for engaging with the legacy of the Enlightenment, which brings us to the second point.

The Enlightenment, as I noted, presents us with a paradox: many of the resources of the Enlightenment are used to contest its legacy.[8] In tragic terms, the positive and the negative are inextricable. Scott argues that "the important point about tragedy is precisely that as a discursive and institutional form it embodied in a compelling way a distinctive capacity for ambiguity and paradox, a capacity to look in several directions at once" (187). In addition, tragedy also "warned of the mind's propensity for theoretical closure" (187; see also Nussbaum 1986, 23-84). The model of tragedy (and particularly, in Scott's use, the tragedy of Oedipus) thus

> makes a contribution to a kind of enlightenment thinking that sustains and even celebrates enlightenment virtues while at the same time opposing enlightenment hubris and the enlightenment drive to normalize and discipline the very subjects it seeks to emancipate and empower. (188)

---

[8]   See Foucault's "What is Enlightenment" (1984) for one instance of attempting to work through this difficulty, in which he seeks to affirm the critical spirit of the Enlightenment, while resisting its hubris.

The ability of tragedy to host paradox, ambiguity and incommensurability thus keeps the irresolvable tension between the Enlightenment's "good" and its "bad" productively alive.

This is then a further advantage of this approach to ethics (both in the novel and in general) for postcolonial criticism, required as it is not only to negotiate the tension between the universal and the particular, but also the "paradox of colonial enlightenment" (131). This is not to say that I am solely concerned with such clear moments of tragic conflict. While this understanding of ethics underpins this study and will be particularly useful in the analysis of Ghosh's *The Hungry Tide*, where there is an explicit conflict of two values, what I am primarily concerned with is the tragic as a figure of ethical impurity. In her lectures *Religion and Literature*, Helen Gardner (1971) provides a useful overview of different understandings of tragedy that will assist in clarifying what I mean. What is common to theories of tragedy, Gardner notes, is that it "includes, or reconciles, or preserves in tension, contraries" (24); the variety in theories of tragedy rests primarily in what each one understands this conflict to signify. For some, of whom the best instance is Hegel, the conflict—as for Nussbaum—exists between ideals and is ultimately comforting:

> that though [tragedy] shows us a world of mutability and irrationality, it shows us in the end a world that has meaning and rationality and is governed by laws. Some with crudity and others with subtlety have attempted to find in tragedy a justification of the universe as ultimately making sense. (25–26)

In this understanding, the conflict expressed in tragedy is revealed as meaningfully part of a greater rationality, rather than exhibiting bare chaos. A somewhat less consoling understanding is located in the work of the "Glasgow School", for whom tragedy "vindicates the universe only in the sense that it displays a universe that provides the opportunity for the existence, and the exercise, of virtue" (28): virtues are not part of a grander rationality, but exist only for themselves. However, the most austere theories are found in Schopenhauer and Nietzsche. For Schopenhauer, "the end of tragedy is to display the 'terrible side of life' and by so doing give us 'a significant hint of the nature of the world and of existence'" (29). Instead of revealing an order that supersedes the chaos of conflict, tragedy exposes something of how the world truly is. Nietzsche's theory is similar, though more "thrilling and beautiful" (30): "Tragedy is to him 'the art of metaphysical comfort', reconciling us to life by showing it as a sublime spectacle, and to the universe as a work of unmoral art" (31). Revealing something of the "unmoral", chaotic character of the universe, tragedy for Nietzsche is comforting—but due to producing acceptance in the viewer, rather than exhibiting a greater rationality that orders the universe.

Gardner concludes her overview with the formula of tragedy she considers the most persuasive, put forward by Beethoven:

> scrawled, perhaps in jest, above the opening bars of the last movement of his last quartet: 'Muss es sein?' [Should it be?] 'Es muss sein.' [It should be] He wrote above the whole movement the words 'Der schwer gefasste Entschluss' 'the Difficult Resolution'. (34)

What differentiates the question and the answer is "hardly more than an inflection of the voice [...] Protest and acceptance are like expressions on the same face" (34). The conjunction of affirmation and rejection, of positive and negative—the *difficulty* of which Gardner speaks here—is what is of interest to me. In the forthcoming analyses there are frequent instances of ethical difficulty where evil and good are not easily decidable, decided upon, or separated: from clashes of values in *The Hungry Tide*, to morally ambiguous characters in *Half of a Yellow Sun*, to the dramatization of ethical failure giving rise to ethical affirmation in *Crossing the River*. And it is in this generalised sense of tragedy as a figure of impurity, that I characterise the ethical explorations in these novels as bearing a tragic character.

There is, then, a generalizable impurity to ethics that can be seen in specific circumstances, from moments of conflicting values, to ethical affirmations that have ethical failure as their condition of possibility. And it is in these terms that I can now clarify what is meant when I speak of the ethical sense of a novel. Rejecting, as Booth (1988) has persuasively shown ethical criticism should, any reductive approach to ethics in the novel, "ethical sense" gestures towards a more complete understanding of a novel's exploration of ethics, beyond any extrapolated "moral". A moral can of course always be extracted, and indeed there is often a discernible central concern in a novel. It is important though, to enrich this by attention to the progression, character development, and narrative detail of the text. The ethical sense is therefore taken to refer to the engagement with ethics, and the explorations of the difficulties of ethical impurity, in the novel as a whole; it refers to the sense of ethical life captured within it. And if there is a discernible "point", neither can the ethical sense be completely reduced to it, nor can it be arrived at without the attention to detail and narrative progression which consequently occupy much of the space in the coming analyses.

In order to bring out the ethical sense, my analyses will focus primarily on the movement of recognition within the text. Recognition is a focal point for numerous general debates: the recognition of human value, the recognition of individual and/or political identity,[9] the recognition of animal value, and the problem of recognizing too easily and completely. Recognition as *anagnorisis*, as a structural feature of fiction, however, is caught up with the particular, and often emotive, aspects of a narrative. Insofar as *anagnorisis* can be characterised as a more dramatic recognition, bringing these two senses of the term into proximity leads to a productive movement between them: structural recognition scenes can be seen to be crucial to thematic moments for the novel's ethical sense, raising the important question of the overlap, or lack thereof, between moral recognitions and *anagnorisis*.

As these definitions suggest, my use of *anagnorisis* takes its bearings from Terence Cave's (1988) extensive study *Recognitions*:

> If anagnorisis *is* still to be used in critical practice, the dispersal of its meanings has to be accepted as a *fait accompli*. In those circumstances, the only way to recover some degree of rigour is precisely to chart the drift and the erosion and use the entire historical purview as an elaborate para-definition, a pluralistic configuration within which one can move from point to point without entirely losing one's bearings. (221–222, emphasis in original)

---

[9] See for this Charles Taylor's (1994) excellent essay "The Politics of Recognition", and Sarah Nuttall (2001) on how need for recognition, as Taylor details it, has played out in theories of reading in postcolonial literature.

In other words, the various ways in which *anagnorisis* has been used within the history of poetics, that is, the different types or objects of recognition, are gathered into a pluralistic definition of the term. Indeed, there is quite a range in the types of recognitions. They traverse from the more strictly Aristotelian recognition of a nominal identity, to the recognition of individual character, through to the even more dispersed "recognition of an obscured or hidden state of affairs" (232).

Central to *anagnorisis* is the question of what is recognised. *Anagnorisis* is a formal feature of fiction, first discussed by Aristotle in the *Poetics* alongside its sibling *peripeteia*. It marks a shift in the plot and is often the cause of the sudden, surprising change of circumstances designated by *peripeteia*. The clearist example is Sophocles' *Oedipus Rex*. In the play, the sudden and unexpected reversal of circumstances (the suicide of Oedipus' mother/wife, his self-blinding, and exile) is brought about by the recognition of his identity and the consequent recognition of his crimes of incest and patricide. The recognition scene here clearly marks a structural shift in the plot. However, *anagnorisis* is not always so dramatic nor always so closely tied to the plot's climax. A good example of more diffuse recognitions would be *The Odyssey*, where rather than a dramatic moment of recognition, there is "an extended anagnorisis and peripeteia" built up over a series of less comprehensive moments of recognition, which effect a "gradual shift from ignorance to knowledge" (41). However, in both the "tragic" recognition of *Oedipus Rex* and the "epic" recognition of *The Odyssey*, "a recognition scene is not conceivable except as *both* a structural shift and the exhibition of some object of knowledge" (225 my emphasis). It is precisely because the recognition scene is always the recognition of something or someone that it is open to being thematically filled by the fiction's concerns—including its ethical preoccupations. As such, the question of what is recognised in a postcolonial novel, the predicate of the characters' revelations, becomes a useful lens through which to consider a novel's engagement with the particulars that constitute its ethical and political concerns.

In addition to this significance for a novel's ethical sense, the recognition scene as a *way* of knowing further yields some important insights. *Anagnorisis*, as Cave argues, is a scandal, and a part of that scandal is due to the undermining the knowledge attained through the means of acquiring it; the figure of recognition as a way of knowing is what Aristotle terms *paralogismos*: false reasoning (39–43). Recognition always requires a proof, some form of evidence, and except for the type which Aristotle considered the highest and best—recognition brought about by the necessary cause and effect of the plot—the proofs are various tokens or signs. Yet the problem is that these proofs are insufficient. The tokens of recognition often lead to both recognitions and misrecognitions. The example of Odysseus is paradigmatic: Odysseus is recognised when one of the servants sees his scar; yet by this reasoning everyone with a scar is Odysseus. The result of this is that even when it is not thematised in the narrative, there is an inherent instability in the recognition scene: it can be seen to call into question the very knowledge it bestows. For this reason, recognitions relying upon tokens and signs were classed by Aristotle as inferior to the more "pure" recognitions arising from narrative cause and effect, without the use of signs (246–247). Rarely, however, do recognitions arise from philosophical reasoning, and this emphasises the contingent and the particular. It is worth quoting Cave at some length on this:

> However skilfully [recognitions] may be integrated into a deductive sequence, they are always contingent in some sense [....] Yet they are seen to work, and their effectiveness often seems to depend on the fact that they emerge accidentally and unexpectedly: the marginal detail triggers the response of recognition where the more general resemblance fails. There could be no more graphic illustration of this than the sequence of recognition scenes in the *Odyssey* where the characters remark on the 'stranger's' resemblance to Odysseus but fail to draw the appropriate conclusion until the accidental discovery of an accidental scar. (250)

The importance of the particular and the contingent in recognition scenes brings them into a productive proximity with the approach to ethics outlined above, not only in the importance of these two features, but also in the significance of the emotions. I have noted, following Nussbaum, that our emotional responses can give rise to recognitions. As such, *anagnorisis* could assist in further displacing the Enlightenment ethical subject, not only through the importance of contingency—and the possible emergence of a "tragic" understanding of ethics—but also through being caused by characters' emotional responses. As Sara Ahmed (1998) notes, this by itself is a fundamental critique of the Enlightenment ethical subject, which is typically male and rejects the value of the emotions as "associated (negatively) with the feminine" (52-53).[10] This, as will be seen, is indeed the case in the works under consideration: repeatedly, characters navigate tragic ethical situations by relying on their emotional responses, which lead them to recognitions that alter their ethical understandings and, in so doing, give shape to the novel's ethical sense.

This approach to ethical criticism is well suited to take account of the ethical concerns raised by postcolonialism. There is one primary objection, however, that needs to be addressed. In discussing Adam Newton and Derek Attridge's approaches above, both of whom draw on the work of Emmanuel Levinas, I noted the concern that the ethics of the image holds for Levinas. It is due in part to this concern with over-determining the other through representation that Attridge, in a move common to postcolonialism, elevates an experience of otherness to the primary value, and that Newton specifies a hermeneutical ethics that grapples with the risks of transforming "person" into "character". In moving away from their approaches, it is important to acknowledge that this is indeed a proper concern, especially for a field of study that is invested in resisting and undercutting colonialist determinations. In positing recognition, and consequently gains in knowledge, as central to my ethical criticism, the question of certainty or of the illusion of grasping the other through recognition must be addressed.

A good instance of Levinas's challenge to literature can be found in his essay "Reality and its Shadow" (1987).[11] As I have detailed, the ethical relationship for Levinas is the face-to-face. The face is the revelation of the other person in their infinity, that is, in my relationship to them even as they exceed every concept of them that I have. Nevertheless, we relate to them and to the rest of the material world, precisely through concepts by which "we maintain a living relationship" (3). Art, however, does not relate to an object through its concept, but through its image. For Levinas,

---

[10] Nussbaum herself notes in an extended footnote this alliance between an Aristotelian understanding of the emotions and feminism. See Nussbaum (1990, 42, n.76).

[11] For an excellent, extended analysis of Levinas' quite ambiguous relationship to literature, see Robins (1999).

every being, every person, "bears on his face, alongside of its being with which he coincides, its own caricature, its picturesqueness". Even as we encounter a person or an object, their very materiality can be lifted like a second skin and made into an image:

> Here is a familiar everyday thing, perfectly adapted to the hand which is accustomed to it, but its qualities, color, form, and position at the same time remain as it were behind its being, like the 'old garments' of a soul which had withdrawn from that thing, like a 'still life'. (6)

As a result, there is a fundamental duality to all beings: "We will say the thing is itself and is its image". The image is different from a sign or a symbol, since "thought stops on the image itself" (6); it is opaque, drawing attention away from a fluid and living relationship to being, and towards the fixity of the "old garments" of its image that it leaves behind. In so doing, artistic disinterestedness, disengagement from the world, "is not the disinterestedness of contemplation but of irresponsibility" (12). Art is therefore caught up in this risk of irresponsibility. In substituting the image for the concept, we exchange the living relationship for one that is static, exchanging it for an "idol" (8). The image is suspended forever in its moment: the Mona Lisa will forever smile, but forever the smile that is about to broaden never will (9). Art is in this way an evasion of reality, of the living relationship to the object inextricably caught in the movement of time, and it is therefore ethically crucial that "the immobile statue [art] has to be put in movement and made to speak" (13); it needs to be returned to the real world. This work is accomplished by criticism, which integrates the image back into the "human world" (12).

We can say, then, that Levinas's position, as Richard Kearney (2002a) puts it, "would appear to be that poetic imagining is fine, as long as it remains answerable to an ethics of alterity" (91). Levinas is also, however, concerned about the fixity of images within the text, which is why he tends to prefer (though not exclusively [93-94]) avant-garde literature that is disruptive of its own representations (91-93)—not dissimilar to what Attridge's argues for Coetzee and can be similarly seen with Sam Durrant's (2004) approach to the same author, though for the latter literature is caught up in mourning rather than being about experiencing otherness *per se*. In addition to the possibility of viewing this book as contributing to the ethically beneficial work of "returning" literature to the "human world", it is worth underlining that not only does *anagnorisis* undermine itself as a form of knowledge and thus circumscribe its certainty, but the recognitions that I consider within the novels are moments of disruption and transformation where the characters' understanding of the world is altered, rearranged in order to make more space for the other. That is to say, the recognitions are not simply about the (racial, cultural, religious) others, but are about the recognising self's relation to them. The certainty of the characters' recognitions does not fix their others in overdetermined categories. Instead it accomplishes the opposite: through their recognitions they undergo a frequently painful and socially disruptive movement towards a more welcoming and open view of those who differ from them.

III

An approach to ethics in world literature that is attendant to the functioning of recognition and how it focalises a novel's ethical sense is thus able to take account of the critical concerns of postcolonialism. Turning now to *The Remains of the Day* (2005), I want to begin by further detailing the understanding of world literature functioning in this book. In my discussion so far I have privileged Damrosch's approach. However, as Robert Young has remarked, "world Literature [...] makes up more a heterogeneous field of critical debate than a constituted canon" (2014, 215). Circulating around the approaches of, most prominently, Pascale Casanova, David Damrosch and Franco Moretti, the contestation that characterises world literature concerns the question of how to limit which texts constitute its corpus. As Damrosch (2003) has commented, "the sum total of the world's literatures can be sufficiently expressed by the blanket term 'literature'", which is to say that the qualifier "world", in order to be meaningful, necessarily needs to designate a "a subset of the plenum of literature" (4). How exactly to define this subset is the focus of the debate, within which three broad positions have been opened up. For Damrosch, world literature consists of those texts which "circulate beyond their culture of origin, either in translation or in their original language" (4), and which, as we have seen, provide insight into foreign cultures (281). For Moretti and Casanova, the focus shifts away from the individual text towards a global understanding of the systems that govern the circulation of, and prestige accruing to, texts: Moretti, departing from close reading, adopts a statistical, quantitative approach to literary circulation and "describes the rise and fall of genres in evolutionary terms" (Porter 2011, 248), while Casanova articulates the social and political conditions within which literatures emerge and compete—with certain geographical centres, such as Paris, holding the literary power to bestow, or withhold, literary status on texts (Casanova 2004).[12] All of these definitions, however, intersect in Ishiguro's *The Remains of the Day*. Ishiguro has been awarded the Man Booker Prize in literature as well as an OBE for contributions in the field of literature and the French Chevalier de l'Ordre des Arts et des Lettres (Faber & faber 2014), evidencing the possession of what Casanova terms "literary capital" (2004, 17); his works have been translated into over 40 languages,[13] showing that his novels have, in Damrosch's terms, circulated significantly beyond their original culture; and both *The Remains of the Day* and *Never Let me Go* each sold over a million copies (Faber & faber 2014), making them particularly prominent in terms of their circulation and Moretti's macro-analysis.

The Remains of the Day can, then, be understood as world literature. Yet, when one begins engaging with the ethical sense of the novel, for which the butler Stevens's moral self-understanding is pivotal, one quickly runs up against the presence of the postcolonial. Early in the narrative, the connections between Stevens and British imperial history begin to emerge. When Stevens decides to take a vacation, he has not progressed far into his motor trip before he takes a break to "take stock, as it were" (Ishiguro 2005, 24). Walking a brief distance along the road, he comes across a local who directs him to climb a nearby hill to see one of the best views in England. Stevens follows the advice and, upon reaching the summit, is met "by a most marvellous view over miles of the surrounding countryside" of "field upon field rolling off into the distance", "bordered by hedges and trees", and in the distance "the square tower of a church" (26). At first glance simply a tranquil, picturesque view, this moment in-

---

[12] See Damrosch (2003), Casanova (2004), Casanova (2005), Moretti (2000) and Moretti (2005). For more on the debates, see also David Porter (2011), David Damrosch (2011), Graham Huggan (2011).
[13] Faber & Faber (2014) place the figure as over 40, while British Council (2016a) place it as over 30.

augurates Stevens's reflections on his (moral) life and connects the complex and nuanced recollections that follow to Britain's history of imperialism. Reflecting later on the vista from the hilltop, Stevens remarks that it is not the most "obviously spectacular scenery". Nevertheless, he locates

> a quality that the landscapes of other nations, however more superficially dramatic, inevitably fail to possess. It is, I believe, a quality that will mark out the English landscape to any objective observer as the most deeply satisfying in the world, and this quality is probably best summed up by the term 'greatness'. (28)

The comparison drawn between the countryside of England and that of "the world" iterates a colonial gesture, not only in the audacity of its scope—revealing his unreliability through the appeal to "any objective observer"—but more specifically in what Stevens specifies as characterising its greatness. "Greatness", he continues, "is the very lack of obvious drama or spectacle [....] its sense of restraint" (29). To speak of a landscape being restrained as opposed to "superficially dramatic" emerges here, as surely such a claim must, from an outlook over farmland: restrained decodes as domesticated. In the same way that Stevens will parallel restraint in a butler to wearing a suit, it is a view of land divided into discreet plots (the "hedges and trees"), that, in an echo of John Locke, is characterised as superior.

The resonance of Stevens's view of the superiority of the English countryside with the work of John Locke—whose arguments in the *Second Treatise of Government*, as Peter Hulme (1990) has shown, were not only used to justify the appropriation of land by colonial settlers but relied for its argumentative force on the idea of the savage in untamed nature, specifically in the Americas—is not accidental. However, Stevens's connection to the colonial enterprise becomes more explicit as his reflections continue. The greatness of restraint that is presented in this vista as rising ineluctably from the English landscape, is, for Stevens, epitomised in the ethic of service and dignity of butlers, and there are three anecdotes that he recounts to explain this. The first is the story of a butler serving his employer in India, who calmly shoots a tiger that has wandered into the dining room just before dinner. Apart from the sounds of gunshots, there is no disturbance and no panic: dinner is served as usual and on time (Ishiguro

2005, 37). The two other anecdotes recount parts of Stevens's father's career as a butler. In the first, Stevens senior prevents guests whom he is chauffeuring from slandering his employer simply by stopping the car and opening the door (40), while the last relates how Stevens senior provided excellent service to the military general responsible for his son's death during the South African War (41–42). Stevens thus concludes:

> The great butlers are great by virtue of their ability to inhabit their professional role and inhabit it to the utmost; they will not be shaken out by external events, however surprising, alarming or vexing. They wear their professionalism as a decent gentleman will wear his suit: he will not let ruffians or circumstances tear it off him in the public gaze; he will discard it when, and only when, he wills to do so, and this will invariably be when he is entirely alone. (43–44)

These characteristics, for Stevens, mean that a butler is essentially English. Continentals—"and by and large Celts, as you will no doubt agree"—are only able to become "manservants" due to their inability to restrain strong emotion: "they are like a man who will, at the slightest provocation, tear off his suit and his shirt and run about screaming" (44). Barry Lewis (2000) summarises the chain of reasoning as follows: "To be English is to be great, like the landscape; to be great, is to possess dignity; and dignity is epitomised by the great butlers" (81).

Stevens's anecdotes reveal, however, that his ethic of dignity and service is one that, as Sim (2006) has shown, is not as autochthonous as Stevens might think. The exemplary dignity displayed by the butler in India situates it on the grounds of the empire rather than in England, with the effect of inscribing the "outside history" of the British empire into the heart of this myth of Englishness that Stevens seeks to embody (137). A similar logic functions with the connection to the South African War, which brings the "greatness" of the gentlemanly houses and the empire "face to face with the fact of ignominious violence" (135), revealing the houses' connections with imperialism. Although Sim's concern is the way in which this "interrogates some new rightist exclusions and ideologemes that emerged in the seventies and eighties" when the book was published (120), these anecdotes reveal the colonial grounds upon which Stevens's ideal of English greatness is founded, and will be important for revealing the wider ramifications of the novel's critique of Stevens's ethical position.

The connection to empire is strengthened by two additional points. The first is the co-incidence of the Suez crisis with the present time of the narrative. John Sutherland (1998) points out that the absence of any direct mention of the crisis is "a vacancy so glaring that it must be intended" (187). Indeed, the dates align almost perfectly, with Stevens travelling during its height, which came to symbolise the decline of the British Empire. When Stevens later mentions that he has met Anthony Eden and was concerned "with international affairs" (Ishiguro 2005, 197), the crisis is powerfully signalled in its absence; it is the hole in the centre of the "doughnut novel" that is *The Remains of the Day* (Lewis 2000, 99). If we add to this Susie O'Brien's (1996) observation that Stevens's ethical code "reflects and supports the model of filial devotion deployed by empire to mask the enforced servitude of its colonies" (790), then not only is it imbricated by empire, but the critique in the novel can be read as corresponding to the waning of empire symbolised by the Suez crisis.

Stevens's further strengthens his link to imperialism through his understanding of the criteria for membership in the Hayes Society, a fictional, elite association of butlers. Stevens notes two criteria that structure his reflections throughout: a great butler must "be attached to a distinguished household" (Ishiguro 2005, 32), and a great butler must "be possessed of a dignity in keeping with his position" (33). Rejecting the Society's exclusion of the newly rich from the first category, Stevens concludes that rather than understanding "the world in terms of a ladder" (121), with royalty at the top and the newly rich at the bottom, it should be understood as a wheel, with some closer to the central, influential positions. The nearer a house is to the "hub" of the wheel, the more (morally) distinguished it is—whether newly rich or not. Stevens states that it would therefore be worthy to serve "a gentleman such as Mr George Ketteridge, who, however humble his beginnings, has made an undeniable contribution to the future well-being of the *empire*" (120, my emphasis). The use of the empire here as a parallel description of the distinguishing features of "furthering the progress of humanity" or "serving humanity" (122, 123), which characterises those at the hub of the wheel, enacts a similar move to the story of the butler in India: it inscribes into the centre that which is considered to lie at a safe distance on the periphery. Stevens's regretful recognitions at the end of the novel, where he begins to allow other values to be counted, thus have a greater significance than simply individual growth. They also critique a certain conception of "Englishness" and Empire, that transnational expression of Englishness (Young 2008). The postcolonial therefore frames the ethical focus of *The Remains of the Day*, making proper attention to it indispensable for a full analysis of the novel. However, the ethical questions that are explored in the novel are not reducible to a question singularity or alterity—though they will still be seen to be of importance for postcolonialism.

The connection of Stevens's moral ideals to colonialism is only part of the picture. These statements of Stevens's values, although accurate, only emerge slowly through the movements of a narrative that is deeply marked by unreliability. Brian Shaffer (1998) suggests that the metaphor of clothing, so important to Stevens's explanation of dignity, "announces one of the novel's chief concerns and controlling metaphors: the literal and figurative ways by which the butler clothes his private self from his own understanding and from the 'public gaze'" (65). Indeed the motif of clothing proliferates: when Stevens later reiterates his understanding of dignity, it "comes down to not removing one's clothing in public" (Ishiguro 2005, 221); he is also preoccupied with his "costume" (11, 20), worries about the possible damage to it while walking across a field to the village of Moscombe (17); and he justifies as a matter of principle his guarded response to Miss Kenton when she surprises him reading a "sentimental love story" (176): a butler "cannot be seen casting [his role] aside one moment simply to don it again the next as though it were nothing more than a pantomime costume" (178). The concealing function of clothing is balanced, Shaffer goes on to note, by its ability to reveal (1998, 66). It is the warp and woof of this concealment and disclosure that constitutes Stevens's unreliability, foundational to which is his ideal of dignity.[14] That Stevens believes he can only relinquish his professional personae when he is "entirely alone" (Ishiguro 2005, 44) means that, as Wall (1994) puts it, "the emotions or emotional turmoil of the private man must not be allowed to interfere with the duty and dignity of the public personae" (26). The emotional turmoil that Stevens experiences at his father's death and Miss Kenton's engagement are thus sublimated under the dignity of the public personae of the butler; or, in Newton's terms, we only

---

14 See Newton (1995, 282), Phelan (2005, 51) and Wall (1994, 25–26).

see Stevens's pain as an "after-image" in these moments that are "defined by the structure of looking away" (Newton 1995, 282).

Through the combination of accidental encounters and a degree of personal integrity which keeps him reflecting on his values despite his growing discomfort (Wall 1994, 37), Stevens slowly approaches his final recognitions when, in Ekelund's (2005) words, the tension is relieved and "narration and reading join in a common moment of anagnorisis as ignorance gives way to full knowledge" (82). These moments are crucial for both Phelan and Newton, who read the different ethical effects of this unreliability on the reader. For Phelan it is Stevens's first major recognition that is the most climatic and important. While Phelan, Wall and Newton concur on Stevens's unreliability, Phelan describes his divergence from Wall as a distinction between a rhetorical and a formalist approach to narrative: "my discussion moves toward the ethics of reading, while hers moves toward the relation between contemporary ideas of subjectivity and unreliability" (2005, 32 n.1). Even though Wall herself does not consider her analysis an ethical one, we will see that Phelan is mistaken in dismissing it as unconcerned with ethics. Phelan is correct, however, in distinguishing between Wall's more intra-textual analysis and his own, which proceeds to the reader's response and the ethics entailed within this move. In this regard Phelan's approach is quite similar to Newton's. The difference between them, as we have seen, lies in Phelan's understanding of the ethics of narration as resting in narrative as an act of communication, while for Newton it resides in the obligations placed upon the reader in the moment of reading.

In the final section of the novel, Stevens comes to the painful realization that he loves Miss Kenton (who has been Mrs Benn for twenty years) and that it is too late for anything to be done about it. Phelan writes,

> As character Stevens is so overcome by commingled feelings of love and loss, recognition and regret that his heart breaks. As narrator, Stevens is so complexly reliable and unreliable that Ishiguro places the authorial audience in a very challenging ethical position. (31)

Phelan agrees with Newton and Wall that, as Stevens proceeds on his journey towards meeting with Miss Kenton, "he shows intermittent signs of recognising the deficiencies of his ideals" (32), but that it is "the meeting itself that leads him simultaneously to recognize and regret just how seriously mistaken his ideals have been and how much he has foolishly sacrificed for them" (32–33). For Phelan, the ethical effect of the novel is caught up in the interplay of reliability and unreliability as it culminates in this interaction with Miss Kenton in a complex "combination of what we might call understating (the character-to-character equivalent of underreporting—they say less than they mean and so convey less to each other) and indirection (they say less than they mean but convey their meaning anyway)" (55). The interchange between Stevens and Miss Kenton at this crucial moment consequently becomes ambiguous, with the ethical question for Phelan pivoting on whether Stevens should have responded as he did, rather than expressing his newly realised love for Miss Kenton.

In the scene, Stevens finally asks Miss Kenton "the first personal question he has ever asked her" (55). Stevens has driven Miss Kenton to the bus stop, when he asks if her husband mistreats her since she has left him several times. Miss Kenton recognises that he is asking more than this and thus rephrases it: "I suppose, Mr Stevens, you're asking whether or not I love my husband" (Ishiguro 2005, 251). Phelan suggests that her own reticence prevents her from rephrasing the question Stevens is truly asking through his indirection, namely, "Do you still love me?" (Phelan 2005, 55). In her reply, Miss Kenton says that she has "extremely desolate moments" when she thinks "What a terrible mistake I've made with my life". It is at such times that she wonders "about a life I might have had with you, Mr Stevens". And it is at such times that she is easily angered and leaves her husband for a short time. She continues:

> But each time I do, I realize before long—my rightful place is with my husband. After all, there's no turning back the clock now. One can't be forever dwelling on what might have been. One should realize one has as good as most, perhaps better, and be grateful. (Ishiguro 2005, 251)

Phelan accurately paraphrases her reply as saying, "I used to love you, and indeed, loved you more than I love my husband now, but my feelings have altered and it's now too late for us to think about a future together" (2005, 55).

Stevens's response is perhaps the most poignant moment in the novel:

> I do not think I responded immediately, for it took me a moment or two to fully digest these words of Miss Kenton. Moreover, as you might appreciate, their implications were such as to provoke a certain degree of sorrow within me. Indeed—why should I not admit it? —at that moment, my heart was breaking. (Ishiguro 2005, 251–252)

In "the moment or two it took to digest" the reply, he is registering, "their subtext" (Phelan 2005, 55), namely, that she is telling him that there is no future for them together. Significantly, the scene is made more moving in that Stevens here shifts from unreliably underreporting his emotions, describing only "a certain degree of sorrow", to full reporting, to fully acknowledging his broken heart (55–56). For Newton, this is one "of only three moments" where Stevens's voice "changes register, as a world of secrets newly discovered wells up from beneath its occluded surface" (1995, 273). In what Stevens goes on to say to Miss Kenton, however, he gives no indication of this shift, no indication of his recognition. He smiles and says that she is absolutely right, that there is no going back and that she "really mustn't let any more foolish ideas come between yourself and the happiness you deserve" (Ishiguro 2005, 251). It is therefore precisely here, Phelan argues, that the "authorial audience" needs to come "to terms with the ethical dimensions of the discrepancy between Stevens's telling and his acting in response to Miss Kenton" (Phelan 2005, 55).

The ethical challenge that the novel presents, for Phelan, is that it leaves two possibilities equally open: on the one hand, there is evidence that Stevens did the right thing in not revealing to Miss Kenton his emotions. On the other hand, it can be read inversely that this is precisely what Miss Kenton wanted him to do, and that in remaining silent he consequently erred again.

In short, we find that we cannot resolve the ambiguity of Stevens's ethical position at this point in the narrative because we cannot clearly determine the implied Ishiguro's relation to Stevens [which is a] direct consequence of the character narration. (58)

Up until this point in the novel, "the narrative [...] has rewarded rather than blocked our efforts to discern Ishiguro's positions behind Stevens's narration" (59), the work that Newton describes as discerning the narrative's after-image. The result is that responsibility thus falls on the readers:

Because Ishiguro's particular use of character narration here blocks our access to conclusive signals about how to respond, the effect of his technique is to transfer the responsibility for disambiguating the scene to the flesh-and-blood reader, and the deciding factor in how we each carry out that responsibility is our individual ethical beliefs as they interact with our understanding of Stevens as a particular character in a particular situation. (60)

The reader needs to make a selection from the "subset of Ishiguro's ethical norms [that] is most relevant to this scene" (60).

Additionally, the progression of the narrative up to this point means that we know more about Stevens's love for Miss Kenton, with the result that the reader has an additional "ethical responsibility": Our "sense of justice" requires that we recognise the fear and hope and confusion that compete with each other in the characters, a "recognition that leads to empathy" and increases "our desire for Stevens to act" (Phelan 2005, 62). We know, however, that he does not act, and thus our desire is frustrated, unfulfilled. Ishiguro does, Phelan argues, give us some satisfaction through the final encounter with the ex-butler on the pier at Weymouth. This figure, Phelan suggests, "is ultimately a stand-in for us", giving Stevens advice that we would like to give, advice that he accepts.

The emotional satisfaction of having Stevens's reality partially conform to our desire and the ethical satisfaction of seeing Stevens resolve to make something of the remains of his days combine to relieve the bleakness of the final situation. His anagnorisis has led not just to his pain but also to a new direction even at this late period in his life. (64)

However, Stevens immediately proceeds to under-regard the value of bantering, leaving his change limited and thus realistic (64–65). Phelan concludes that "Ishiguro's communications to us [...] are a generous offer to share human warmth", a communication that through presenting the narrative of a character that loses that warmth, shares Ishiguro's concerns of the ways we as readers might miss it.

And that sharing is one that implies a deep trust in our ability to read the disclosures behind his many strategies of indirection— and, in the key moment of the narrative, to fend for ourselves. *The Remains of the Day*, in that respect, is itself an ethical act of the highest order. (65)

For Newton, on the other hand, the ethical import of the novel rests in the "responsibilities incurred" when reading, when responding to the demands of the text (1995, 19). It is thus primarily the warp and woof of revelation and secrecy throughout the narrative that is of importance for him, rather than the final recognitions (of which Phelan only considers the first, but more on that in a moment), although they are not irrelevant. Newton argues that Stevens's unreliability instructs the reader "a little in the art [he] calls 'good waiting': 'that balance between attentiveness and the illusion of absence'. This is the art not of occlusion but of double vision: keeping two surfaces co-present" (284). Throughout the process of reading *The Remains of the Day*, the reader has had to keep in sight both the surface of the world through which Stevens "discreetly and courteously escorts us" (270), and the surface of that world's "after-image" (282), which "emerges [...] mostly unbeknownst to him, through a sort of discursive double exposure" (270). And since, as we have seen, the mechanism of the narrative is this "looking away", according to which it is constructed and its after-image emerges, Newton argues that corresponding to this in the reader is "a kind of sympathy, as sympathy itself involves what Robert Unger has called a 'recognition of comic incongruity'" (269). The art of "good waiting" in which the novel instructs us, therefore, is "the tactful capacity for recognition, for seeing 'comic incongruity'" (284).

The responsibility that for Newton is involved "when selves represent or are represented by others" is "learning the paradoxical lesson that 'getting' someone else's story is also a way of losing the person as 'real,' as 'what he is'" (18). In other words, there is the risk of relating to an entirely knowable image, instead of to the ungraspable individual. The "double vision" in which *The Remains of the Day* instructs us corresponds to this need to both "get" and "not to get" Stevens's story. It is thus important for Newton that Ishiguro's novel "contain[s] the sign of remainder" in its title. Not only are Stevens's recognitions—and thus the reader's—limited, but there is also an excess in "the day which is still left to enjoy": in the novel "something is left over, inaccessible, unexposed" (284). Newton therefore concludes, "And so, reading sometimes demands the contrary sign of looking away, of stopping short, of realizing that texts, like persons, cannot entirely be known, that they must keep some of their secrets. It is, finally, the sign of interruption", that is, the negotiation of indirection and maintaining double vision, "which identifies the reader's share in the act of telling the self to others, the dialectic of revelation and concealment, of leaving home and looking away, of knowing and acknowledging, that is narrative ethics" (285).

For both Phelan and Newton, then, the unreliability of Stevens is the crucial element of the novel that gives rise to its ethical force: for Phelan, an ethically ambiguous situation at the conclusion of the novel leaves the final ethical judgement to the reader while highlighting the importance of human warmth; for Newton, it provides a type of training in negotiating double meaning and the art of looking away while reading,[15] of refusing absolute knowledge of the characters in a text. As such, both locate the impact of the novel in the ethical response required from the reader. However, both neglect to consider the full implications of Stevens's recognitions on the understanding of ethics, and in this case the ethical subject in particular, within the novel itself.

I have noted that Phelan distinguishes his approach from Wall's, designating hers as concerned with the understanding of subjectivity that underpins unreliability, rather than with ethics. This corresponds of

---

[15] There are affinities here to Spivak's argument that literature "allows you to train for [moving toward the other]" (Damrosch and Spivak 2011, 482).

course to Wall's own description of her goal in her essay. Her description of the relation between unreliability and the understanding of subjectivity is nevertheless ethically salient, and worth quoting at length:

> The standard definitions of an unreliable narrator presuppose a reliable counterpart who is the 'rational, self-present subject of humanism,' who occupies a world in which language is a transparent medium that is capable of reflecting a 'real' world. But if 'subjectivity [...] is precarious, contradictory and in process, constantly being reconstituted in discourse each time we think or speak', then we are forced to think about the issue of unreliable narration as a matter of degree rather than as the moral aberration of more traditional definitions. (1994, 21–22)

What has emerged from the above discussion, is that Stevens is precisely this kind of narrator. He is discovering himself as he speaks, interrupted by himself, disjointed from himself. Stevens is continuously recovering the ground of his memories, coming to a new understanding of himself in the process, which has implications for his ethics.

The question to be asked is does Stevens's recognition at the end of the novel further the decentring of the rational, fully self-aware subject identified by Wall? At the close of the novel, Stevens is sitting on a pier, and shares with a stranger his second major recognition:

> Lord Darlington wasn't a bad man. He wasn't a bad man at all. And at least he had the privilege of being able to say at the end of his life that he made his own mistakes. His lordship was a courageous man. He chose a certain path in life, it proved to be a misguided one, but there, he chose it, he can say that at least. As for myself, I cannot even claim that. You see, I trusted. I trusted in his lordship's wisdom. All those years I served him, I trusted I was doing something worthwhile. I can't even say I made my own mistakes. Really—one has to ask oneself—what dignity is there in that? (Ishiguro 2005, 255–256)

The flow of this passage needs to be considered carefully. Stevens is here still responding to the understanding of dignity that he had encountered the previous night in Moscombe, where dignity is synonymous with freedom of thought and conscience (196). At that time, he had reiterated his position on serving Lord Darlington and asked, "what is there 'undignified' in this?" (211). Here, he realises that in not expressing his own opinion, as Harry Smith had put it, he did not decide what was or was not worthwhile to do; committed to serving Darlington in whatever course he chose, he "trusted" that it was worthwhile. Having finally acknowledged the previous night that Darlington's work had turned out not to be so, he now inverts his defensive question into an accusation that echoes Smith: "what dignity is there in that?". Implied in this moment, then, is also a confirmation of the regret and shame against which he was fighting the previous night; indeed, the tone of the scene and his tears indicate that this is what he is feeling.

That his recognition, which is itself something of an ethical achievement, produces a distinct change is clear from Stevens's determination to pursue "human warmth" (257–258). However, before turning to that, what critics seem to have passed over is Stevens's final *defence* of Lord Darlington. In this moment of clarity, when he realises that his trust in and service to Darlington did not deliver the value and worth he had hoped for—in other words, in a moment when Stevens would be most open to not defending Darlington—he nevertheless asserts that "Lord Darlington wasn't a bad man. He wasn't a bad man at all". To what extent is this another instance of Steven's unreliability? Contrary to what seems to be a general consensus on Darlington's grave moral failing and betrayal of Stevens, I want to suggest that the novel actually presents Darlington in a somewhat ambiguous light, and that Stevens at this moment is not entirely unjustified. This is supported by the fact that two characters outside of Stevens's daily life make the same point about Darlington.

First, senator Lewis, at the conclusion to the 1923 conference, describes Darlington and his companions as gentlemen, but political amateurs:

All you decent, well-meaning gentlemen, let me ask you, have you any idea what sort of place the world is becoming all around you? The days when you could act out of your noble instincts are over [....] If you don't realize that soon you're headed for disaster. (106–107)

And it is precisely Darlington's noble instincts that lead to his destruction: it is his sense of honour towards a defeated enemy that leads to his support for Germany. This is confirmed, secondly, by the young Mr Cardinal (who dies fighting in the war, making him something of a sympathetic character) who diagnoses Darlington's problem to Stevens on the night of the secret conference, the same night that Miss Kenton announces her engagement:

He's a gentleman, and he fought a war with the Germans, and it's his instinct to offer generosity and friendship to a defeated foe [....] And you must have seen it Stevens. How could you not have? The way they've used it, manipulated it, *turned something fine and noble into something else*—something they can use for their own foul ends? (243, my emphasis)

This is not to excuse in any way the significant error of Darlington's anti-democratic sentiments, or the seriousness of Darlington's act of anti-Semitism when he dismisses the two Jewish servants. Rather, it is to suggest a more nuanced and complex view of Darlington within the novel: to re-emphasise his regret for the dismissal and to mention his motive—a mistaken concern for "the interests of the guests staying here" (155)—since it is in these that Stevens at the end tries to find refuge.

Stevens therefore recognises Darlington's good intentions, and his courage in following his chosen path, even as he recognises that this path was the devastatingly wrong one to take and ended in disaster—for both Darlington and himself. What is important, though, is the close parallel between Darlington and Stevens at this moment. Stevens's description of Darlington could be applied to himself: "He chose a certain path in life, it proved to be a misguided one, but there, he chose it, he can say that at least" (255–256). Although Stevens did, as it were, sign over to Darlington his future decisions, he made that decision by himself. And although he does not put it in these terms, we can see that Stevens discerns this, and rapidly retreats to it:

> what can we ever gain in forever looking back and blaming ourselves if our lives have not turned out quite as we might have wished? The hard reality is, surely, that for the likes of you and me, there is little choice other than to leave our fate, ultimately, in the hands of those great gentlemen at the hub of this world who employ our services. What is the point in worrying oneself too much about what one could or could not have done to control the course one's life took? Surely it is enough that the likes of you and me at least try to make a small contribution count for something true and worthy. And if some of us are prepared to sacrifice much in life in order to pursue such aspirations, surely that is in itself, whatever the outcome, cause for pride and contentment. (257)

This has often been commented upon as a reversion by Stevens to his old habits. In some ways that is true: despite having realised the indignity of not pursuing his own opinion and thoughts, of not making his own mistakes, he is unable to abandon his view of the world as a wheel. Yet this passage is nonetheless saturated with his recognition: he does not renege on his assessment of Darlington's failure, that he did not in the end serve a man who advanced humanity. However, Stevens has rephrased his description of Lord Darlington and applied it to himself, though on a smaller scale: "it is enough that the likes of you and me at least try to make a small contribution".

The last line of this passage references his loss of Miss Kenton. He most certainly has "sacrificed much in life in order to pursue" his "aspirations" of making a contribution. We can thus see him sublimating the pain of his earlier recognition with Miss Kenton (the likely cause of this recognition, considering it is the only significant event between this point and his defence of his values in Moscombe) into his newly qualified ethical framework of the importance of trying to make a difference. In doing this, Stevens oversteps his recognition, pushing his new knowledge further than it should go: although there may be something of value in the sacrifice, it is not something of which to be proud and content. Nevertheless, his position has shifted and, considering his deeply ingrained emotional reticence, significantly so as he commits himself to pursue human warmth.

Unfortunately for Stevens, it is at this point that the accrual of connections to empire throughout the novel, especially the imbrications of the great houses with imperialism, becomes pertinent. Stevens's retreat from his culpability into his good intentions, anchored as it is in Darlington's good intentions, are, unbeknownst to him, indissociable from what some try to argue were the "good intentions" of colonialism. The framing of the novel therefore not only indirectly critiques colonialism through Stevens's recognition of the failure of his ethical code which was so intertwined with imperialism, but also undercuts Stevens's recourse to his good intentions even as it presents it in a sympathetic light. The reader at this moment of recognition is left with a carefully developed exploration of agency and responsibility and its implications for ethics more broadly: to what extent do good intentions remove culpability for wrongdoing? It seems that Stevens does not consider Darlington's good intentions as absolving him from his failure, which is confirmed by the framing of the novel and the implicit critique of colonialism. Yet Stevens swiftly moves from acknowledging his own failure to congratulating himself for his good intentions.

The beginnings of an answer to the question thus posed by the ending of the novel can be found in Stevens's new ethical position and its relation to the understanding of the human subject. For one, his recognition is only partially effective. He maintains his view of the world as a wheel, and he pushes his recognition too far so as to give himself peace. Even in his moment of *anagnorisis*, he is a limited, in-process subject, who lacks any pure autonomy despite his constant referencing of his pursuit of virtue. There is also the fact that it is his pain at the loss of Miss Kenton that leads him to this recognition—rather than the arguments of others, which he shores himself up against—leading to the further question of the role of the emotions in rational thought. Yet the crucial point is that just as his gain in self-knowledge is in large part the result of luck—the constant accidents and diversions from his planned itinerary throughout his vacation—he finds that his moral excellence is similarly affected by luck. That is, as Nussbaum uses the term, "what does not happen through his or her own agency, what just happens to him, as opposed to what he does or makes" (1986, 3). At the start of the closing section, Stevens is in precisely this position. He did not make his own mistakes, but is feeling regret and shame. While this is to a certain extent because of his own decision to serve Darlington, his own suspension of autonomy as it were, he nevertheless seems to consider himself culpable for mistakes that he did not choose to make. He sidesteps this quandary by reverting to that decision to suspend his own decision making, and importantly references the motives for that decision, leaving intact something like the Kantian idea of the good, and invulnerable, will. However, that this is itself undercut by the framing of the novel as well as symptomatic of his continued unreliability, leads to the final position of the novel being that his moral goodness is indeed vulnerable to that which is beyond his control.

While Newton and Phelan's readings of *The Remains of the Day* are insightful and valuable, a focus on the ethical sense of the novel as it is structured around moments of recognition is productive for reading the text as a nuanced exploration of an ethical argument. The ethical concern that it considers in this case is the question of culpability in situations and outcomes beyond our control, that is to say, the question of moral luck and the vulnerability of the good. *The Remains of the Day* only suggests an answer to the question, opening it to the reader for further thought. Nevertheless, it is a subtle exploration of the question through a moving account of the particular, contingent details of Stevens life, and which comes into focus through moments of recognition and the importance for them of the postcolonial.

IV

The larger question that is at stake in *The Remains of the Day*, and which has been a thread throughout this introduction, is the question of humanism. A highly contested term—and indeed, as Tony Davies (2008) points out, an incredibly polyvalent one—it is a major locus of the postcolonial critique of the Enlightenment,[16] and one of the three ethical themes considered throughout this book. It should be clear from the discussions above that the approach I take to ethics in world literature is deeply influenced by the need to rework and reconstruct, to use Césaire's phrase, "a true humanism—a humanism made to the measure of the world" (quoted in Young 2001, 270). A similar conviction will be seen across the selected authors—all of whom find that the possibility of a common humanity is essential to their work. A critical part of exploring this possible humanism, is questioning the boundaries between humans and animals. Most explicitly addressed in the work of Ghosh and Coetzee, animal ethics interogates the division between human and animal so fundamental to the Enlightenment subject. The works of Ghosh and Phillips focus more directly on this figure of the (ethical) subject, and present one who is semi-autonomous, vulnerable and embodied. In Phillips, as also we have seen in Ishiguro, there is the exploration of a more radical conception of a subject who is additionally dislocated from themselves, lacking full self-awareness. Even in the work of Adichie, where this question is not overtly thematised, the navigation of difference that she portrays can nevertheless be understood as requiring the underpinning of a common humanity. This question of the idea of the human (a questioning that is part of the theorizing of what is often termed the posthuman) is futher developed by Smith, who introduces the related question of beauty and aesthetics—or, in Levinas's terms, the question of the image. The authors collected here are therefore engaged in precisely the tension that I have outlined above: the need for universals—primarily a common humanity, a humanism—balanced against the need for speciificity, for a recognition and welcoming of difference.

The two additional themes—the remembrance of violence and religion—although separate have close connections to the question of

---

[16] See, for example, Gandhi (1999), Durrant (2004), Scott (2004), and Spivak (1999).

humanism. Postcolonialism, as Durrant (2004) and Gandhi (1999) argue, is a matter of remembrance and mourning, of recovering lost and suppressed pasts—a suppression and loss that is inextricably tied to the violence of European humanism. It is primarily as a concern with recovery that the theme of history or remembrance is engaged in the work of Ghosh, particularly *The Hungry Tide*. In Adichie and Phillips, however, the central ethical question is *how* to remember. When the past is violent and traumatic, what is the relationship between the freedom of art and the obligations of commemoration? This is first introduced primarily with Adichie's novel on the Biafran war, *Half of a Yellow Sun*, and is taken up again in both of Phillips's novels. Phillips's engagement, however, is the more nuanced. Navigating this ethical tension that surrounds remembrance, his carefully constructed narratives also expose the silences in the historical archive and thus return us to the question of lost and suppressed histories—with the notable difference that these gaps are left shrouded in silence.

The theme of religion is perhaps the most unevenly engaged across these authors. A possible sub-category of the first theme, it is the work of Adichie that shifts it to the fore as an ethical concern in its own right. In Ghosh, we see religion deployed as either an alibi for colonial violence, or as a non-modern, hybrid discourse that is disruptive of attempts to totalise out knowledge of the other. For Smith, religious tolerance opens up possibilities for connecting with others, while in Phillips's work religion is brought forward into a more discursive role, shaping the thought-lives and discursive possibilities of the characters. In Adichie, however, it is presented as a feasible mode of engaging with the world. A part of this is a necessary undermining of inhospitable and violent forms of religion—a central concern for the ethical sense of *Purple Hibiscus*. We also see in Adichie a way of being in the world that rejects some fundamental Enlightenment distinctions, primarily the separation of the secular and the sacred, a rejection that faces us with an aporia: the increasing rise of fundamentalism makes an assertion of secularism imperative, yet the idea of secularism is caught up in the binaries fundamental to the Enlightenment understanding of Man. Although this is beyond the purview of the current analysis, the potential productivity of this aporia is worth noting.

This book is structured, then, along a trajectory that marks a gradually evolving complexity of thematic ethical engagement. While all three themes are present in most of the selected authors, there is an alternating emphasis between them in the movement from Ghosh to Adichie, with Phillips engaging all three in a more complex and nuanced way—though with religion, as it were, bringing up the rear—Zadie Smith developing the role of aesthetics in realizing our animal vulnerability, and J.M. Coetzee engaging the idea of the human in relation to the animal. In the chapters to come, the central function of recognition in a novel's ethical sense is tested through the differing styles and concerns of the chosen authors. The ethical concerns that are explored in each text are postcolonial in focus, and, insisting upon ethics and the commitments of postcolonialisim, I insert them through the consideration of form, into world literature.

Chapter One
Anagnorisis and the Clash of Values

> I came back to the houseboat with my head in a whirl: when Jodu's eyes met mine, in the Consoo House, it was as if our lives had changed. A strange and powerful thing is recognition!
>
> (Ghosh 2015, 266)

I

Amitav Ghosh, more than any of the other authors considered in this book, has invested in the idea and power of recognition. As the epigraph reflects, recognition enters his work as an explicit theme in the final book of the Ibis Trilogy. Ghosh's work is thus an excellent point at which to begin refining the approach to ethics in world literature outlined in the introduction. I will focus my attention on two of his works, namely *The Hungry Tide* (2005a)[17] and *Sea of Poppies* (2008), as both deploy *anagnorisis* as a narrative mechanism, as well as engaging all three of the ethical themes that I have introduced. Least directly engaged, however, is the question of religion. In his study of Amitav Ghosh, Anshuman Mondal (2007) argues that Ghosh's engagement with religion and secularism are caught up in his negotiation of the tension between modernism/humanism and postmodernism. While the "authoritarianism, violence and coercive reflexes" of the postcolonial State need to be criticised, the "Nehruvian vision of a secular, democratic nation-state that accommodates India's 'diversity' into a syncretic unity" nevertheless remains essential for Ghosh as a "bulwark against the forces of religious and ethnic chauvinism" and the political and ethical risks these entail (28). The accuracy of this assessment is borne out by the observation that religion in these two novels tends to be either a syncretic fusion of different languages and beliefs, as in the Bon Bibi myth in *The Hungry Tide*, or is subjected to critique when used as an alibi for violence and coercion, which we see with Mr Burnham's Christianity in *Sea of Poppies* (Hoydis 2011, 329). Ghosh's negotiation of religion in these novels is not, however, an

---

[17] First published in 2004. All references refer to the 2005 Harper Collins Publishers paperback edition.

engagement with religion as such, and therefore functions more, as it were, as a prelude to the engagement in the work of Chimamanda Adichie that will be observed in the next chapter—at which point I will explore more fully questions of the relationship between religion and colonialism.

Of greater concern to Ghosh are the themes of history and humanism. The meticulous historical research that characterises his oeuvre has been well documented by critics. Mondal and Hoydis both observe that Ghosh is most concerned with histories or stories that fall beyond the pale of historical narratives, involved as they are with the grand narrative of "modernity, development and Progress"; his interest is in "'fragments' of human experience that have been occluded from the historical record, and which find no place in such grand designs" (Mondal 2007, 21).[18] It has been observed that Ghosh challenges traditional historiography on two levels. Noting the proximity of Ghosh's work to that of the Subaltern Studies collective, Mondal argues that a consideration of the necessarily increasing self-reflexivity of Subaltern Studies clarifies the effectiveness of Ghosh's fictionalizing of history. "Indeed, it could be argued that Ghosh [as a writer] has the licence to explore areas of the Subaltern Studies project that the historians themselves are prohibited from by virtue of their investment in 'historiography'" (27). The two novels under consideration here continue this concern with elided and forgotten narratives.[19] In each case, there is a "forgotten history" that is fictionalised. With regard to *Sea of Poppies* Ghosh comments, "The Ghazipur and Patna opium factories between them produced the wealth of Britain. It is astonishing to think of it but the Empire was really founded on opium" (quoted in Hoydis 2011, 330). It is this "forgotten history" of the fundamental importance of opium to the British Empire—and its devastating effects on her subjects—that Hoydis argues Ghosh seeks to recover. Similarly with *The Hungry Tide*: though less directly connected to colonialism, in this novel it is the incident of the Morichjhāpi massacre in the Sundarbans that is recovered,

---

[18] See also Hawley (2005) and Tomsky (2009).
[19] It is important to emphasise that this is not imply that Subaltern Studies can be reduced to a concern with forgotten histories. See Chatterjee (1993). For the extent to which *Sea of Poppies* is invested in this project, see the description of the archive drawn upon for the Ibis Trilogy in the 'Epilogue' in *Flood of Fire* (Ghosh 2015).

an event that until the publication of the novel "had all but lapsed into oblivion" (Tomsky 2009, 57).

To limit Ghosh's engagement with history to the recuperation of forgotten stories would, however, produce an impoverished understanding of his work. Ghosh's concern with history exceeds a recounting of events, of cause and causality (Bose 2003, 18). The second challenge that Ghosh directs towards traditional history resides in his humanizing it, which brings us to the third ethical theme and the main focus in this chapter. In an interview with Vijay Kumar (2007), Ghosh comments that what he finds useful in his research is the recreation of singular "predicaments":

> I think what is interesting about, say, history in terms of a novel is that history gives us particular predicaments which are unique predicaments, not repeatable in time and place. So that's what is really interesting to me [....] So for me the research part of it that is interesting is to recreate that predicament faithfully, to re-create the details of that predicament. (101)

The primary interest of these predicaments, he continues, is "the structure of emotion that accompanies" them (101). It is within this interest in the human experience of singular locations and historical events, that we can situate Ghosh's concern to do justice to "cultural difference", the representation of non-normative perspectives, while simultaneously emphasizing "the underlying similarity of human experience across both space and time" (Mondal 2007, 29). As will be seen, this tension is particularly present in *The Hungry Tide* where, alongside a strong affirmation of a common humanity, the reader negotiates, together with the main characters, encounters with singular differences which "dispute the valorization of elite mobility" (Mukherjee 2010, 116).

As this implies, Ghosh's novels are all ethically engaged and can be productively read in ethical criticism: the epic historical tapestry of *The Glass Palace* (2001) that reveals the complex imbrications between the colonial and the postcolonial, and the difficulties of navigating these shifting, unstable complexities; the ethics of memory and identity in *The Shadow Lines* (2005b) as these unfold across the instituted boundaries of nations and within the imagination. Each novel is ethically intricate and valuable.

My privileging of *Sea of Poppies* and *The Hungry Tide* is due to two main points: the centrality of *anagnorisis,* and the engagement with ethical concerns addressed by this book. *Sea of Poppies* presents Ghosh's most explicit positing of a universal humanism, which is expressly accomplished through the interplay of concealment and revelation characteristic of *anagnorisis*. *The Hungry Tide*, for its part, raises a challenging ethical paradox that attends to environmental ethics and the question of the posthuman, a field that is rapidly growing within postcolonial criticism.[20] That this is again addressed through moments of recognition marks these two novels as well suited for an initial testing of the approach to ethical criticism that I have adumbrated.

Sea of Poppies opens in India in 1838, just before the Opium Wars between England and China, and follows diverse characters as they either come to be indentured servants or to escort those servants on their transportation to the Mauritius Islands. Throughout, most of the main characters hide their identities in some way in pursuit of new lives, "escaping one life for another" (Schine 2009), with the result that multiple social divisions become problematised. As Hoydis points out, in *Sea of Poppies* "Ghosh's concern with border-crossing between castes, races and cultures" is presented "in a nutshell" (2011, 328). That it is largely through the interplay between the concealing and revealing of nominal identities that this is accomplished, makes moments of recognition fundamental for the novel's challenge to the permanence of cultural divisions and difference. Interestingly, the predominance of recognitions of identity makes this almost an "orthodox" use of the recognition scene. As I noted in the previous chapter, Aristotle was primarily concerned with recognitions of family and political relations, of nominal identity. Importantly, the "severance from origins" that characterises this kind of recognition plot, "provides the narrative grounding for the ever-present possibility of a monstrous transgression: killing or mating a close relation. Incest and parricide, the themes of the Oedipal paradigm, are at least potential themes in most types of recognition narrative" (Cave 1988, 227). Ghosh exploits this intimate connection between recognition and transgression, destabilizing heteronormative relationships along the lines of caste, race, culture and

---

[20] See Huggan and Tiffin (2010) and Mukherjee (2010).

gender.[21] For several of the characters in the novel, such as Deeti's uncle-in-law, the breaking of these social barriers is indeed a "monstrous transgression". It is for this reason that Deeti and Kalua, who have broken the rules of caste, must hide their identity and flee their village. Similarly, Paulette hides her identity—a white French woman, she successfully passes as Indian—in order to secure passage aboard the *Ibis*. In part through the intimacy of focalization, however, the novel is quite clear that these transgressions are positive; and instead of revealing an accidental transgression, Ghosh's characters intentionally deploy its potentialities. Much of the tension in the novel results from the possibility of exposure, and it is in the climactic revelation of these multiple duplicities and transgressions, when all of the characters are fully revealed while at sea aboard the *Ibis*, that the ethics of this problematizing of social divisions becomes explicit.

The idea of a common humanity, though it becomes explicit towards the end of the novel, underpins the multiple transgressions of cultural norms. It will emerge that in neither *Sea of Poppies* nor *The Hungry Tide* does Ghosh present a simple, or easy, recognition of a common humanity. In keeping with the tension between postmodernism and humanism that Mondal has observed in his work, Ghosh does not minimise the power of social categories—neither in defining one's sense of self, nor as present social realities. Nevertheless, the emphasis in *Sea of Poppies*, more so than in *The Hungry Tide,* is on humanism. There are several relationships in the novel that engage this theme: those between Deeti the pious widow of an opium factory worker and Kalua the low-caste ox-cart driver, Paulette the French botanist's daughter and her Indian childhood companion Jodu, Neel the zamindar and Ah Fatt the opium-addicted prisoner from Canton, and Zachary the American mixed race son of a freed slave and Serang Ali the leader of the lascars and wanted by the law. Throughout the novel, the imagery of rebirth or transformation as concurrent with breaking out of the moulds of social categories and as opening up possibilities for new life, is pervasive and is centred upon the figure of the frigate, the *Ibis*, a ship that has itself undergone a transformation, being refitted from a slave ship to one more fitted for ostensibly freer cargo, namely indentured servants and prisoners. As Hoydis describes it, the *Ibis* is "an

---

21 My focus here is on the norms surrounding caste, race and culture. For an analysis of the destabilising of gender as a result of, in the terms of my analysis, the interplay of concealment and recognition, see Leverton (2014).

equalitarian melting-pot" (2011, 334),[22] establishing what Shao-Pin Luo (2013) terms a "vernacular cosmopolitanism" (379), where the mixing and switching of linguistic codes reflects the "displacement and dislocation, [...] 'unnatural' intermingling and transgression, [...] radical reinvention and transformation" experienced by the characters aboard the *Ibis* (382).[23]

The first transgression of social norms occurs when Deeti recognises Kalua is an individual human being, and not just a shadowy, if intensely embodied, member of a lower caste. Deeti, as a member of a high caste in India, should avoid any physical or eye contact with Kalua who is an untouchable. Their interactions are entirely governed by the rules of caste, a point which is carefully emphasised by the narrator. Thus, when Deeti's opium-disabled husband is climbing onto the ox-cart which Kalua drives to make his living, we are told that Kalua does not help him "and was careful to keep his face hidden from him: he was of the leatherworkers' caste and Hukam Singh [Deeti's husband], as a high-caste Rajput, believed that the sight of his face would bode ill for the day ahead". This is not to say that there are no interactions between the castes. Indeed, Hukam and Kalua converse "amicably enough", but this conversing is completely determined: they do so with "never exchanging glances" (Ghosh 2008, 4).

Circumstances come together in such a way, however, that Deeti violates the rules of caste. One night, walking to the Ganga to refill her water pot, she stumbles across Kalua who is about to be shamed and violated by local landowners. Kalua is a towering, powerful figure, "a man of unusual height and powerful build" (49), but of a "peaceable disposition" (50). Some prominent landowners from their region, using their power and influence, persuade him to wrestle for them—a skill that later in the trilogy will be crucial for sparking another recognition (Ghosh 2015, 372).[24] Mak-

---

[22] For an interesting analysis of the imagery of the ocean within the novel, and its "capacity to liberate the oppressed and to turn land-based assumptions on their head", reinforcing the transformative experience of the passengers of the *Ibis*, see Eckel (2014).
[23] See also, Han (2013).
[24] Ghosh's intentional play with the potentialities of recognition becomes even more overt in this later episode in the trilogy. Kalua is wrestling a soldier whom he doesn't realise is Deeti's brother. Having a sudden moment of recognition, Kalua stops wrestling properly and allows Kesri to win. The nar-

ing the landowners rich and a name for himself, there is soon an invitation to wrestle the champion of "His Highness, the Maharaja of Benares" (50). It is a fight that Kalua loses due to his humiliation by a prostitute the night before. The scene that Deeti stumbles upon is the landowners' moment of exacting revenge.

Hidden among the poppies but witnessing the events, Deeti experiences a powerful emotive resonance between herself and Kalua. Deeti's husband from her arranged marriage is handicapped and an opium addict, with the result that he shows no sexual interest in her whatsoever. Having no clear memories of her wedding night as they are covered by an opium-induced haze, she is nevertheless convinced that her husband did not father her daughter—that in fact she was drugged and then raped by her brother-in-law with the collusion of her mother-in-law. As she watches from her hiding place, the trauma of her rape resonates with the humiliation to which Kalua is being subjected:

> Ever since the night of her wedding, Deeti had been haunted by images of her own violation: now, watching from the shelter of the poppy field, she bit the edge of her palm to keep from crying out aloud. So it could happen to a man too? Even a powerful giant of a man could be humiliated and destroyed, in a way that far exceeded his body's capacity for pain? (53)

As the narrator shifts into narrated monologue we see something of the impact of Deeti's recognition of her own violation in Kalua's;[25] and it is precisely the commonality marked by "too" that gives expression to the reason for Deeti's powerful urge to cry out aloud. In what seems to be a variation, if not a near inversion, of the kind of recognition common in Re-

---

rator's comment: "The reversal of fortune was so inexplicable that it left Kesri feeling strangely grateful to the lascar [Kalua]" (Ghosh 2015, 372), is too close to the link between *anagnorisis* and *peripeteia* (the reversal of fortune) I noted previously to be entirely coincidental.

[25] "Narrated monologue" is Dorrit Cohn's (1983) term, which she prefers over "free indirect style" as it restricts the focus on the narration of characters' interior monologue. She writes, "By implying the correspondence to a (potential) quoted monologue, the more specific name pinpoints a more specific 'thing'" (110).

naissance romances, where knights "prove their personal, chivalric or spiritual identity by performing special feats" (Cave 1988, 228), Kalua's human identity—his commonality with Deeti—is revealed to her through being subjected to an ordeal similarly traumatic to what she herself experienced. In this moment of shared trauma Kalua moves from being determined for Deeti by caste, to being an individual to whom Deeti has a common, emotional link.

The recognition is completed once Deeti has managed to thwart the landowners' plans for Kalua by secretly frightening their horses. She moves over to the unconscious Kalua to check that he is alive. Overcoming the internal resistance of the ingrained norms of caste, Deeti touches Kalua to check for a pulse. She finds one, and, ready to run at the first hint of a return to consciousness, takes a closer look:

> She saw now that his size was deceptive, that he was quite young, with no more than a faint feathering of hair on his upper lip; lying crumpled in the sand, he was no longer the dark giant who called at her home twice a day, without speaking, or allowing himself to be seen: he was just a fallen boy. (54)

Through the emotive commonality of violation, Kalua was first, to Deeti, powerfully ripped out of a general, caste-determined background; here this move becomes more explicit to Deeti's consciousness. No longer is he a vague figure; he is now recognised as a fellow human being. The result is that Deeti proceeds to clean the horse dung off him, an act of care and generosity that contrasts sharply with her usual avoidance of contact, and then lays her hand upon his exposed groin. Soon, though, she realises what she is doing and recoils, returning to the shelter of the field.

The opening created by this emotive, particular disruption of social norms, the recognition of Kalua as a specific individual, is thus closed, but only partially since the moment continues in Deeti's memory, her mind "sharpening the details and refreshing certain particulars" (54). Her act of helping and touching Kalua was also not without consequence; this moment marks a crucial shift in the plot. Unbeknownst to Deeti, there is a mutual affective connection between the two of them, and later Kalua also acts against rules of caste by rescuing Deeti from her husband's funeral pyre and fleeing the community with her, thus setting the two of them on their trajectory towards the *Ibis*. Therefore, in a pattern that will be repeated in the novel, the recognition of Kalua's moral identity—his equal humanity with Deeti—results in the concealing of their nominal identities.

The dissidence in which Deeti and Kalua are involved is importantly characterised in the novel as liberatory. Once Deeti realises that she is still alive, we are told that she

> did not feel herself to be living in the same sense as before: a curious feeling, of joy mixed with resignation, crept into her heart, for it was as if she really had died and been delivered betimes in rebirth, to her next life. (163-164)

Deeti is free to pursue a life without an opium-addicted husband and the continual proximity of her rapist. Despite this sense of rebirth, Deeti and Kalua's transgression of social rules and subsequent exile is difficult and painful. Most obviously, the fact that Deeti must leave her child behind is devastating. There is also a powerful sense of dislocation. When Deeti and Kalua join the barge of indentured servants, she needs to introduce herself, and gives her proper name: Aditi. This is initially a positive moment: "this is who she was—Aditi, a woman who had been granted, by a whim of the gods, the boon of living her life again" (216). When it comes to specifying her caste, however, it is much more difficult. In needing to give a lower caste—Kalua's—she is "confronted with the prospect of cutting herself loose from her moorings in the world"; her caste has always been "as intimate a part of herself as the memory of her daughter's face—but now it seemed as if that too were a part of a past life" (217). It takes several tries for her to designate herself as a different caste, showing the inherent power of social categories to define Deeti's sense of self. Her breaking caste is a painful and dislocating experience, even as it gives her hope and rebirth.

Whereas Deeti and Kalua's freedom is clouded through their becoming indentured servants, the possibility of a new life is more obvious with Zachary, "the charismatic, curly-haired [...] pale-skinned son of a black Baltimore 'freedwoman' and her former master" (Thompson 2008). Having initially joined the crew of the *Ibis* as a carpenter, numerous misfortunes during the voyage result in his elevation through the ranks up to the level of first mate, and he finally arrives in Calcutta as the acting Captain of the ship. Zachary is marked on the ship's manifest as "black". However, Baboo Nob Kissin Pander (another employee of Mr Burnham, Zachary's employer and an important figure for Ghosh's deployment of the thematic of religion, to which I will turn in a moment) causes this knowledge to be temporarily lost through recognizing Zachary as a Guise of Krishna. About to enter the Captains' cabin to request the ship's manifest, Baboo Nob Kissin hears what he thinks to be a flute. Having "been filled with premonitory foreboding" (Ghosh 2008, 133) that his spiritual awakening is at hand he reads the sound of the flute as a sign:

> Was it really a flute, Lord Krishna's own instrument that had started to play [...]? It seemed impossible, but there could be no denying it—just as there was no denying that the tune [...] was set to Gurjari, one of the most favoured ragas for the singing of the Dark Lord's songs. (133)

In this moment of false reasoning, the method by which so many recognitions occur (Cave 1988, 42), Baboo Nob Kissin concludes that whoever is playing the flute—in this case Zachary—is a Guise of Krishna. We have here the recognition of a spiritual identity, although Baboo Nob Kissin begins to have some doubts when he sees that Zachary has pale skin: Krishna's name means "black", and his "darkness had been celebrated in thousands of songs, poems and names" (Ghosh 2008, 134). As with Deeti though, the recognition of a spiritual or moral identity leads to the displacement of a nominal one. Baboo Nob Kissin's confirmation of his spiritual recognition that obscures Zachary's race: when Baboo Nob Kissin reads on the ship's manifest that Zachary is categorised as "black", it was "with a sigh of quiet jubilation that he rested his eyes on the scribbled word that revealed the hand of the Dark Lord" (152–153). The ship manifest, and along with it the knowledge of Zachary's racial categorization, vanishes into Baboo Nob Kissin's possession. The racism that Zachary would have suffered is thus averted, opening up new possibilities: he goes on to become the official second mate of the *Ibis;* another liberatory breach of the divisions of society is achieved.

The lot of Neel Rattan Halder, "an erudite raja brought low by the racist injustices of British rule" (Thompson 2008), and his friendship with Ah Fatt, focuses another bridging of cultural divisions. Although the liberatory aspect is clouded, as with Deeti, due to Neel's imprisonment, there is, nonetheless, a rupture with his moorings in life which is caught up in the figure of rebirth. The recognition of the rebirth in this case is not Neel's own but that of Baboo Nob Kissin (356), though the strong friendship between Neel and Ah Fatt, their refusal to "overmaster" each other (353), in violation of the usual expectations of their captors, does give him something of a glimpse into the new life that Baboo Nob Kissin discerns. It is when we witness in Neel another instance of the strength of cultural determination, however, that we also see most clearly his renewal. Upon his imprisonment, Neel is faced for the first time with the prospect of eating food "prepared by hands of unknown caste" (246). Although he had always professed that he did not believe in caste, and had laid claim to a "lineage of egalitarianism" that stretched through "Buddha, the Mahariva, Shri Chaitanya, Kabit" (246), yet his body resists ingesting the food. Forcing himself to swallow it, he felt "as if he had ingested a handful of burning embers, for he could feel each grain blazing a trail of fire through his entrails", yet he continued eating "until his very skin seemed to be peeling from his body". It is this physical trial of breaking caste that leads to his new life, although he does not expressly recognise it himself, considering his dreams to be "plagued": "That night his dreams were plagued by a vision of himself, transformed into a moulting cobra, a snake that was struggling to free itself of its outworn skin" (247).

Neel is slightly different to Zachary, Deeti and Kalua, as well as Paulette, however, in that there is no overt veiling of his nominal identity. What makes Paulette stand out, in her turn, is that her disguise is the most elaborate, and that she willingly breaks the norms of race and gender in sneaking onto the *Ibis* as an Indian indentured servant. For her, as with Zachary, the benefit is obvious—the ability to escape her restricted life. In her case also, there is the figure of rebirth which she herself provides. The veiling of nominal identities, often the result of the recognition of more spiritual ones, leads these variously oppressed or restricted characters through multiple breaches of societal division and onto the *Ibis*, the looming figure of their transformation. As Paulette and the other women approach the ship, Paulette says to Deeti, "From now on, and forever afterwards, we will all be ship-siblings—*jahazbhais* and *jahazbahens*—to each other. There'll be no differences between us" (328). Deeti's response is important:

This answer was so daring, so ingenious, as to fairly rob the women of their breath. Not in a lifetime of thinking, Deeti knew, would she have stumbled upon an answer so complete, so satisfactory and so thrilling in its possibilities. [...] Yes, said Deeti, from now on, there are no differences between us; we are [...] all of us children of the ship. (328)[26]

"No differences between us": here we have, with their arrival at the *Ibis*, the beginning of the birth to which the breaches of societal divisions and norms were the labour pains. As one reviewer put it, the *Ibis*

is the slave vessel that brings Zachary, the son of a slave, his status in a white world [....] It is the jail that finally frees Neel. It is in the hold [...] that a Frenchwoman finds her true identity in an Indian disguise and that an oppressed Indian victim of rape is transformed into a woman of courage and leadership. (Schine 2009)

The escape from the divisions of this world is an image that is repeated several times aboard the *Ibis* through the recognitions of the hidden identities, primarily Zachary's. There are two people who recognise his identity, both of whom learn the fact through Baboo Nob Kissin. The first, and earlier in the narrative, is Paulette, though she keeps her knowledge secret until her later conversation with Zachary. In the final sequences, as she is disclosing her knowledge to him, which is for Zachary a double recognition (of Paulette as well as of her knowledge of him), Baboo Nob Kissin reveals Zachary's secret, accidentally this time, to Mr Crowle the first mate. These multiple recognitions in quick succession, occurring shortly after the exposure of Deeti and Kalua's nominal identities, are the final revelations in the novel's climax and bring matters to a head between Mr Crowle and Zachary—who now knows that Zachary is cate-

---

[26] That it is Paulette (as an educated European) who suggests the idea, echoes the challenge noted in the introduction of negotiating the legacy of colonialism in the use of humanistic, Enlightenment ideals. That it is not soley a legacy of colonialism, however, is reflected in Neel's Indian "lineage of egalitarianism" (246).

gorised as "black" and intends to use the information to bend him to his will—as well as between Zachary and Paulette.

What is significant is the subversion of what Baboo Nob Kissin calls the "illusory differences of this world" (Ghosh 2008, 461). Through the interplay of concealing and revealing identities, the recognition of moral or spiritual identities resulting in the concealment of nominal ones, numerous cultural divisions are bridged. The results are affective connections that defy societal norms: Deeti and Kalua get married; romance blossoms between Paulette and Zachary; a friendship flourishes between Zachary and Serang Ali; and Neel and Ah Fatt become strong friends, defying the expectations of their guards. Part of Paulette and Zachary's conversation is salient with respect to this, building upon the conversation between the women noted above. The two of them are speaking in Zachary's cabin, after his double recognition. Paulette offers the following insight:

> What does it matter, Mr Reid? [...] Are not all appearances deceptive, in the end? Whatever there is within us—whether good, or bad, or neither—its existence will continue uninterrupted, will it not, no matter what the drape of our clothes, or the colour of our skin? What if it is the world that is a duperie, Mr Reid, and we the exceptions to its lies? (459)

Zachary does not agree at this point. As we have seen, the experiences of the individual characters show that it is precisely not the case that "whatever there is within us" continues "uninterrupted". This is also confirmed through the organizing metaphor of rebirth: the bridging of cultural divisions and categories has been a matter of transforming the characters' sense of self. We might say, then, that the qualified version presented by the novel is that the self can continue, but somewhat altered due to very real interruption. And indeed, shortly after this, Zachary comes to a similar, if slightly less idealistic, realization in his encounter with Mr Crowle, when he is struck by the "delirium of the world" in which a single word, "black", "could be invested with so much authority" (465).

Freedom from cultural differences is repeated by Baboo Nob Kissin moments later as he rejoices in becoming "the key that could unlock the cages that imprisoned everyone, all these beings who were ensnared by the illusory differences of this world" (461). This understanding is continually reiterated while the characters are aboard the ship. And while the bridging of cultural categories of difference is not as easy as Paulette seems to think, the main characters nevertheless have some measure of success in doing so. The relationships and possibilities that are birthed on the *Ibis* are aptly described by Zachary's insight into his relationship with Serang Ali:

> he saw now that it was a rare, difficult and improbable thing for two people from worlds apart to find themselves linked by a tie of pure sympathy, a feeling that owed nothing to the rules and expectations of others. He understood also that when such a bond comes into being, its truths and falsehoods, its obligations and privileges, exist only for the people who are linked by it, and then in such a way that only they can judge the honour and dishonour of how they conduct themselves in relation to each other. (403)

Adumbrated here is a fluid and contingent relation to the other person, not specified by the "rules and expectations of others" or the "illusory differences of the world", but by the relationship itself. At the close of the novel we have seen a "slave ship bringing freedom to an unlikely group of people" (Schine 2009), variously dispossessed and forming a transformed, undetermined group; each remains burdened, but also possesses the possibility of self-regeneration.

In her analysis of the novel, Hoydis argues that "the repeated emphasis on the *Ibis* as an equalitarian melting-pot and Ghosh's use of the metaphor sometimes scratches the borders of the pathetic or the too obvious" (2011, 334). Indeed, it does seem at first that Ghosh is being rather heavy-handed in his treatment of the transformation of his characters. A more nuanced unfolding of characters' passing through transformative experiences is achieved in *The Hungry Tide* (Hoydis 2011, 334). However, this neglects a crucial element of the novel. I noted above that when Ghosh addresses the question of religion, it is usually either in terms of syncretism or a critique of hypocrisy. The latter is certainly present in *Sea of Poppies*: When Burnham is speaking about the possibility of invading China in order to secure the continued openness of Chinese markets to opium, he says,

> It will be for a principle: for freedom—for the freedom of trade and for the freedom of the Chinese people. Free Trade is a right conferred on Man by God, and its principles apply as much to opium as to any other article of trade. (Ghosh 2008, 106)

The complicity of religion with colonialism is thus rendered quite explicit, and is consequently critiqued throughout the novel. An instance of this is Captain Chillingworth's denouncement of the war: "The truth is, sir, that men do what their power permits them to do. We are no different from the Pharaohs or the Mongols: the difference is only that when we kill people we feel compelled to pretend that it is for some higher cause. It is this *pretence of virtue*, I promise you, that will never be forgiven by history" (242, my emphasis). In addition to this, Hoydis suggests that the *Ibis* itself is "a symbol of religious syncretism" because of the babble of prayers from numerous faiths that "resonates" throughout the ship when it enters the open seas (Hoydis 2011, 332).

While I concur that *Sea of Poppies* continues Ghosh's previous approach to religion, the novel also possesses something of a mythic character. Opened by Deeti's vision of the *Ibis* and of Zachary aboard her, it closes with Zachary locking eyes with Deeti for the first time and recognizing her. Alongside this symmetry there is, as Hoydis notes, "much greater authorial control" than in Ghosh's other novels, which makes the often traumatic events that befall the characters seem "purposeful rather than as random coincidences" (Hoydis 2011, 336); indeed, one might rephrase Hoydis' point to say that the characters are made to seem subject to fate, rather than chance. This picture of fate and visions is filled out further when we consider the character of Baboo Nob Kissin. Throughout the narrative, he is beginning to manifest his deceased female guru Taramony. This process comes to fruition aboard the *Ibis*: "Now that Taramony's presence was fully manifest in him, it was as if he had become the key that could unlock the cages that imprisoned everyone" (Ghosh 2008, 461). I have already noted that Baboo Nob Kissin's declaration of the "illusory differences of this world" is one of the ethical points of the novel. Yet what is intriguing is that he is completely correct: crucial as he is for bringing the characters together and in freeing those who were imprisoned, he is indeed "the key".

These features of the novel work to cast Ghosh's metaphorical heavy-handedness in a new light: it can be understood as part of this mythic quality of the narrative. And that the novel is structured in this way adds an additional layer to its ethical sense: a tale of transformation and of a common humanity that endures the differences of the world, it is told in a manner that resonates with religious discourse. That is to say, although the humanism that is conveyed is fairly proximate to the secular ideal, it is presented in a way that unsettles secular, modern discourse. In a fashion not dissimilar to what will be observed in *The Hungry Tide*, Ghosh renders the form of the novel somewhat "improper" (Mukherjee 2010, 121), imbuing it with a form of syncretism that, while congruent with Ghosh's earlier engagement with religion, also opens up fascinating possibilities for ways in which to negotiate the conflict between the affirmation and simultaneous critique of Enlightenment thought outlined in the previous chapter.

II

The Hungry Tide, as with *Sea of Poppies*, is concerned with the question of a common humanity. Crucially, however, it includes two ethical concerns that are not present in *Sea of Poppies*. As Julia Hoydis (2011) rightly notes, the distinguishing feature of *The Hungry Tide* in Ghosh's oeuvre is the concern with the clash between human interests and nature, and as such it poses a question "most often sidelined in conservation drives" (Anand 2008, 35), namely the impact of conservation on local people. At the core of Ghosh's exploration of this dilemma are the events of the 1979 Morichjhāpi massacre.

The Sundarbans, where Morichjhāpi is located, is a vast archipelago of mangrove forests, covering "an area of 10,000 square kilometres, sprawling across India and Bangladesh" (Anand 2008, 25). Nirmal, one of the central characters of the novel, describes it as "interposed between the sea and the plains of Bengal [...] the islands are the trailing threads of India's fabric, the ragged fringe of her sari, the *āchol* that follows her, half-wetted by the sea" (Ghosh 2005a, 6). It is a place of continuously shifting geography, the countless channels and rivers in their meeting and parting giving evanescent shape to thousands of islands, submerging nearly all of them at every high tide; "some have lasted through recorded history while others were washed into being just a year or two ago" (7). The Indian part of the region is home to about 245 tigers and seven million people, and was declared a tiger reserve in 1973, becoming a national park in 1984 (Anand 2008, 25). It is an area of extreme poverty; as Upamanyu Mukherjee (2010) puts it, the "*Sundarbans* of majestic tigers and mysterious forests", exists alongside the "*Sundarbans* of unremitting poverty, human and non-human immiseration, government neglect and oppression" (108).

In 1978 around thirty thousand low-caste refugees from Bangladesh settled on Morichjhāpi (Anand 2008; Mukherjee 2010). Although it was the rhetoric of the Communist Party of India (CPI[M]) that had encouraged the refugees to settle there (Anand 2008, 31), upon ascending to power in 1978 the CPI(M) effected a "fast and vicious reversal of its line on the refugees", demanding that they evacuate from the region (Mukherjee 2010, 110). The official reason for the demand was that Morichjhāpi was a part of the protected forest and tiger reserve, which the settlers were violating. That this alleged environmental concern merely served as an alibi can be seen in that the

> Island of Morichjhāpi was part of the Sundarbans Forest Reserve, but the mangrove vegetation was cleared in 1975 by the Congress government to make way for the revenue-generating coconut and tamarisk plantations. The island was also not part of the core area of the tiger reserve. (Anand 2008, 31)

Nevertheless, in early 1979 the government instituted a blockade of the island in an attempt to starve the settlers out. On 14 May 1979, when the settlers still refused to leave, the government ordered the police force, together with hired thugs, to forcefully remove them (Anand 2008, 32; Mukherjee 2010, 111). Over the next two days, this force "moved in on Morichjhāpi, systematically raping, killing and burning houses" (Mukherjee 2010, 111). Due to unreliable data and the lack of an official inquiry it is impossible to know how many people were killed; estimates range from five to fifteen thousand (Mukherjee 2010, 111; Anand 2008, 33).

While the government's motives for ordering the evacuation of Morichjhāpi are suspect, the novel is constructed in such a way so as to present the massacre as the confluence of environmental protection initiatives and the deadly fight for survival between humans and tigers within the Sundarbans. The novel tells the story of Piya Roy, an American cetologist of Bengali descent, and Kanai Dutt, an Indian middle-class translator and businessman from Delhi, as they journey into the Sundarbans and their separate lives intertwine. Piya is in search of an endangered species of river dolphin, the *Orcaella brevirostris* or the Irrawaddy dolphin, while Kanai is en route to visit his aunt Nilima who lives on the (fictional) island of Lusibari in order to read through some papers left for him by his late uncle Nirmal. That Piya is a conservationist begins to bring this conflict between human and non-human to the fore; that the papers left for Kanai, which form a substantial sub-narrative to his own, is Nirmal's diary of the events leading up to the massacre in the name of conservation, makes it explicit (Anand 2008, 24). Piya and Kanai thus establish the two sides to this conflict as formally constitutive of the novel. Thematically, we learn from Piya that the dolphins are suffering a "dramatic deterioration" of their habitat (Ghosh 2005a, 266), and we witness the killing of a tiger by the inhabitants of one of the villages in the area as it preys on their livestock. Additionally, Nirmal writes in his diary,

> I remembered how when I first came to Lusibari, the sky would be darkened by birds at sunset. Many years had passed since I'd seen such flights of birds. When I first noticed their absence, I thought they would soon come back but they had not. I remembered a time when at low tide the mudbanks would turn scarlet with millions of swarming crabs. That colour began to fade long ago and now it is never seen any more. Where had they gone, I wondered, those millions of swarming crabs, those birds? Age teaches you to recognize the signs of death. (215)

The Sundarbans are in an ecological crisis, and the novel gives vivid representation to both the plight of the humans and the non-humans. As Anand astutely notes, the idea of hunger in the title signals the locus of this conflict: "Whose hunger is to be privileged? The hunger of the poor, who are struggling to eke out a living [...] or the tiger, losing its habitat, threatened by poaching and on the verge of extinction?" (2008, 35).

With the massacre as central to the novel, *The Hungry Tide* further raises the question of the ethics of remembering historical trauma and violence. As with *Sea of Poppies*, the main thrust of this ethical concern, as Terri Tomsky suggests, is "to recuperate suppressed subaltern histories and to advance their calls for social justice" (2009, 54). After having occurred, the incident slipped below the horizon: there was very limited coverage of the tragedy, the Prime Minister of the time failed to pursue the matter, and the Scheduled Castes and Tribes Commission, "responsible for ensuring the well being of the lower castes" concluded that "there were no human rights violations or atrocities committed in Morichjhãpi even though their file contained newspaper clippings, petitions and names and ages of 236 men, women, and children killed by the police at Marichjhapi prior to the massacre" (Anand 2008, 33). The novel can, therefore, quite rightly be seen as engaged in remembering neglected stories, of "writing historically about pasts that could not have been articulated through historical discourse in the first place" (Mondal 2007, 162). However, this work of remembering extends beyond the recollection of the incident itself to an engagement with the validity of a different understanding of and epistemic approach to the world, an engagement that is crucial to the transformation of the elite characters in the novel. I will spend some time on these transformations, focusing particularly on Kanai and Nirmal, which will, in turn, return us to the recognition of a common humanity and the tragic conflict of values seen in the tension between the human and the non-human.

The importance of transformation to the ethical sense of the novel is implied in the description of the Sundarbans, which is itself in a constant state of flux, of transformation: "There are no borders here to divide fresh water from salt, river from sea" (Ghosh 2005a, 7); borders in the Sundarbans are transient, the islands shifting their shape and size according to the water's flow. And it is not only between land and water, salt water and fresh, that the borders are porous and shifting. The tide country, as it is called, is simultaneously a place of despair and of hope; the rankings of caste or religious demarcations are nearly non-existent; and the myth of Bon Bibi, which articulates the area's fear and hope, is a hybrid result of the confluence of various languages and belief systems. This rural, poverty-stricken place is, in fact, remarkably cosmopolitan (Johansen 2008), and this hybrid, fluid nature of the tide country serves as the image for this central concern. As Saswat Das (2006) puts it, the "river [...] respects no boundaries or culture, washing ashore myriad possibilities only to dissolve them in its abysmal depth" (181).

A further reinforcement of this theme of transformation can be seen through Nirmal's citations of Rilke's *Duino Elegies*. Hoydis argues that the tension between despair and hope, that I suggest is mythologised in the legend of Bon Bibi, is also reflected in the poems which "comprise the novel's main themes in a nutshell" (2011, 309). Of particular importance is when Nirmal's reading of Rilke coincides with the fluctuating nature of the Sundarbans. Recounting a journey with Kusum, Fokir and Horen to the island of Garjontola in order to visit a shrine to Bon Bibi, Nirmal begins to realise the discursive richness of the jungle. Rather than being "an emptiness, a place where time stood still", it is in fact the opposite:

> What was happening here, I realized, was that the wheel of time was spinning too fast to be seen. In other places it took decades, even centuries, for a river to change course; it took an epoch for an island to disappear. But here, in the tide country, transformation is the rule of life: rivers stray from week to week, and islands are unmade in days [....] It is as if the whole tide country were speaking in the voice of the poet: 'life is lived in transformation'. (Ghosh 2005a, 224,225)

This continuous transformation, in Hoydis's words, "becomes Nirmal's credo" (2011, 309). It also extends beyond Nirmal's private reflections as each of the privileged characters in the novel undergoes transformation. Crucial for this, and more significant than Rilke's poetry, is that they "encounter a series of heterogeneous cultural texts—songs, folk tales, oral histories and, most crucially, *Jatra* [a hybrid form of folk theatre]"; it is, in part, through encountering "challenging counter-narratives" that their transformation is achieved. (Mukherjee 2010, 122) It is also, as Tomsky (2009) argues, through powerful emotional responses.

Mukherjee and Tomsky both consider the (connected) transformations of Nirmal and Kanai. For Mukherjee, Nirmal's transformation consists in learning "to imagine himself through the eyes of others—human and non-human" (2010, 123). His conversations with Horen play an important part in accomplishing this. In reading to him about European adventures in Bengal, "Nirmal assumes he is enlightening the illiterate Horen about the ebbs and flows of history as they are charted by the canonical knowledge contained in a European text". Horen, however, continuously interrupts Nirmal's reading with his own accounts of the same territory. Over time, Nirmal's position shifts to the realization that "he can learn more from people like Horen and Kusum than from liberal imperialists" (122), a shift that is later confirmed before the blockade of Morichjhāpi. During a journey with Kusum, Horen and Fokir to visit the shrine on Garjontola, he listens to Horen pray to Bon Bibi at the shrine and is amazed at "hearing these Arabic invocations" (Ghosh 2005a, 246); his amazement deepens when he is given a pamphlet from which the prayer is taken: "the pages opened to the right, as in Arabic, not to the left, as in Bangla. Yet the prosody was that of much of Bangla folklore" (247). What seems to be crucial for Mukherjee in this moment is Nirmal's admission that he was completely taken by his recognition of the complex hybridity of the Bon Bibi myth (Mukherjee 2010, 123). As such, it marks and confirms a crucial shift in Nirmal's way of thinking.

While this seems to be correct, it is necessary to supplement it with Tomsky's observations. Of interest to her is the emotional aspect of Nirmal's involvement with Morichjhāpi. Nirmal's intellectual recognition is crucial, but there is an important emotional corollary to it: Kusum. Nirmal describes her as his "muse", rivalling his desire for his life with his wife: "I felt myself torn between my wife and the woman who had become the muse I'd never had; between the quiet persistence of everyday change and the heady excitement of revolution—between prose and poetry" (Ghosh 2005a, 216). Nirmal is a poet and idealistic socialist, making his choice to identify with the refugees not entirely surprising. What Tomsky (2009) notes is the role of Nirmal's emotions for this: "One might ask whether the cause of Morichjhāpi would energize Nirmal in the same way if he were not nostalgically attached to the idea of revolutions, or infatuated with Kusum". While she agrees the novel establishes as important that "one's own sedimented norms are [...] perceived and then overturned", this is tightly knit with and enabled by his "complex affective experiences that arise from [Kusum's] proximity and his exposure to the galvanizing atmosphere and energies of Morichjhāpi's community" (59).[27]

---

[27] See also Hoydis (2011, 313–319).

Through Nirmal's notebook being passed on to Kanai, it is he "who most explicitly assumes the burden of Nirmal's experience" (Mukherjee 2010, 123). While Kanai is reading the notebook, we are told that he recollects seeing in his childhood a *Jatra* performance of the same Bon Bibi myth that Nirmal heard and read. The Nirmal of Kanai's childhood memory is very different from the Nirmal of the notebook, as he denigrates the story as telling of "imaginary miracles of gods and saints" which diverts the locals' attention from "the true wonders of the reality surrounding them" (Ghosh 2005a, 102). For the young Kanai, however, the experience of the *Jatra* is a riveting, emotional one that is marked by the same realization of hybridity and complexity as Nirmal's later one. Although we can surmise that the performance had a minimal lasting impact on Kanai when he first saw it, Mukherjee suggests that the recollection sparked by Nirmal's notebook has a transforming effect: "Like Nirmal, these memories of a multicultural, polyglot *Jatra* lead Kanai to accept that the culture of the *Sundarbans*, like its geography, is composed of diverse worldly currents that dispute the contemporary Euro-centric notions of modernity and globalization" (2010, 124).

The difficulty with Mukherjee's argument here is that at this moment of recollection Kanai remains largely unchanged. He has only just begun reading his uncle's notebook, and the recollection is presumably sparked by Nirmal's plea for him to read the account: "If not for my sake, then for [Kusum's], read on" (Ghosh 2005a, 69). Later, when Piya and Fokir arrive in Lusibari, we witness the continued presence of his perceived (metropolitan) superiority to (the rural) Fokir in the condescending manner in which he addresses him: "it was the kind of tone in which someone might address a dim-witted waiter, at once jocular and hectoring" (210). Rather than being transformed through his recollection of the *Jatra*, it seems more likely that the memory is caught up in the powerful effect of Nirmal's account of his own: it is shortly after this revealing meeting with Fokir that Kanai reads Nirmal's account of his wonder at the Bon Bibi story. As Tomsky argues, the notebook has a transforming, interrupting effect on Kanai since it "carries within it an affective surplus that leaves its distinctive imprint on Kanai, as it communicates a traumatic history" (2009, 60).

The importance of both the intellectual and emotional impact of the diary on Kanai becomes clearer shortly after he has completed reading it: Kanai's "hands were shaking" when he is finished reading (278), revealing the diary's emotional impact upon him. And it is only after finishing it that Kanai's moment of recognition occurs, when Fokir takes Kanai to Garjontola, the same island of Nirmal's own epiphany. Whereas Nirmal's experience of the island was peaceful—though laced with fear of encountering a tiger—Kanai's is rather more dramatic, what Giles (2014) describes as an experience of the postcolonial sublime because language fails Kanai when he is confronted with the inexpressible reality and fear of the tiger (232). Mukherjee describes the situation succinctly when he notes, "For Fokir, the island holds no fear for those who are pure at heart, but the impure are sure to be punished by the servant of the forest deity—the tiger" (Mukherjee 2010, 128). When Kanai becomes enraged at Fokir he is revealed as holding within himself what was implied in his earlier condescending tone toward Fokir: "the master's suspicion of the menial; the pride of caste; the townsman's mistrust of the rustic; the city's antagonism towards the village" (Ghosh 2005a, 326). As such, the island becomes the scene of his judgement and self-recognition:

> In Kanai's professional life there had been a few instances in which the act of interpreting had given him the momentary sensation of being transported out of his body and into another. [...] it was exactly this feeling that came upon him as he looked at Fokir: it was as though his own vision were being refracted through those opaque, unreadable eyes and he were seeing not himself [...] but a great host of people—a double for the outside world, someone standing in for the men who had destroyed Fokir's village, burnt his home and killed his mother; he had become a token for a vision of human beings in which men such as Fokir counted for nothing, a man whose value was less than that of an animal. [...] Fokir had brought him here not because he wanted him to die, but because he wanted him to be judged. (327)

I will return to this critical moment in more depth further on, but here we can note that Kanai recognises himself as complicit with the "vision of human beings" that enabled the Morichjhāpi massacre to occur; he recognises his complicity with the injustice, and has it forcefully driven home by feeling himself to be judged. And indeed, in his terror, in a "flood of pure sensation" (328), he sees the custodian of judgement: a tiger.

Mukherjee argues convincingly that this scene (among others) bears some formal characteristics of *Jatra*, namely "heightened emotive language, mythic morality and judgement, the forest goddess and the tiger" (2010, 128). Their effect is to render the form of the novel "improper" (121), producing in the readers an effect similar to seeing the performance of a *Jatra*—indeed, it is almost as if Kanai has in this scene entered the story of Bon Bibi. As a result of the "formal mixture of psychological realism [...] and the highly melodramatic and theatrical", there is a "shifting of the privileged normative cosmopolitan or metropolitan point of view in the novel to that of the local or provincial", a shift that needs to be negotiated by the reader for whom the possibility is thus opened up to learn the "same lesson" (129) as Kanai, namely, "Learning to see oneself with other eyes, eyes that belong to the lost and the broken" (128).

While Kanai's lesson is important, before discussing it I want to stress what Mukherjee calls the scene's psychological realism. What makes this moment intriguing, and emphasises the emotive aspect of Kanai's feeling of being judged, is that this is not his first realization of complicity. In the time between reading Nirmal's notebook and this recognition scene, Piya and Kanai witness a village killing a tiger. In the resulting debate, Kanai argues that he and Piya are complicit in enforcing wildlife protection that has no thought or regard for the large number of human lives taken by tigers and affected by the conservation: "It's not hard to ignore the people who're dying—after all, they are the poorest of the poor" (Ghosh 2005a, 301). Kanai can thus be seen to already possess a certain amount of self-recognition as the result of reading Nirmal's diary. On Garjontola, however, it emerges that this is only the first step to his more powerful, emotionally dramatic recognition which includes his personal complicity in the more heinous offense of the Morichjhāpi incident, and is focused not on a general category of "the poorest of the poor" but on the specific person of Fokir, indicating the importance of affective connections for recognition.

The importance of Fokir for Kanai's *anagnorisis* brings us to the ethical theme that underpins all of the transformations in the novel. As has been noted before,[28] *The Hungry Tide* presents a form of humanism, a common humanity, that enables the bridging of differences between people as the transformation of Nirmal and Kanai illustrate. An important scene where this becomes overtly thematised occurs early in the novel. As a result of the misfortunes that mark Piya's first days in the region, she finds herself sharing a small boat with a local fisherman and his son, Fokir and Tutul, respectively. Neither of them can speak any English, the only language that Piya knows, making verbal communication impossible. They nevertheless manage to strike up a form of communication through gestures. There are two moments of importance. The first is shortly after Fokir has rescued Piya from the river. As the launch with the corrupt forest guard, from which she fell into the river, begins to disappear, the shock of her experience sets in and she is suddenly shaking hard enough to rock the small boat:

> There was a touch on her shoulder and she turned sideways to see the child [Tutul], standing beside her. He put his arm around her and clung to her back, hugging her, trying to warm her body with his own. She closed her eyes and did not open them again until the chattering of her teeth had stopped. (63)

Tutul's gesture of warmth and assistance is remarkable, cutting across any barrier or hesitation that might be expected between strangers. The child's unconditional acceptance is distinct from Fokir's, and we are quickly made aware that it is Tutul's presence that helps Piya to trust Fokir; she describes him as her "protector" (64).

It is not long, though, before this changes, a crucial moment for which is Piya's realization of Fokir's own recognition of their fellow humanity. Fokir creates a small enclosure on his canoe for Piya to change in, and she finds the gesture particularly moving:

> It was not just that he had thought to create a space for her; it was as if he had chosen to include her in some simple, practised family ritual, found a way to let her know that despite the ines-

---

[28] See for instance Hoydis (2011), Rollasson (2011), Huggan & Tiffin (2007), and Hawley (2005).

> capable muteness of their exchanges, she was a person to him and not, as it were, a representative of a species, a faceless, tongueless foreigner. But where had this recognition come from? He had probably never met anyone like her before, any more than she had ever met anyone like him. (71)

Hoydis argues that Fokir's concern for Piya here expresses "a 'humanism of the other' in Levinas's sense", primarily because it "seems to precede comprehension" (2011, 314). This is unconvincing, however, since although Fokir's action precedes *familiarity*, it does not precede comprehension: from the moment that he engaged with Piya and the forest guard their relation would have been comprehended in terms of power relations, and class and linguistic distinctions, precisely those barriers that are overcome through characters' transformations. A Levinasian understanding locates the ethical relation of the face-to-face as preceding—but not chronologically prior to—this determination of their interactions, and present only as a trace. Nevertheless, while this passage is not strictly a Levinasian moment as Hoydis thinks, she is right in noting the acknowledgement of Piya's singular personhood; Fokir's recognition here is remarkable precisely because he consciously relates to Piya as a fellow person, resisting the determinations of which the contours of Piya's surprise—"not, as it were, a representative of a species, a faceless, tongueless foreigner"—shows that she is aware.

This recognition of a common humanity is not, as has sometimes been suggested,[29] simply straightforward and uncomplicated. Hawley (2005) argues that *The Hungry Tide* reveals the "transient nature of the division between individuals" (132). However, the ease that is implied here is misleading. As in *Sea of Poppies* the "illusory differences of this world" are not painlessly discarded or overcome (Ghosh 2008, 461). What is required to bridge the division between individuals is a frequently painful change—on the part, especially, of the metropolitan elites (Mukherjee 2010, 117). Thus, Kanai dramatically and somewhat traumatically moves from viewing Fokir as a hindrance to his wife and son as they seek to advance in the world, to his recognition noted above which ultimately leads him to restructure his business so that he can move to Kolkata to write

---

[29] See Hoydis's discussion of Rollasson (2011).

Nirmal's story. There are also two further moments of recognition, however, that complicate the idea of a common humanity as such.

The first of these occurs between Kanai and Kusum, the first time they meet. It is during a gathering of the women of Lusibari and one woman is recounting a story of brutal violence suffered at the hands of a father-in-law and his family. Kanai is eavesdropping, and remains undetected except by Kusum:

> Kanai and Kusum held each other's gaze, and for the duration of that moment it was as though they were staring across the most primeval divide in creation [...] it seemed scarcely imaginable that here, in the gap that separated them, lay the potential for these extremes of emotion, this violence. (Ghosh 2005a, 91)

The context of gender violence in which this occurs suggests that "the gap" is, in one sense, the difference of gender. While the violence that results from the distance between individuals has definite gendered dimensions, what I understand to be recognised here is something more fundamental—namely, the ultimately unbridgeable dissonance between selves that leads Levinas to describe the relation to another self as a relation to infinity: the other person always exceed the idea you have of them in the same way that infinity always exceeds whatever conception you have of it. In Kanai and Kusum's case the "mystery" of "the gap that separated them" awakens their curiosity (91). Yet there is a recognition that it is the ultimately unbreakable silence between selves which can give rise to "these extremes of emotion, this violence"; there is always the possibility for the spaces between individuals to be bridged by violence rather than by recognition and compassion. Confirmation of this deeper recognition can be seen when Piya concludes that her mute relation to Fokir is, in its silence, more honest.

> In contrast [to the way that for dolphins "to 'see' was also to 'speak'," "to exist was to communicate"], there was the immeasurable distance that separated her from Fokir. What was he thinking about as he stared at the moonlit river? [....] Whatever it was, she would never know: not just because they had no language in common but because that was how it was with human

> beings, who came equipped, as a species, with the means of shutting each other out. [...] and wasn't it better in a way, more honest, that they could not speak? [...] speech was only a bag of tricks that fooled you into believing that you could see through the eyes of another being. (159)

Speech cannot break this epistemic silence between people, cannot successfully bridge the gap; it can only give the illusion of doing so.[30] That Piya's reflections here are general also problematises Victor Li's (2009) argument that *The Hungry Tide* seals its subaltern characters into an impenetrable silence through their deaths, thus ensuring "that the idea of subalternity may live on in a non-subaltern future" (290). Li's argument here is part of a larger critique of works "in which the loss or death of subalterns leads in turn to the immortalization of the dead subaltern as representing the idea of resistance and utopian difference"—a pattern he dubs a "logic of sacrifice" (282): the subaltern characters do not survive into the new future. While he is correct in noting the silence between the metropolitan and subaltern characters, what is missed, apart from the fact that Fokir is not the only subaltern character, is that in Piya's experience with Fokir he does not simply represent unreachable difference. Rather, the difference which he does represent reveals to Piya the broader reality of the gap which exists between all individuals—hence, her insight that language only gives the illusion of true connection. Throughout the novel, then, there is the experienced necessity of recognizing an individual as specific, and the related need to bridge the gap between persons with transforming recognitions and compassion, alongside a simultaneous recognition of the limits of knowledge between other people, of the impossibility of ever truly grasping another self, and the consequent possibility of violence that ultimately haunts each relation. The novel thus does not represent a naïve move towards a more humanistic understanding of

---

[30] This doubles back, of course, onto Kanai's recognition discussed earlier, where he sees himself through Fokir's eyes. That Piya's reflections here suggest this might not actually be what Fokir is thinking/seeing is, however, irrelevant. Kanai's self-recognition succeeds because he recognises himself in what he thinks Fokir sees—regardless of whether that is accurate or not. In other words, Fokir's state of mind is not the predicate of the recognition, just part of the "false reasoning", in Aristotle's terms, that sparks it.

relating to another person; there is the awareness that this relation can be undone by the very same gap that makes it possible and necessary.

These recognitions and transformations that I have detailed are closely connected to the Morichjhãpi incident, and are thus central to the novel's framing ethical theme of conflict between the human and the non-human. I argued above that the novel establishes a clear conflict, despite the duplicity of the government in citing environmental protection as their reason for clearing Morichjhãpi. A number of critics, in addition to Anand who I discussed above, have commented on this tension. The most prominent are Anshuman Mondal (2007) and Graham Huggan and Helen Tiffin (2007; 2010). In both readings of the novel, there is a distinct lack of a resolution to the conflict that is so vividly evoked.[31] Both also consider a crucial moment of the conflict between human and non-human, which will provide a good place to begin.

Piya, Kanai, Horen and Fokir are together on the river when they learn of a commotion in a nearby village. A tiger has entered the village and clawed its way through the roof of the hut that is the livestock pen in order to feed on a newly born calf. The villagers realise that

> for the few minutes it was in the pen, it was vulnerable, because to make its escape it would have to leap vertically through the hole in the roof. Even for a tiger, this would not be a simple feat, not with a calf in its jaws. (Ghosh 2005a, 292)

This tiger has killed two people from the village and has been successfully preying on the villagers' livestock for a long time. Seizing their opportunity, the villagers trap the tiger in the hut with nets and begin to stab into its interior with sharpened staves, trying to kill it. It is not long before someone sets the pen alight, proceeding to burn the tiger alive. As Huggan and Tiffin comment, this is "a traumatic scene of death and torture that the reader is forced to witness through Piya's horrified eyes" (Huggan and Tiffin 2007, 5). This is not, however, an unbalanced portrayal, which weights the novel in favour of the tiger. The vividness of this violence against the tiger is matched when Kusum recounts to a young Kanai that

---

31 For examples of other critics who likewise consider the conflict largely unresolved, see Anand (2008) and Hoydis (2011).

she witnessed her father's death by a tiger. Although she shut her eyes, she still heard everything:

> the roar that froze her father; she heard his cry for help—*bachao!* She heard the sound of his bones cracking as the animal swiped a paw across his neck; she heard the rustle of the mangrove as the animal dragged the corpse into the forest. (Ghosh 2005a, 109)

When it is thus reported that two people from the village have been killed by the tiger, Kusum's trauma is recalled. What we have in this scene of the tiger killing, then, is a representative moment of the clash between the human and non-human.

For Huggan and Tiffin, Piya's horror at the brutal killing of the tiger, and her attempted intervention, is "based, it is suggested, on a sentimentality that fails to take into consideration the large number of people whose lives have been taken by tigers in the past". They therefore conclude that for Ghosh, "People [...] must necessarily take precedence over animals" (Huggan and Tiffin 2007, 5). While Huggan and Tiffin are, to a certain extent, correct, it is not this scene that suggests such a reading. Mondal is surely right to assert that Ghosh at this point actually sharpens the conflict (Mondal 2007, 177–178). While Kanai does say that Piya fails to understand what is transpiring, the two of them debate the topic again the next day. It is crucial moment, where the two narrative threads that I noted earlier—Piya expressing the conservationist perspective and Kanai, through Nirmal, the villagers'—enter into explicit dialogue. In the debate, Kanai reiterates his argument that Piya does not appreciate that the tiger killed by the villagers had been preying on them and their livestock. Piya's retort that "everywhere in the world dozens of people are killed every day—on roads, in cars, in traffic" is countered by Kanai's confession of complicity noted above in discussing his recognition (Ghosh 2005a, 301): there are so many deaths because conservation efforts are pushed through without thought for the human costs. Piya's own response is to assert that the importance of conservation is fundamentally connected to humanity's well being, especially those who Kanai is concerned about:

Just suppose we crossed that imaginary line that prevents us from deciding that no other species matters except ourselves. What'll be left then? Aren't we alone enough in the universe? And do you think it'll stop at that? Once we decide we can kill off other species, it'll be people next—just the kind of people you're thinking of, people who're poor and unnoticed. (301)

The debate ends soon after this, seemingly with no final conclusion, though Piya has had the final word.

For Mondal, the inconclusiveness of the debate shows that the "the novel does not offer a resolution; its position is ambivalent, but this lack of resolution is precisely what opens up the ethical debate" (Mondal 2007, 178). It is, he argues, because Ghosh does not wish to subsume the ethical under the political, under the need for decisive action, that he leaves the debate open (173), and this ambivalence is "the register of an ethics that recognises the inescapable duality and impossible paradox of the post-colonial predicament" (174). The ethics that Mondal outlines here is quite close to what I argued for in the introduction, primarily in the need to navigate the inescapable ethical tragedy that characterises the postcolonial situation. It is nevertheless necessary to qualify Mondal's reading. Firstly, his argument for the ambivalence that he locates seems to imply that this clash is *fundamentally* irresolvable, that is, that it is a logical paradox, a case of "either or", both sides of which Ghosh affirms. However, Huggan and Tiffin in their criticism of *The Hungry Tide* inadvertently present a reason for rejecting this assessment, revealing, in addition, that it is inaccurate to characterise the novel as not providing a resolution.

For Huggan and Tiffin, we saw, Ghosh seems to prioritise human over animal life. Nevertheless, their assessment is in one respect similar to Mondal's. They find that the difficult question of the clash between the human and non-human is never directly addressed; ultimately "neither a practical nor philosophical management of the problem [of the clash] is offered" (2007, 5). Rather, it is avoided: in making Piya's work the conservation of the river dolphin, "the real clash of interests is peculiarly—and perhaps deliberately—displaced" (5).[32] There is no difficulty with dolphin conservation because dolphins do not prey upon people. Huggan and Tif-

---

[32] Huggan and Tiffin's argument is reiterated in their more recent book. See Huggan & Tiffin (2010).

fin go on to make an argument very similar to Piya's cited above: Ghosh's privileging of the human over the animal repeats the ideology that authorises the killing of non-human others as well as of other humans by categorizing them as animalistic. This, they argue, is a fundamental part of the ideology of imperialism: "In assuming human ethical and material priorities over those of other animals, we continue to repeat the ideology of imperialism, condemning ourselves to Ghosh's perpetual impasse of tiger versus human" (6). The flaw in this position is that the "impasse of tiger versus human" exists precisely because the traditional privileging of human over animal interests has been removed. If human interests trumped those of the tigers, there would be no impasse. Thus, in agreement with Mondal, I suggest that *The Hungry Tide* holds human and tiger interests in tension with each other, not prioritizing one over the other, as Piya's last word in the debate suggests. But, in opposition to Mondal, this is not a fundamental paradox; the two values are contingently incommensurable. And it is in making this clearer that Piya's concern with the dolphins, rather than displacing the issue, is absolutely crucial to it.

What Piya's conservation of the Irrawaddy dolphin shows us is that it is possible for conservation and the interests of local people to coincide. We see this not only in Huggan and Tiffin's point that dolphins do not eat people, but also in the detrimental effect new fishing methods are having on the ability of the villagers in the Sundarbans to feed themselves. At one point, Kanai is talking to Moyna, Fokir's wife, when she mentions that Fokir's way of life is not sustainable because

> in fifteen years the fish will be gone [as a result of] new nylon nets, which they use to catch [...] the spawn of tiger prawns. The nets are so fine that they catch the eggs of all the other fish as well. (Ghosh 2005a, 134)

It is safe to assume that the destruction such fishing wrecks on the natural habitat of the dolphins would be of concern to Piya, and as such that it serves as a common point of interest for conservationists and locals. Rather than sidestepping the issue, Piya's conservation works to reinforce the simultaneous affirmation of the value both of the human and the non-human in a way that asserts two *contingently* conflicting values, rather than a fundamental paradox. And as such, the "practical" way forward that Huggan and Tiffin discern in the novel—namely "no conservation without local consultation and participation" (2007, 5)—gains more validity than they ascribe to it.

In bringing this analysis to a close I want to return to my comment above that Huggan and Tiffin are to a certain extent correct in arguing that Ghosh privileges the human over the animal. As I elaborated in the introduction, moments of incommensurability demand a decision; and a decision that is thoroughly condemned by the novel is the one which precipitated the Morichjhāpi massacre. It is significant in this regard that Kanai's powerful recognition occurs not only in relation to Fokir, but to Morichjhāpi. As we saw, Kanai in that moment realised himself as complicit with a "vision of human beings in which men such as Fokir counted for nothing, a man whose value was *less* than that of an animal" (Ghosh 2005a, 327, my emphasis). This judgement is not a matter of valuing humans as intrinsically higher than animals, but of valuing them less; of viewing "men such as Fokir"—the poor and disposed—as expendable. For it seems to me that the challenge in undoing the hierarchy of value between human and non-human, as I have argued Ghosh does, is not to invert the hierarchy, an inversion that would make the already marginal even more vulnerable. What is clear is that the novel, in its judgement of Kanai, judges the privileging of the tiger over the human *in this particular* conflict that was Morichjhāpi. Thus while the novel is in one sense ambivalent as it upholds both of the conflicting values, it is also insistent upon the action that should have been taken in the concrete situation which it considers.

III

In both of these novels we have seen the importance in Ghosh's writing of moments of transformation, where characters bridge the differences—racial, cultural, or linguistic—that separate them. We have also seen that these connections and transformations are grounded in a common humanity. Explicitly presented in *Sea of Poppies,* such an understanding of humanity is also at work in *The Hungry Tide.* While in both cases Ghosh's humanism is qualified by the constitutive effect of cultural categories to our sense of self, it is in *The Hungry Tide* that we see the idea that bridging differences holds within it its possible undoing. At this moment Ghosh becomes almost Derridean in his representation of the fundamental silence between individuals as the condition of (im)possibility for connecting across difference. Nevertheless, Ghosh seems to follow several prominent theorists, such as Hallward and Appiah, in asserting the importance of maintaining a form of humanism while simultaneously showing its limits and undermining it.

In *Sea of Poppies* the possibilities of recognition are both thematically and formally deployed, with the interplay of recognitions reinforcing the ethical sense of an enduring, common humanity. Repeatedly, the recognition of spiritual or moral identities that transcend the cultural differentiations on which nominal identities are based results in the temporary elision of those nominal identities. This in turn further enables a transgression of social boundaries, allowing and fostering affective connections which, in the climactic concatenation of recognitions, is seen as the main ethical thrust of the novel: the recognition of the illusionary differences of the world. In all of this, *anagnorisis* is central. Although not thematically deployed in the same way in *The Hungry Tide*, recognition retains its importance in this novel as well. The individual transformations are moments of recognition, all of which pivot around Kanai's dramatic recognition on Garjontola. They are, additionally, dependent upon emotional responses in a way that was only visible in *Sea of Poppies* in Deeti's recognition of Kalua's equal humanity. It was Kanai's dramatic recognition, however, and the results of Piya's own transformation, that enabled a recalibration of the central ethical clash between the human and the nonhuman in the terms of a tragic (contingent) conflict of values.

These two novels have, then, provided an initial crystallizing of what it means to read the ethical sense of the novel in the terms for which I have argued, presenting good examples of both the importance of *anagnorisis*, the importance of the emotions for this, and the tragic conflict of values. They engage directly with the ethical question of humanism, problematizing the classical division between human and animal, and I have also noted their lesser engagement with questions of religion and the remembrance of violent histories. Actively recuperating forgotten and marginal histories, Ghosh's engagement with history can be seen as an ethically motivated work of the recovery of stories that are either politically suppressed or would otherwise fall beyond the pale of traditional historiography. He presents an ethical challenge to historiography by "humanising" it, and resisting, to some extent, its drive for "complete, accurate historical representation" (Hoydis 2011, 58). The ethics of representing past trauma in narrative, however, is less of a pressing concern: when the past is particularly traumatic and violent, what is the relationship between the obligations of memory and the creative freedom of art? In the work of the Nigerian writer Chimamanda Adichie, who has dramatised scenes of civil and domestic conflict in her first two novels and short story collection, this question is of pressing importance. She will also introduce more overtly the ethical theme of religion, and I turn now to consider her work.

Chapter Two
Religion and the Ethics of Remembrance

> The rawness of Edna's grief made her helpless, brought the urge to stretch her hand into the past and reverse history. Finally, Edna fell asleep. Olanna gently placed a pillow beneath her head and sat thinking about how a single act could reverberate over time and space and leave stains that could never be washed off. She thought about how ephemeral life was, about not choosing misery.
>
> (Adichie 2007a, 245)

I

Chimamanda Adichie is one of the new generation of Nigerian authors, often dubbed the third generation, and the two texts on which I will be focusing—*Purple Hibiscus* (2005) and *Half of a Yellow Sun* (2007a)—correspondingly shift our focus from India to Nigeria. Turning to Adichie allows me to retexture my argument that the world novel often grapples with the intricate ethical legacy of the tragedy of colonial Enlightenment. Adichie's novels draw out a further aspect of this complexity through bringing into view an important ethical concern which Ghosh only engages with indirectly. As a self-confessed, though doubting, Catholic, Adichie has an interest in religion, particularly Catholicism, as a viable ethical framework in contemporary Nigeria. Christianity, as I will discuss below, came to southern Nigeria as a result of intensive missionary work in conjunction with colonialism. Its subsequent pervasiveness thus constitutes an embedded colonial legacy that raises, among others, questions of hospitality to different beliefs, the inculturation and/or syncretization of formerly alien beliefs, and religious fundamentalism—a field of enquiry which has recently been receiving a much needed increase in attention. For these reasons, Adichie's work provides a valuable opening into negotiating this legacy. Adichie does not focus exclusively on Christianity. While it is central in *Purple Hibiscus*, a novel that lends itself to an overtly Christian interpretation (see for instance Chennells [2009]), in *Half of a Yellow Sun*, Adichie's interest in the ethics of belief is both broader and more dispersed, surfacing in the intersections of a rational, secular understanding of the world with traditional, Christian and Islamic understandings.

The different emphasis on belief in the novels, while in part due to the author's changing relationship to Christianity (Tunca 2013), also results from the fact that *Half of a Yellow Sun* is a different kind of novel to *Purple Hibiscus*. Where the latter is a *Bildungsroman* that narrates the spiritual growth and major transition in Kambili's life, namely her changing understanding of Catholicism, the former is a more complex, mainly historical novel. Concerned to recount the Biafran war (1967–1970), it does so through narrating its effects and the years preceding it on the level of the everyday, romantic lives of its focalisers. Thus John Marx (2008) comments that the novel "has a lowbrow cousin who can be found in the 'historicals' section of the romance-novel shelf" (612). Adichie complicates this, though, by incorporating aspects of the *Bildungsroman* in the narrative of Ugwu: whose education and growth echoes on a number of points that of Triton in Romesh Gunesekera's *Reef* (1998), one of Adichie's favourite novels (Tunca 2005). The interweaving of these different narrative forms results, as will be seen, in a nuanced representation of the Biafran war and a corresponding widening of the ethical scope beyond the interactions of different belief systems, though this still remains important.

My approach to the novels, as in the previous chapter, will be by way of their recognitions, drawing out how their ethical sense unfolds through them. However, the shaping of the novels by their generic forms and the geographical and historical settings to which I have just gestured is a simultaneous shaping of the recognitions that are found in them. This in turn affects the relationship between the ethical knowledge to which the characters come and the ethics of the novels as a whole. For instance, in both *Purple Hibiscus* and *The Hungry Tide* there are recognitions that pertain to the moral self of a main character. In the former, Kambili comes to both a spiritual and an ethical awakening regarding her Catholicism and her relationship with her father, while in the latter Kanai has a psychically disturbing recognition regarding his affiliation to a class of people that regards the poor as irrelevant and dispensable. The narrative structure of *The Hungry Tide*, as we have seen, draws this crucial recognition into the wider ethical shape of the narrative, namely the injustice of the massacre at Morichjhãpi and the complexity of navigating between conflicting values. In *Purple Hibiscus*, however, Kambili's recognition and consequent change forms the predominant ethical shape of the narrative, to which the other recognitions in the narrative are subordinated. As a result, the recognitions are, as in the example of *The Odyssey* discussed in the introduction, more dispersed, accruing over time to bring about the main realization and transformation in the narrative. In this regard, *Half of a Yellow Sun* has more similarities to *The Hungry Tide* as it is likewise concerned with a historical event. It is here that the shaping effect of geographical and historical context on the recognition's predicate will be important. Before considering the details of the novels, then, it is necessary to fill in some of that context, namely the history of Islam and Christianity in Nigeria, going into specific detail with Christianity, which is Adichie's primary concern. This will lead me to introduce the ideas of inculturation and syncretism, as well as to reflect upon Adichie's citation of Achebe, a common occurrence in much contemporary Nigerian writing (Boehmer 2009).

II

Adichie's short story "The Headstrong Historian" (2009b), a rewriting or appropriation of, in particular, Achebe's *Things Fall Apart* (Tunca 2012; VanZanten 2015), opens up the question of her engagement with her predecessor as well as the history of Christianity in Nigeria. The story tells us of the life of Nwamgba, an Igbo village woman born (we suppose) in the late nineteenth century. We learn of her happy marriage to Obierika, her multiple miscarriages, and the finally joyful birth of her son Anikwenwa. Upon Obierika's suspiciously early death, however, what looked to be a promising future is suddenly threatened as Obierika's jealous cousins (whom she suspects of poisoning him) begin to appropriate parts of her late husband's estate. As time passes, Nwamgba feels increasingly threatened by them, fearing that they might dispose of Anikwenwa by secretly selling him into slavery. Her only solution is to act on the stories she's been hearing about the white man, about his courts and his missionary schools: she sends Anikwenwa to school. Going first to an Anglican mission, Nwamgba ends up taking her son to the Catholic mission instead when she learns that the Anglicans teach in the vernacular: Nwamgba went to the missionary school "in search of English" so as to empower Anikwenwa to reclaim what is rightfully his (Adichie 2009b, 208). While the Catholic missionaries are brutal in their punishments, Anikwenwa learns well and is, after a time, able to reclaim from Obierika's cousins what belongs to him. However, the school does more than Nwamgba thought it would, and soon Anikwenwa eschews the food and way of life of his tribe as respectively tainted and idolatrous. Sorrowful, Nwamgba rests her hopes on the Igbo belief in reincarnation, believing that Obierika will be reborn in her grandchild. Her first grandchild follows his father's ways, but in her granddaughter, Afamefuna, the headstrong historian of the title (named Grace by her father), Obierika's spirit is indeed reborn. In Afamefuna there is a return to the traditions of her ancestors as she rejects her father's and brother's dour, sanctimonious ways. And we learn that in her future she will become an acclaimed historian, working to restore the dignity of the Igbo through rewriting the history of their colonial encounter. We learn this in a prolepsis, however, and the narrative closes with the teenaged Afamefuna holding her grandmother's hand as she passes away.

This is a rich story, not least in its citations and adaptations of Achebe. What I want to dwell on now is what can be discerned in the story of the history of Christianity. The first white men that Nwamgba sees are Catholic missionaries "from France, far across the sea. They were all of the Holy Ghost Congregation; they had arrived in Onicha in 1885 and were building their school and church there" (Adichie 2009b, 205). Contact with Europe through trade along the west coast had been present since the late fifteenth century. Though there had been a number of attempts to spread Christianity, both Catholic and Protestant, in West Africa since then, there was no substantial, lasting Christian presence until the advent of modern missions in the nineteenth century due to the natural barriers of desert and forest that hindered the spread of Christianity from North and East Africa where it has been present since shortly after its founding (Isichei 1995; Parrinder 1969). In the nineteenth century, missionary attention moved progressively around the western coast of Africa, turning first to Sierra Leone in 1792 with the arrival of more than a thousand African settlers from Nova Scotia (Isichei 1995, 160; Parrinder 1969, 124), and then to the Gold Coast, now Ghana, where the modern missionary enterprise began with the arrival of the Basel missionaries in 1828 (Isichei 1995, 160; Parrinder 1969, 126). In Nigeria there were two early encounters with Christianity. In 1842 Thomas Birch Freeman preached in Badagry near the western limit of present-day Nigeria, while the first Christian contact with the Igbo specifically was a year earlier, in 1841, during the

Niger River Expedition which stopped over at the village of Abo (Ubah 1988, 75; Ifemesia 1980). It was indirectly from this mission, as a result of the presence of Samuel Crowther, that the first permanent Christian presence in Nigeria would eventually come. Crowther was a catechist at the time of the failed Niger Expedition, but became the first African Anglican bishop and was crucial in spreading Christianity further inland than managed by others at that time (Parrinder 1969, 132–133). In 1857 he led a Church Missionary Society (CMS) mission that "established a permanent station at Onitsha" (Ubah 1988, 75), but advancement from there was slow. As Achebe (2009a) puts it,

> The first missionaries came to the Niger River town of Onitsha in 1857. From that beachhead they finally reached my town, Ogidi, in 1892. Now, the distance from Onitsha to Ogidi is only seven miles. Seven miles in thirty-five years: that is one mile every five years. That is no whirlwind. (7)

This was a common feature of missions in West Africa, and "by 1900, western and Christian influences had touched only the fringes of [West African] cultures" (Isichei 1995, 155), with Christians remaining in the minority even where their presence had been long-established. Nevertheless, in 1885 the CMS mission at Onitsha was joined by another: the Holy Ghost Fathers of Adichie's story (Ubah 1988, 75).

When Nwamgba sees the Holy Ghost Fathers, she is the first person to ask a question and, rather than ask about Christianity, she quite naturally queries after the stories that she has been hearing about other white men: "Had they brought their guns by any chance, the ones used to destroy the people of Agueke, and could she see one?" The missionaries respond "that it was the soldiers of the British government and merchants of the Royal Niger Company who destroyed villages; they, instead, brought good news" (Adichie 2009b, 205). The missionaries are, strictly speaking, correct. However, the connections between the missionaries and the colonial enterprise do not allow for a complete separation. As Ogbu Kalu (1980) comments, "both the government and the missions looked upon the civilization of the black man as their paramount goal" (182), and this common goal was strengthened by practical considerations: the government provided practical services "on which survival and evangelism depended" while the missionaries, in turn, acted as "agents provocateurs for western civilisation" (183). The two enterprises were sufficiently separate, however, for there to be points of conflict between them, though there were never any public incidents. Afigbo (1980) identifies three main conflicts. One was the brutality that the colonial government showed in its treatment of the local populace, and against which the missionaries spoke out: an endeavour that won them some esteem and trust. However, while the missionaries may have attempted to prevent the poor treatment of Africans, they were on a collision course of their own with the local culture. The missionaries wanted either to eradicate or totally reform local social norms, which they saw as godless and evil, while the colonial government wanted to shore them up. On the one hand, the colonial government did not want the locals becoming too westernised, and on the other they wanted to institute indirect rule (Kalu 1980). Furthermore, as Ubah points out, the government was highly concerned with the maintenance of law and order and wanted to avert the conflicts that arose between the new Christian order and the old one; a concern of enough importance that missionaries were only allowed to work in a town if they were welcomed by the warrant chiefs (1988, 78–79).

It is what Afigbo notes as the third point, however, that was the source of greatest conflict, and is an important theme in Adichie's story: education. The missionary schools had been running for a number of decades before the government was in a position to turn its attention to education. Isichei notes that in "1942 [the missions] controlled 99 per cent of Nigeria's schools, and 97 per cent of all students were in mission schools" (1995, 270). The conflict over the schools arose due to very different goals. For the missionaries, education was the primary means of evangelization and conversion. For this reason, it was limited and not very advanced. The colonial government, meanwhile, wanted administrators and clerks and so attempted to take control of the schools, primarily through funding pressures that required them to meet a certain standard in order to qualify for grants (Isichei 1995, 270–272); they never quite succeeded. However, as Adichie's short story depicts, the schools were successful among the Igbo because of the prestige, power, and potential material benefit that were associated with any level of western education. Nwamgba sent Anikwenwa to the school seeking the power that speaking the coloniser's language would bring, only to wonder later, upon seeing him Christianised and westernised, if she "had meddled with his destiny" (Adichie 2009b, 212). This illustrates an important practical alliance between colonial rule and missions: colonial rule increased the allure of western education leading to higher attendance, while the mission schools provided western education and converted those who attended. It is in part due to this that there was a sudden, massive spread of Christianity throughout southern Nigeria, particularly among the Igbo, in the first half of the twentieth century (Ubah 1988; Isichei 1995).

Anikwenwa goes to the missionary school, becomes a catechist, and rejects as much of his mother's way of life as he is able. The ethical concern raised here of relating to a culture and a spirituality different from your own is central to *Purple Hibiscus*, as is the legacy of "a self-perpetuating tradition of severity, verging on brutality" in the schools (Isichei 1995, 270). But it is in Afamefuna and the choices that she makes that an echo of the movement made by Kambili in *Purple Hibiscus* can be heard. With her faith unspecified and her deep respect for the ways of her ancestors (both suggestive facts, raising the question of syncretism and inculturation, but more on this later) it is in her, as her grandfather's spirit reborn, that the continuance of her people is ensured, engaging the interplay of generations and the existence of the past in the future in a way similar to *Purple Hibiscus* (Chennells 2009, 23; Walder 2011, 129). I will return to these themes in detail.

Christianity was not, however, the only religion in Nigeria to benefit from colonialism. While the spread of Islam was not tied to the colonial project after the manner of Christianity, British colonial policy nevertheless played a crucial, if partly unintended, role in spreading Islam to its present level, in addition to enforcing the divisions between the north, west and the east along religious lines. As Parrinder details, Islam came to Africa in 640, shortly after the death of the Prophet Mohammed, with the conquest of the "Byzantine fortress of Babylon" near the location of present-day Cairo, and the surrender of Alexandria, Egypt, the following year (1969, 171). So began the spread of Islam in Northern Africa through conquest by Islamic empires, eventually covering the whole of North Africa and replacing Christianity as the dominant religion (171–181). West Africa, however, due to forest and desert, was isolated from "the great Islamic empires in the North" (183), and it was only through the journeys of Muslim traders following the routes southwards down the coast from Morocco that Islam began to enter the region some four hundred years later. Initially, it spread only among some of the elite, and in the eleventh century there were in the Kingdom of Gana "twelve mosques and Muslims were among the court officials" (182). An important event in the further spread of Islam in West Africa occurred in 1076 when the capital of Gana was sacked by the Almoravids. The Tuareg (the inhabitants of Western Sahara) followers of Ibn Yasin sent his people on a holy war, conquering Morocco as well as Gana. With the fall of Gana, the kingdom of Mali rose in its place. Its rulers were Muslim, and Islam spread gradually among the elite (the rulers and traders) of the region, assisted by the successive influence of the Mali and the Songhai empires. This was further aided by the importance of Islam for trade links to North Africa, and of Arabic for literacy and as a lingua franca (183–186).

It was only in the nineteenth century that the greatest spread of Islam in West Africa occurred. Where, before, Islam had "been fragmented [...] surviving only by fitting into African ways of life" (raising, again, the question of inculturation) there were now "great urges towards the formation of Islamic states, ruled by the law of Islam imposed upon older forms of society" (197), and a number of Islamic leaders in West Africa lead holy wars to this end. Among them was 'Uthman dan Fodio, a Fulani, who led a jihad against the Hausa in Northern Nigeria, conquering Zaria in 1805 and Kano in 1809. Only Bornu, which had its "own religious military leader" was able to fend off 'Uthman's forces (189). Islam was subsequently imposed upon the Hausa, and when the British arrived only about half of them followed Islam and 'Uthman's empire was declining and partially fragmented (189). With the arrival of the British, however, Christian missionaries were prevented from entering the north, and the colonial administrators, unaware that in many regions Islam was prevalent mostly only among the elite, backed and consolidated the power of the emirs and made Islam the official religion, with the result that "tribes where a majority followed traditional religion were subjected to Islamic rule" (206). This is not, of course, to deny the resistance of the northern tribes to the colonisers. Nevertheless, the result of colonial policy was a sharp increase in the number of Muslims in the north, though there was also a large, more organic spreading of Islam "among the Yoruba who were beyond Fulani rule in western Nigeria" (206). In any case, by the time of the civil war in the sixties, the setting of *Half of a Yellow Sun*, Nigeria was divided along religious and regional lines, with Muslims in the north and west, and Christians in the east.

The religious context and history of Nigeria sharpens the ethical significance of the interactions between faiths and the importance of inculturation. Islam spread in West Africa through a combination of force and a more organic extension through channels of usefulness and opportunity, while Christianity largely lacked the inculturation and tolerance that was often exhibited by the early Christians in North Africa. It is only in later generations, as with Afamefuna in "The Headstrong Historian", that a return to more traditional ways of life is achieved. Not by a return to a "pure" past but rather, in her case, through something of a non-religious form of inculturation. The term inculturation, Gallagher (2003) notes, developed in sociology where it mainly designated the process of "socialisation", that is, how people "[learn] the ways of the group through social formation" (118). It has come to have a "specifically [Christian] theological meaning", designating the belief that "evangelisation, echoing the incarnation itself, demands 'the insertion of the Gospel into the very heart of culture and cultures'" (118–119). This would then give rise to "original expressions of Christian life, celebration and thought" (quoted in Chennells [2009, 18]). This theological understanding will be of particular relevance for my reading of Adichie and so warrants some further explication.

There is much that could be said about inculturation and the debates surrounding it, but what is salient here are two of its theological underpinnings. The most important is the incarnation (Gallagher 2003; Manathodath 1990): In a similar way that within Christian theology Jesus is understood to have been incarnated into Jewish culture, so the Gospel is to be inculturated into various other cultures. As Gallagher (2003) explains it, "inculturation imitates, so to speak, that embracing of humanity by God in Christ, in order to give flesh to the gospel again in different cultures" (122). There are limits to this model, however. It needs to be supplemented by the acknowledgment of the need for the redemption and change of all cultures, the difficulty of the process of inculturation, as well as the recognition that what is inculturated is not simply the transcendent Word of God but an (always) already inculturated faith (122–124). Nevertheless, the incarnation remains as the pivotal theological basis, and opens on to the second, which it implies: the value of all cultures and religions. Explicitly addressed by the Catholic Church for the first time in Vatican II

(Manathodath 1990, 95), it acknowledges that non-Christian religions, in the words of that council, "reflect a ray of that truth which enlightens everyone" (Vatican Council II 1990, 969), and that each religion is worthy of respect due to it being the product of man striving after God (Manathodath 1990, 94–99). As such, inculturation as a movement within Christianity rejects the approach to traditional cultures that was exhibited by the Christian missionaries in Nigeria in the nineteenth and early twentieth centuries. And in so doing, it brings to the fore a question with which Adichie engages: what would an inculturated Catholicism in Nigeria look like? The ethics of the different approaches to traditional culture and religion, and the different forms of Christianity that they represent, are explored in *Purple Hibiscus*, constituting the central axis along which Kambili's narrated journey progresses.

Adichie's short story positions this question in relation to the work of Chinua Achebe. Written from a female perspective, it is, in VanZanten's (2015) words, a "*supplemental transformation*" of Achebe's first novel (89, emphasis in original), rather than an adaptation (a version of the same story in a different form) or an appropriation (a critical parody, subversion or contestation of an earlier text). The most explicit citation of *Things Fall Apart* in the story is Afamefuna's school textbook chapter that shares, almost exactly, the title of the District Commissioner's book from the end of Achebe's book: 'The Pacification of the Primitive Tribes of Southern Nigeria' (Adichie 2009b, 215). The result, as Daria Tunca (2012) has observed, it to challenge "Achebe's rather depressing conclusion" to his novel by making it the District Commissioner's work that is reduced to a single chapter (246), rather than the story of Okonkwo and the village of Umuofia. More generally, however, Adichie's wider work is, as Boehmer (2009) notes, "stamped with numerous filiative gestures towards Achebe" (148), and not only with reference to his first novel. Adichie also parallels *No Longer at Ease* (1960) in her short story through having the engagement with tradition and the negotiation of a mixed heritage (both colonial and traditional)—in "The Headstrong Historian" and *Purple Hibiscus*—undertaken by a later generation.

In addition, Achebe is referenced in *Purple Hibiscus* with its opening line: "Things started to fall apart at home when my brother, Jaja, did not go to communion and Papa flung his heavy missal across the room and broke the figurines on the étagère" (Adichie 2005, 3). Later in the novel we see Kambili, the narrator, going to stay with her Aunty Ifeoma who lives on Marguerite Cartwright Avenue in Nsukka, the same road on which Achebe lived for a number of years. In *Half of a Yellow Sun* (2007a), additionally, Adichie mimics Achebe by unexpectedly inverting the reader's understanding in a similar manner to the ending in *Things Fall Apart*: having been led to suppose that the book *The World Was Silent When We Died* is written by Richard, the novel closes with the revelation that its author is, instead, Ugwu. There are many untranslated Igbo words in both novels (see Cooper [2008]), while in *Half of a Yellow Sun* there is incorporated into "the configurations of plot and character" the motif of twins (Boehmer 2009, 148). Such citation of Achebe is fairly common among, though certainly not exclusive to, contemporary Nigerian writers (Boehmer 2009; Osinubi 2009). Osinubi, commenting on this trend in "third generation" Nigerian authors specifically, argues that "*Things Fall Apart* returns in these new narratives because they deal with new crises of language and ideology" (2009, 160). This certainly seems to be the case here, as *Purple Hibiscus* and *Half of a Yellow Sun* are both organised around moments of crisis and their accompanying recognitions.

What is particularly salient with regard to Adichie's citation of Achebe, to bring these contextual and introductory comments to a close, is her incorporation of Achebe's concern with Christianity into *Purple Hibiscus*. When Christianity first arrives in Umuofia in *Things Fall Apart*, it is not unanimously hostile to the local religion and culture. One missionary, Mr Brown, is singled out for admiration by some of the "great men" in the village. The reason for this admiration is that Mr Brown "trod softly on [the clan's] faith". His approach fosters dialogue and mutual understanding:

> Whenever Mr Brown went to that village he spent long hours with Akunna [one of the great men] in his *obi* talking through an interpreter about religion. Neither of them succeeded in converting the other but they learnt more about their different beliefs. (Achebe 2009b, 101)

Ill health forces Mr Brown to leave, and his successor "condemned openly Mr Brown's policy of compromise and accommodation" (104). Consequently, the missionaries and converts become increasingly antagonistic towards the clan's faith, which culminates in the clan razing the church. We have briefly seen this hostile manifestation of Christianity in Adichie's "The Headstrong Historian", though there is also a Mr Brown equivalent in Father O'Donnell (Adichie 2009b, 213). In *Purple Hibiscus*, Kambili's crisis of faith and filial love sees her making an ethical choice between these different manifestations of Christianity, and moving away from a colonial, intolerant form of Catholicism into an inculturated one in which some elements of traditional Igbo spirituality continue to exist. As I turn now to consider the novels, first *Purple Hibiscus* and then *Half of a Yellow Sun*, we will see that these moments of crisis—shaped by the influence of Achebe and the Christian legacy of colonialism—are navigated through particular ethical recognitions which often precede and, to some extent, resolve them.

III

The opening section of Adichie's *Purple Hibiscus*— "Breaking Gods: Palm Sunday"—contains the novel's moment of greatest change. Kambili's brother, "Jaja, did not go to communion and Papa flung his heavy missal across the room and broke the figurines on the étagère" (Adichie 2005, 3). This apparently simple defiance is highly significant and rich in imagery, though the reader only discovers its full meaning in the analepsis that makes up the majority of the novel. Kambili and Jaja's father, Eugene, is an abusive man tyrannically ruling his family in accordance with an intolerant, Eurocentric Catholicism, and Jaja's defiance is the first open resistance to his rule from within the family. The result is a transformation of familial relations: when Jaja later defies his father for a second time that day, Kambili notices "a shadow clouding Papa's eyes, a shadow that had been in Jaja's eyes. Fear. It had left Jaja's eyes and entered Papa's" (13). No longer does Eugene rule over Jaja. The implications of this opening moment begin to unfold when we learn that the shattered figurines had served as Kambili and Jaja's mother's refuge after being beaten by her husband, when she would meticulously clean each figurine. Eugene in his anger destroys the coping mechanism that sustains Beatrice through his abuse. However, rather than the devastating event one might expect it to be for her, it is a moment of liberation.

The knowledge that this moment at which things fall apart is positive and not a disaster as the citation of Achebe's title initially implies, comes to Kambili through two entwined recognitions. Upon learning that her mother will not replace the figurines, Kambili thinks,

> Maybe Mama had realized that she would not need the figurines anymore; that when Papa threw the missal at Jaja, it was not just the figurines that came tumbling down, it was everything. I was only now realizing it, only just letting myself think it. (15)

The "now", also recurring in the second recognition, marks the moment of realization. Reaching it through witnessing the continued and unpunished defiance of Jaja, the predicate of Kambili's recognition begins as the figurines and broadens to include the *peripeteia* itself, the extent to which the moment of Eugene breaking the figurines has changed everything. This recognition is given pre-eminence in the novel through its position as the opening, and as the organizing principle of the narrative as a whole: part two is titled "Speaking with our Spirits: Before Palm Sunday", while part three completes the circle, "The Pieces of Gods: After Palm Sunday". It is only with the brief, closing part four that "Palm Sunday", the day of this recognition, ceases to be the organizing term.

The structuring of the narrative around a Christian feast adds a further resonance to the breaking of the figurines: what Eugene throws at Jaja, and which breaks the ballerinas, is his leather bound missal, a book containing the liturgy for the mass and the different Christian feasts and seasons (Thurston 1911). The suggestive image of the Catholic liturgy breaking Beatrice's source of comfort and marking the end of the order of things in which they were needed foreshadows (and, chronologically, encapsulates) the crucial role that an inculturated Catholicism, distinct from Eugene's, will be seen to play in bringing about this change. And this is additionally signalled by the substance of Jaja's defiance—he refuses to take communion—bringing into play from the outset the ambiguity of Catholicism in the narrative as both that which can be oppressive, and must be resisted, as well as that which can be liberating.

The meaning of Jaja's defiance constitutes the predicate of the second recognition in this opening section. Immediately after the first, Kambili's understanding continues to shift: "Jaja's defiance seemed to me now like Aunty Ifeoma's experimental purple hibiscuses: rare, fragrant with the undertones of freedom [...] A freedom to be, to do" (16). When Jaja first defies their father, Kambili is distressed. Unable to bear the tension, she leaves the room and passes an anxious few hours, scared about how their father will punish Jaja. When Jaja proceeds to defy him again at lunch, her terror intensifies: "This had never happened before in my entire life, never. The compound walls would crumble, I was sure [...] The sky would cave in. The Persian rug [...] would shrink. Something would happen" (14). But nothing does. And it is only later that evening that she "now" begins to realise the afternoon's significance: that rather than being a cause of distress and fear of what their father might do in response, Jaja's defiance is, in fact, the fragrance of freedom.

For Brenda Cooper (2008), in her study *A New Generation of African Writers*, the throwing of the missal signifies rather differently. Cooper argues that Kambili's moment of suffocation where the furniture seems to be bearing down on her, and her fear that the compound wall will fall down or that the Persian rugs will shrink, are the work of the spirits, the *mmuo* that we encounter later in the novel, as they appear "in all the moments of stress or emotion in her life" (133). From this perspective, which argues for a more syncretic form of Catholicism, the figurines "are Mama's protecting spirits" and the "étagère was Mama's shrine" (116). The *mmuo* consequently "play havoc with the family [...] in response to Papa's onslaught on their sacredness, when he throws his leatherbound church records book at Jaja, which smashes the figurines they inhabit" (133). Rather than signifying the liberating potential of Catholicism, Cooper understands this moment as representing the conflict between Catholicism and traditional spirituality. The difficulty with this, however, is that, on the one hand, this reading does not quite seem to fit. For instance, it fails to explain Kambili's fear that the sky will cave in. Wedged between her other fears of that moment, presumably the vengeful manipulations of the *mmuo*, it is suggestive that Cooper cites all of them except this one (113). More significantly, though, the argument hinges on understanding the scene with the *mmuo*, the masquerade, as recognizing their veracity; we will see that this important moment of recognition should instead be understood as accomplishing the opposite.

The scene with the *mmuo* is one of four key recognitions in part two of the novel, and which, taken together, result in Kambili's recognition on Palm Sunday. The first two that I will consider have as their predicates different forms of spirituality and religion. Kambili comes, first, to recognise a tolerant form of Catholicism, and as she is immersed within it she comes to understand, second, the vitality and value of her grandfather's spiritual life. Her grandfather, Papa-Nnukwu, is crucial for the subsequent recognition in which Kambili realises his value for her life personally and, importantly, that her father's Catholicism has robbed her of it. In the final recognition Kambili realises an important difference between her and her cousins' upbringing. While the ethical impact of each of these gains in knowledge might appear minimal, their importance for Kambili's initial (or final) recognition of freedom is what provides its ethical shape and potency: they reveal the order of things that falls apart on Palm Sunday as one of an intolerant Catholicism which has robbed Kambili of a valuable relationship with her grandfather, is blind to the value in other traditions, and is horribly abusive. The transition that Kambili goes through in her recognition of the disintegration of that order as freedom is therefore a powerful, ethical rejection of her father's way of life for one that is better; one that is inculturated, hospitable, respectful and nurturing. A large part of the narrative features Kambili detailing for us how things came to this point, how the red hibiscuses in the garden came to be mixed with the rare, purple hibiscuses—themselves a product of biological inculturation, as it were—which bloom as the brother and sister begin to experience the "freedom to be, to do" (Adichie 2005, 16).

The Eurocentric strain of Catholicism that I have traced in both Achebe's work and Adichie's short story is vividly represented in Kambili's childhood, where it is represented by the European style church of St Agnes, with its stained glass windows, blonde Mary, and racist priest for whom Igbo can only be used for songs during the ofatory. "[Father Benedict] called them native songs, and when he said 'native' his straight-line lips turned down at the corners to form an inverted U" (Adichie 2005, 4). This attitude towards Igbo extends into daily life, where Eugene insists on his family only speaking English in public. Unsurprisingly, this Catholicism—and Eugene as its practitioner—is hostile to both non-Christians and non-Christian spirituality. Even Eugene's own father, Papa-Nnukwu, is avoided if possible and, if not, is treated as tainted. Eugene himself never visits him. In contrast to this, Kambili tells us of her maternal grandfather, who was treated with deep respect. A very light-skinned man, "almost albino", he "determinedly spoke English, always, in a heavy Igbo accent. He knew Latin, too, often quoted the articles of Vatican I, and spent most of his time at St Paul's, where he had been the first catechist" (67).

The reference to the first Vatican Council signals the novel's exploration of Catholicism as positioned within the shift in doctrine between Vatican I and Vatican II (the latter of which Adichie describes herself an "enthusiast"(quoted in Stobie 2010, 422). While Catholicism, despite the centralised dogma of the councils, is richly diverse, these two ecumenical councils establish the poles between which Kambili transitions. Vatican I was convened at the height of imperialism (1869–1870). 'Canons 1' states: "If anyone denies the one true God, creator and lord of things visible and invisible: let him be anathema" (Vatican Council I 1990, 809). Although the declaration of "one true God" is common to Christianity in its many permutations, and the formulae "If anyone... let him be anathema" is common to all the Church Councils from Nicaea to Vatican 1 (Catholic Online 2010a), there is an element of exclusion which in Eugene's understanding of Catholicism is applied to all of life rather than to the spiritual blessings that are administered to the Christian by the Church. The Greek word *anathema* designates the most extreme form of excommunication. While in Old Testament usage it meant being separated off and marked for complete destruction (and could be used to designate a thing, an animal, or, indeed, a person), in the New Testament and the earliest Church Councils it ceases to entail death and is synonymous with complete exclusion from the community of faith. From the sixteenth century onwards a further distinction is made and *anathema* is placed at the extreme end of degrees of excommunication:

> minor excommunication, formerly incurred by a person holding communication with anyone under the ban of excommunication [this was formally abolished in 1884 (Catholic Online 2010b)]; major excommunication, pronounced by the Pope in reading a sentence; and anathema, or the penalty incurred by crimes of the gravest order, and solemnly promulgated by the Pope. (Catholic Online 2010a)

Those who are *anathema* are thus entirely excluded from any form of relationship with Christians, and it is this exclusion that Eugene extends indiscriminately, trying to protect his life from what he perceives as the tainting influence of the heathen.

Nearly a hundred years after the first Vatican Council, the second Vatican Council (1962–1965) provided a corrective to this interpretation, an intervention which made it, as already mentioned, the first ecumenical council to address non-Christian religions directly. Explicitly rejecting the form of Catholicism which Eugene exemplifies, it takes a decisive step towards inculturation as an important spiritual practise. It exhorts Catholics to engage with non-Christians, allowing the liturgy to be celebrated in the vernacular. The tolerant, inculturated Catholicism envisaged by this post-imperial council is what we see in Eugene's sister's family and, in particular, their priest, Father Amadi. He helps to care for Papa-Nnukwu, sees Christ in the faces of the impoverished boys whom he coaches in football, and uses Igbo during Mass. Additionally, Daria Tunca (2014) has observed how his use of Igbo proverbs and the respect thus shown for "ancestral Igbo wisdom" illustrates the "potential reconciliation" between Catholicism and traditional spirituality (34, 35). Kambili will only meet Father Amadi properly (he had once visited St Agnes previously) when she and Jaja go to spend some time with their aunt Ifeoma in Nsukka.

It is through the influence of Ifeoma and her family that Kambili reaches the recognitions that lead to her liberating understanding of Jaja's defiance. Ifeoma first appears in the narrative when her family joins the Achike family for Christmas in Abba, and we are immediately presented with a contrasting picture of family life, where the children, though Catholic, enjoy a rich relationship with their grandfather. The difference of relationship to Papa-Nnukwu is critical, and I will return to it. However, these divergences between the two families quickly become centred on the children's participation in the nearby *mmuo*, the masquerade. Promising Eugene that she will take the children sightseeing and avoid the *mmuo*, Ifeoma takes the children to see it anyway, picking up Papa-Nnukwu en route and bringing us to the first of Kambili's recognitions. When they arrive at the masquerade, "cars lined the road almost bumper to bumper" and the people crowded around the cars so densely that "there was no space between people and they blended into one another" (Adichie 2005, 85). The procession of *mmuo* has already begun and Papa-Nnukwu begins to explain each spirit as it passes by. Suddenly, and demonstrating the patriarchal shape of his beliefs, he shouts, "Look away! Women cannot look at this one!", when the most powerful spirit passes by. The response of the others is revealing: "Aunty Ifeoma looked amused, but she turned her head away. 'Don't look girls. Let's humor your grandfather,' she said in English. Amaka had already looked away. I looked away too" (86). Brenda Cooper comments that this is an instance in which "the novel distances itself from Papa's rejection of Igbo beliefs and customs as 'devilish folklore'" (2008, 113). Cooper is referring to the moment when, as they are pulling up at the masquerade, Kambili recalls that "[papa] said that the stories about the *mmuo* [...] were all devilish folklore. *Devilish Folklore*. It sounded dangerous the way Papa said it" (Adichie 2005, 85). There is, indeed, a distancing from this attitude. Ifeoma's amusement, coupled with the revelation that Obiora, her eldest son, has been through the *ima mmuo* or, "the initiation into the spirit world"—which Eugene forbade Jaja from doing because "Christians who let their sons do it were confused, [and] would end up in hellfire" (87)—begins to disturb Kambili's acceptance of her father's view of the *mmuo* as dangerous and tainting.

It is, however, precisely because Ifeoma does not believe the *mmuo* to be real that she can be amused at Papa-Nnukwu's injunction to look away and can allow Obiora to go through the initiation. Ifeoma describes looking away as "humor[ing]" Papa-Nnukwu, a position that is in sharp distinction from the women who "turned and dashed into nearby compounds" (Adichie 2005, 86). Coupled with the fact that she speaks in English so that Papa-Nnukwu cannot understand, the effect is to undermine the *mmuo's* veracity. As Chennells remarks, "Ifeoma's tolerant amusement and use of English distance herself and the children not only from Papa-Nnukwa [sic] but from those in the crowd to whom the masks are objects of awe and reverence, and her words reduce the masks to picturesque remnants of a tradition". Chennells goes further, arguing that Ifeoma's response is, in fact, more sceptical than Eugene's, for whom the masquerade has the real "possibility of diabolical power" (2009, 20). Eugene's description of the *mmuo* as "devilish folklore", however, seems to suggest the contrary. The potential power which the masquerades hold for Eugene rests not in their spiritual reality, but in their "heathen", non-Christian quality; his designation of them as "folklore" suggests that he considers them no more real than does Ifeoma. As Father Benedict (whose interpretation of doctrine Eugene appears to follow) instructs Kambili later during confession: "Pagan rituals are *misinformed superstition*, and they are the gateway to Hell" (Adichie 2005, 106, my emphasis). What we see, then, is that both Ifeoma and Eugene understand the masquerade as lacking spiritual reality, viewing it either as tradition and safe, or as devilish folklore and therefore dangerous and to be avoided. Ifeoma's hospitable attitude towards it means that in addition to Kambili recognizing "the supernatural power that tradition once accorded the masks" (Chennells 2009, 20), she also has her first recognition of a different, more ethical way of relating to a non-Christian spirituality.

This scene sits in counterpoint to the pilgrimage that Kambili, Amaka, Ifeoma and Father Amadi later make to Aokpe, where it is reported that the Virgin Mary is manifesting. There are a number of parallels between the scenes: there is the same mass of cars, the same crowd "packed so close that the smell of other people became as familiar as their own" (Adichie 2005, 274), all of whom have likewise come to experience something spiritual. Instead of tolerant amusement, however, at this point Kambili experiences the presence of the "Blessed Virgin": "Then I saw her [...] an image in the pale sun, a red glow on the back of my hand, a smile on the face of the rosary-bedecked man whose arm rubbed against mine. She was everywhere" (274–275). It is an important scene in which, Stobie (2010) observes, the "feminine spiritual principle" is privileged and challenges the "'infallible' patriarchy" that is evident in both Eugene's Catholicism and Papa-Nnukwu's traditionalism (430). It does not place both religions on entirely equal footing, however. While it is not specified whether the others in the car experienced anything, as they are driving away Ifeoma remarks, "Kambili is right [....] Something from God was happening there" (Adichie 2005, 275).

Ifeoma thus bestows a spiritual reality on the manifestation of the Virgin Mary which she seems to withhold from the *mmuo*. Nevertheless, these two scenes do draw an inexorable parallel between two distinct religious traditions. As such, it is unsurprising that Ifeoma does not reject all of Papa-Nnukwu's beliefs. The first indication of this is while they are driving to the masquerade. Ifeoma and Papa-Nnukwu are talking about Eugene, whose neglect of his father Papa-Nnukwu blames on the missionaries. Ifeoma asks in response, "Did I not go to the missionary school, too?". In answer, Papa-Nnukwu conveys his gratitude for her exemplary care, going on to say, "My spirit will intercede for you, so that *Chukwu* will send a good man to take care of you and the children." To which Ifeoma immediately asks him to pray for her "promotion to senior lecturer" instead (83, emphasis in original). There is, as Chennells notes (2009, 22), an ironic interplay of different traditions here, not least in Ifeoma's resistance to the assumption that she needs a man to look after her (see also Stobie [2010, 424]). What is pertinent, however, is that Ifeoma acknowledges the reality of Papa-Nnukwu's prayers, and it is this that becomes the predicate of Kambili's second recognition.

While Kambili and Jaja are staying with Ifeoma in Nsukka, she instructs Kambili one morning to watch Papa-Nnukwu complete his "itu-nzu, his declaration of innocence" (Adichie 2005, 166). Kambili does so, watching as he systematically gives thanks for the morning, health and prosperity, declare his innocence from evil, and ask for blessings for his family members. It is an enlightening experience, leading her to recognise the vitality and joy present in a different spiritual tradition. Her initial surprise is due to his magnanimity: he prays for Eugene "with the same earnestness that he prayed for himself and Aunty Ifeoma" (168). But as Kambili watches him tie his wrapper once he is finished, what strikes her most is the fact that he is smiling, which she never did after her prayers (169). In a moment that nuances her rejection of the *mmuo*, Ifeoma tells Kambili that "sometimes what was different was just as good as what was familiar, that when Papa-Nnukwu did his itu-nzu [...] it was the same as our saying the rosary" (169). Kambili, watching her grandfather, recognises that "something from God", in Ifeoma's words from Aokpe, happens in other religions, or, as Vatican II puts it, that they "frequently reflect a ray of the truth which enlightens everyone" (1990, 969).

The equivalence between Papa-Nnukwu's itu-nzu and the Catholic rosary thus shows Kambili that the spiritual boundaries between religions are not as rigid as Eugene thinks—but not completely porous either as indicated by the rejection of the *mmuo*. While this aligning of the two traditions opens up the question of psychological explanations, which we will see in *Half of a Yellow Sun*, it is nevertheless these two recognitions—of the life and joy that can be present in a different spiritual tradition and of a different way of relating to such a tradition—that start Kambili along the path which culminates with her realization of the intolerance and injustice of her father's way of life. The key to this final realization, however, is her recognitions about her familial relationships. The Catholicism that Kambili encounters in Nsukka is an inculturated Igbo Catholicism which, in the words of Pope John Paul II, "brings forth from its own living tradition original expressions of Christian life, celebration and thought" (quoted in Chennells 2009, 18). It is being immersed in this hospitable, inculturated Catholicism that enables Kambili to spend time with Papa-Nnukwu in a way entirely unavailable to her before, and which changes her life completely.

Kambili's relationship with her grandfather is a series of moments of exclusion, of recognizing the absence of a real, emotional connection. Already during the drive to the *mmuo* over Christmas, Kambili begins to realise the richness of the relationship that her cousins have with her grandfather, and to wish that things were different for her and Jaja. However, although this feeling is heightened when they are living in the same house as him, particularly when he tells stories to which they do not know the correct patterns of response, the most poignant moment of Kambili's longing for a connection with her grandfather is the day before he dies. Watching her cousin paint a portrait of him, Kambili "felt a longing for something [she] knew [she] would never have" (Adichie 2005, 165). The experience is one of exclusion circumscribing desire, and sharpening it. When Papa-Nnukwu dies the next day, she feels unentitled to mourn him and begins to recognise the role of her father in it: "I did not have a right to mourn Papa-Nnukwu with [Amaka]; he had been her Papa-Nnukwu more than mine. She had oiled his hair while I kept away and wondered what Papa would say if he knew" (187). With the irrevocable loss of Papa-Nnukwu, Kambili begins to understand that she has been deprived of something good and valuable in her life.

As Kambili is packing her bags to return to Enugu, Ifeoma gives Jaja the symbolic purple hibiscuses to plant in their garden, while Amaka gives her the nearly finished painting of Papa-Nnukwu. She cherishes it, stealing glimpses only when she knows that her father will not see. One afternoon a few days later, Kambili is showing the painting to Jaja when Eugene walks in and sees it. Both of them claim it as theirs, when

> Papa snatched the painting from Jaja. His hands moved swiftly, working together. The painting was gone. It had already represented something lost, something I had never had, would never have. Now even that reminder was gone, and at Papa's feet lay pieces of paper streaked with earth-tone colors. [....]'No!' I shrieked. I dashed to the pieces on the floor as if to save them, as if saving them would mean saving Papa-Nnukwu. I sank to the floor, lay on the pieces of paper. (210)

The absence of her grandfather in her life, something she had never had and now would never have, is brought sharply into focus by the destruction of the last remnant symbolizing the object of her longing. What she had begun to know through her emotional responses to Papa-Nnukwu is now fully and powerfully brought into consciousness in this moment of recognition, overwhelming her fear of her father and causing her to act against him for the first time in a desperate attempt to claim the last, now destroyed, remnant of Papa-Nnukwu; an action that leads to Eugene kicking her repeatedly until she is hospitalised. Discharged into Ifeoma's care, she returns to Nsukka, and shortly after this the purple hibiscuses start to bloom.

I have traced how the inculturated Catholicism in which Kambili is immersed in Nsukka, its hospitality to different spiritualities, made it possible for her to be exposed to Papa-Nnukwu and to recognise both the vitality of his spiritual life and that Eugene has wronged her, and indeed her entire family, through preventing a meaningful relationship with him. In the time that Kambili spends with Father Amadi, she comes to the fourth recognition. Although Father Amadi represents, as already indicated, a more tolerant Catholicism, the recognition that he sparks concerns her relationship with her father, who emerges as the key focus of the tragic complexity of Kambili's ethical situation. Throughout the novel, Kambili can be seen to love her father fiercely, as well as to fear him deeply. In the opening section, on Palm Sunday, we are introduced to a habit of Eugene's: whenever he pours himself some tea, he offers Jaja and Kambili a sip.

> A love sip, he called it, because you shared the little things you loved with the people you loved [...] The tea was always too hot, always burned my tongue, and if lunch was something peppery, my raw tongue suffered. But it didn't matter, because I knew that when the tea burned my tongue, it burned Papa's love into me. (8)

The pain of the love sip and the simultaneous joy of having the love burn into her, captures the dual relationship between Kambili and her father. Whenever Eugene is praised for his generosity to the church and charity organizations, for his courageous use of his newspaper to fight for liberal democracy in a time of military rule—for which "*Amnesty World* gave him a human rights award"—Kambili "would sit with [her] knees pressed together [...] trying hard to keep [her] face blank, to keep the pride from showing, because Papa said modesty was very important" (5, emphasis in original). This intense longing to do what pleases her father is seen throughout, even when she begins to move away from his form of Catholicism. So intense is this desire that she becomes jealous when someone else wins his approval, and feels "as though [her] mouth were full of melting sugar" when she herself does so (26).

The burn of the love sip, however, presages Eugene's physical abuse of his family which culminates with him literally burning her, pouring boiling water over her feet as a punishment for staying in the same house with Papa-Nnukwu for a week; and then only a few days later nearly kicking her to death. Although these worst instances occur later in the narrative, Kambili has a deep fear of displeasing her father, of provoking his anger. When she is watching Father Amadi in Nsukka train some of the local Nsukka boys in high jump, he raises the bar a notch behind their backs believing that they can clear it. At that moment she recognises the difference between how her and her cousins were raised:

> It was what Aunty Ifeoma did to my cousins, I realized then, setting higher and higher jumps for them in the way she talked to them, in what she expected of them. She did it all the time believing they could scale the rod. And they did. It was different for Jaja and me. We did not scale the rod because we believed we

could, we scaled it because we were terrified that we couldn't. (226)

This marks an important shift in Kambili's relationship with her father, taking place shortly after being discharged from hospital. Combining with the previous recognitions, it enables her to distance herself from him and his abusive and intolerant ways, to recognise them for what they are. It is not long after this that she realises, in part one, the collapse of the old order as liberating.

The change can, however, already be discerned soon after the recognition. Previously, her father had laid down the rule of right and wrong: what he says is sinful, is sinful; what he sets out in her daily programme for her to do, she will do. We can see this over Christmas: before the drive to the *mmuo* Ifeoma asks Kambili if she would like to change into shorts. She responds, "I'm fine Aunty", and wonders "why I did not tell her that all my skirts stopped well past my knees, that I did not own any trousers because it was sinful for a woman to wear trousers" (80). There is no distance between Kambili and the view articulated here. It is only the parallels to Eugene's manner of speaking ("it was sinful") that reveals, as Daria Tunca has shown in other moments in the novel, that Kambili "has no critical distance vis-a-vis her father's teachings and weaves his speech into hers" (2014, 56). After her recognition, however, this changes. Attending Mass in Father Amadi's church, in a parallel scene, Kambili notices that many of the women do not have their hair "properly covered", and "others wore trousers, even jeans". Observing this, Kambili thinks to herself, "Papa would be scandalized. A woman's hair must be covered in the house of God, and a woman must not wear a man's clothes, especially in the house of God, he would say" (Adichie 2005, 240). Placing "he would say" at the end rather than the beginning of the sentence results the reader initially reading this as another ventriloquism of Eugene's views, only realizing at the conclusion of the sentence what has changed. The fact that it is "Papa" who "would be scandalized" and that "he would say" that it is wrong signifies a critical distance and thus a major shift in Kambili's relation to her father, and his ethics.

An important element in all of these recognitions, particularly of the importance of Papa-Nnukwu to her, is Kambili's emotional response. After the events of Palm Sunday, Kambili expresses her love for Father

Amadi, which has been steadily growing throughout the narrative. The primary impact that Father Amadi has on Kambili, or rather, the way in which he is so influential with her, is in drawing her out of the shell in which her father has kept her, bringing her out of the silence imposed upon her and into an enjoyment of laughter and curiosity. On the way back to Ifeoma's flat after their first afternoon alone together, Kambili replays the afternoon in her mind: "I had smiled, run, laughed. My chest filled with something like bath foam. Light. The lightness was so sweet I tasted it on my tongue, the sweetness of an overripe bright yellow cashew fruit" (180). This image is quite different from the description of her pleasure at gaining her father's approval. Where previously her mouth felt full of melting sugar, the imagery here is also of sweetness, but is combined with lightness: the single word "light" slipping between the physical quality of weightlessness and optic brilliance. As a result, it is a more embodied, powerful image, and Kambili's love for Father Amadi, as is the case with erotic love, is likewise more powerful than that for her father: it consumes her to the point that she envies the water he drinks.

This love gives her the motivation to overcome her silence. She begins to sing Igbo choruses with Father Amadi in his car, and when she returns to school before being hospitalised, she, unusually, plays with the other children, hearing Father Amadi's voice encouraging her. It is Father Amadi that gives her the courage to make use of the freedom which opens up for her at the end of the novel, and it is because of this that in the final section he retains his importance. Eugene is dead, poisoned by his wife; Ifeoma and her family move to the United States; and Father Amadi, in poetic moment of reversal, is sent to Germany as a missionary. Once Eugene is dead, Kambili still loves him, "offers Masses for [him] every Sunday", and wants "to see him in my dreams [...] so much I sometimes make my own dreams" (306). Yet she has completely moved away from his Catholicism. She attends St Andrews in Enugu where the priest is a Blessed Way Missionary Father like Father Amadi, and carries Father Amadi's letters around on her person, "because they remind me of my worthiness, because they tug at my feelings" (303).

Kambili's emotions also signal the tragic ambiguity that exists in Eugene. I have noted that Kambili's love and respect for her father in large part reflects his work to keep publishing politically critical articles in his newspaper, despite the pressure of the government; her fear of him reflects his devastating failure as a father and a husband. The effect of this mixture of responses is to problematise the rejection of Eugene's abuse and Catholicism that is carried out in the novel. Cooper accurately observes that "while Papa should be uncompromisingly condemned for the emotional and physical abuse he heaps on his family, he should also be appreciated, to some, albeit limited, extent, for the political stance he takes publically" (2008, 126). By extension the same applies to his Catholicism: the oppressive and intolerant strain of Catholicism that is rejected in the novel is what educated both Eugene and Ifeoma, and motivates both his political stance and his massive, secret donations (which are only discovered after his death) to hospitals and charities. This tension is cast by Cooper in terms of personal redemption; that is, whichever action is more ethically weighty defines the situation and Eugene's character, which in this case runs the risk of redeeming him. And it is a risk for Cooper, as Eugene's crimes are irredeemable (127–128). Although this might often be a necessary judgement to make, Eugene can be more productively read as an instance of the tragedy of the colonial legacy. Not an example of contingently conflicting values, as was the case in *The Hungry Tide*, Eugene rather embodies what I decribed in the introduction, where the negative and positive ethical aspects of a situation or person are folded into one another and do not necessarily synthesise into a single conclusion. There is something worth salvaging from Eugene's life and Catholicism while there is simultaneously an urgent need to reject much of the same.

The dispersed recognitions that occur throughout the narrative, recognitions in both the more general sense of gaining knowledge and narrative shifts, bring about and shape Kambili's primary recognition, the moment of *anagnorisis*, and the transition and growth through which she moves in the novel—a transition that constitutes the novel's intervention into the ethical question of the interactions between different faiths and the value of inculturation. Nevertheless, the rejection of the form of Catholicism which Eugene represents is no simple matter, caught up as it is in the embedded, tragic character of the legacy of colonialism. As I turn now to consider *Half of a Yellow Sun*, we will see that Adichie's concern with the ethics of belief remains pertinent as the setting of the novel brings to the fore the relationship between Christians and Muslims. There is also, as noted earlier, a widening of the ethical scope beyond the relatively narrow focus of *Purple Hibiscus*, to the ethics of remembering violence.

IV

The recognitions in *Half of a Yellow Sun* differ from those in *Purple Hibiscus*. In the latter I tracked the progression of four dispersed recognitions that together shaped and brought about the primary ethical recognition in the novel. In the former the recognitions, while still interconnected, are in a different relation to the narrative's ethical concerns. *Half of a Yellow Sun* is set in the decade of 1960, covering the years before the Nigerian Civil War, as well as and primarily, the years of the war itself. As such, the ethics of the novel are immediately cast, at least partially, in terms of remembrance. What makes *Half of a Yellow Sun* interesting is that the ethical recognitions that occur in it are often not to do with the war at all. Instead, the narrative foregrounds the everyday, particularly the romantic, details of the characters' lives, and it is along this axis that many of the recognitions take place. Nevertheless, the narrative makes a poignant, ethical remembrance of the Biafran war. It is precisely in the interplay between the war and daily life, and the way the recognitions in the novel are folded into it, that the novel's ethics is developed.

A further distinction is the role played by the emotive aspects of the novel. In *Purple Hibiscus,* the role of the emotions in bringing about some of Kambili's recognitions and in highlighting the tragic ambiguity of Eugene emerged. This will be particularly relevant in *Half of a Yellow Sun*, primarily due to the form which Adichie utilises, namely, the romantic novel that, together with works that (ethically) remember horrors of the past, emphasises the importance an emotional response. I will first discuss *Half of a Yellow Sun* on a more general level, sketching the combination of genres in the narrative, and the interplay between them and the remembrance of the war. In subsequently turning to the details of the recognitions themselves, which mostly follow the personal relationships and crises, I will map the ethical sense that emerges and, linking back to *Purple Hibiscus*, how different belief systems intersect with this. This will return us to the ethics of remembering violence, and I will close with a consideration of how the ethical sense is shaped by the recognitions in the novel.

A number of the novels set during the Nigerian Civil War have tended to focus on its horrors and injustices. For instance, Cyprian

Ekwensi's *Divided We Stand* (1980), narrated by the Igbo journalist Isaac Chike, emphasises the slaughter of innocent victims: the war is genocide in the name of unity, sponsored and caused by Britain and the west. Festus Iyayi's *Heroes* (1986) is similar. Also narrated by a journalist, one Osime Iyere, it likewise emphasises the brutality of the war—though in this class focused account both sides are committing horrors (an acknowledgement that we also find in Adichie), and those who are to blame are the Nigerian elite, again on both sides. They are the source of the lies and manipulations that caused the pogroms in the first place, and they are the ones that profit from the mutual slaughter of tribes where before there was friendship and brotherhood. I am not here going to get into the details of these novels. I mention them to mark the fact that Adichie is less concerned with portraying the horrific violence of the war than some previous representations of it have been. There is a precedence, however, for the kind of novel that Adichie has written. In her acknowledgments, she notes Chukwuemeka Ike's *Sunset at Dawn* (1976) and Flora Nwapa's *Never Again* (1975) as "indispensable in creating the mood of middle-class Biafra" (Adichie 2007a, 435). As this implies, both of these novels approach the war more obliquely, as Adichie does, with a corresponding shift away from a preoccupation with the violence. Nevertheless, *Sunset at Dawn* still focuses on the violence, particularly the unrelenting bombing of non-combatants. Flora Nwapa's novella, on the other hand, is quite distinctive, especially among the early civil war novels, in representing almost no direct fighting at all, and through this creating a remarkably tangible sense of the fear and perpetual threat of violence that pervaded civilian life during the conflict.

It is this aspect of her heritage on which Adichie draws in limiting the amount of violence in the narrative. Discussing the novel, John C. Hawley (2008) remarks that it is one "that some might criticize as too heavily laden with love stories and with comparatively little gore" (21). Interestingly, these scenes of conflict come under criticism for the opposite reason to what Hawley imagined. Brenda Cooper, for instance, argues that the intense clarity of the portrayals of violence plays into the stereotypical tropes of Africa as brutal and violent, "add[ing] to the archive of negative images". She asks of these scenes: "when families are butchered and cut up in the novel, when good men participate in gang rape [...] what is added to our knowledge of Africa?" (2008, 139). While Adichie does, perhaps, run a risk of reinforcing a negative view of the continent, Cooper is asking a misleading question here. If we ask, instead, what these scenes of violence add to our knowledge of the Biafran war, the implied answer is quite different.

While it is possible to write a story of the war without any violent details, as Flora Nwapa did (though it is doubtful whether it is possible in a work of greater length), there is an ethical basis for not doing so: it is important to remember those who were brutalised (Kearney 1999). Cooper has up until this point in her work been engaged in analysing the excellent use to which Adichie puts her "richly depicted" details of everyday life (2008, 134), in both *Purple Hibiscus* and *Half of a Yellow Sun*. Rather than, as Cooper argues, this characteristic feature of Adichie's writing getting "hijacked by being sucked into the tropes of dominant discourse" in the scenes of violence (143), it seems that the texture of description remains constant across scenes both of violence and of the non-violent daily life. The rich, detailed and sensuous descriptions, which Cooper admires, are unflinchingly extended into the more unpleasant moments, making them more traumatic. The result, as Dennis Walder (2011) argues in his discussion of Cooper's reading, is that the details "provide the novel with a sense of *witnessing* what has happened, rather than merely remembering or recording it" (134). The few (and there are, as I have emphasised, comparatively few) representations of violence that are included in the novel can therefore be understood as an ethical (and necessary) part of the remembrance of the war.

That there is a restriction on the violence represented in the novel is due to the use of a limited, extra-diegetic narrator, none of whose focalisers (except for Ugwu towards the end) are directly involved with the fighting. The use of a limited perspective, Hugh Hodges (2009) observes, creates a persuasive sense of the human scale of the conflict: "we learn only as much about Nigerian air raids on Umuahia (or the uses of traditional magic in modern Nigeria, or the starvation caused by Nigeria's blockade of Biafra) as we can by observing characters experiencing them" (8). To have utilised an omniscient narrator that provides the reader with facts far beyond the characters' knowledge (as in, for instance, Buchi Emecheta's *Destination Biafra* [1982]) would shift the focus onto the events of the war and away from the particular experience of living through them. In using a limited narrator, Adichie foregrounds the lives of the characters as they live the run-up to, and the difficulties of, the conflict—only bringing into focus suffering and ethical challenges as they are individually experienced. As my discussion of violence in the novel suggests, Adichie's focus on the characters' lives rather than the events of the war does not relegate the war to a static backdrop. Hodges notes that unlike a few other civil war novels—his example is Kalu Okpi's *Biafra Testament* (1982), a civil war novel in the form of a spy/war thriller with scenes that could be transposed into any other spy/war thriller context—the war in *Half of a Yellow Sun* has a profound effect on the characters' lives and senses of self. In the words of Hawley, the war is "a vortex that threatens to pull [Adichie's] characters to pieces" (2008, 23).[33]

Adichie's characters are primarily involved in a number of love stories, which occupies much of the novel, and through which most of the recognitions occur. Before considering them in detail it will be useful to discuss at a more general level the interaction between the romantic lives of the characters and the war. The narrative is divided into chronologically disordered parts ("early sixties", "late sixties", "early sixties", "late sixties") with the result that the first section dealing with the events of the war (part two: the late sixties) introduces the reader to an unexplained baby. It is also scattered with references to a resolved relationship crisis about which the reader only learns the details in the next section. The effect is that within the narration of the devastating, haunting events of the massacres of the Igbo, the mass migration south, the secession, and the early stages of the war, a curiosity about the characters' relationships prior to the war is kept alive. The narrative shifts to this moment of crisis in part three and then returns, in part four, to the years of the war. Commenting on this structure in an interview, Adichie remarked that she "wanted [the reader] to remember the times when life was fairly peaceful and all these characters had to worry about was who was sleeping with whom" (Mundow 2006, n.p.). This shifting in time accomplishes more than this, however. It also results in the haunting of the peaceful times in part three by the gruesome fates that some of the characters, we know, will meet and have already met in part two. As Cooper comments, "when we observe characters involved in the minutiae of their daily lives before the war, characters who we have already seen brutally massacred during

---

[33] See also Adichie's comments on this in an interview for the Boston Globe (Mundow 2006).

the war, the meaning of the everyday within its supposed ordinariness is de-familiarised" (2008, 134–135). The characters' lives while at peace and while at war are thus tightly interwoven and this double effect, of the concerns of peacetime shadowing the time of war and the horrors of war haunting the concerns of peacetime, creates a sharp sense of the human cost of the war. Both the limited narrator and the non-linear structure of the novel are, in these ways, crucial to the sense of the war that is conveyed. As I turn now to the relationship plots and their recognitions, this double influence of war on life and life on war will be of continued significance, though the war itself will momentarily drop from view as many of the recognitions occur in the years preceding it. Its implications will be seen again, though, in one of the more important realizations towards the close of the novel.

The web of relationships is introduced to us in part one through the three focalisers. The first, and perhaps most significant due to his central position in relation to the others (Akpome 2013, 28), is Ugwu, a young boy who moves to Nsukka from his village to work as a houseboy in Odenigbo's home. Through Ugwu we learn that Odenigbo, a professor of mathematics at the university, is in a relationship with Olanna, the second focaliser and the daughter of the very wealthy Chief Ozobia. Olanna moves to Nsukka to take up a lectureship at the University and to move in with Odenigbo. Through Olanna, in turn, we meet Kainene, her maternal twin sister who, in part one, begins what is to be a serious relationship with Richard, the third focaliser and a white Englishman who has recently moved to Nigeria. When part one comes to a close, we are familiar with these five main characters in an apparently stable web of interconnection.

The crisis in these relationships begins with Olanna's recognition of Odenigbo's infidelity. Part three opens with Olanna spending some time away from Nsukka in London. While she is away, Odenigbo's mother visits from the village for a couple of days with a young woman, Amala, in tow. The details of her two visits will be considered below. However, during this first substantial absence of Olanna from Nsukka, Odenigbo betrays her and sleeps with Amala. Returning unawares, Olanna meets Odenigbo's mother and Amala as they are leaving Odenigbo's house, and, illustrating the frequent reliance of recognitions on "marginal detail[s]" (Cave 1988, 250), begins to notice signs that everything is not as it should be. The first indication is Odenigbo's greeting: when they hugged, "his body did not relax against her and the brief press of his lips felt papery" (Adichie 2007a, 222). Olanna becomes concerned when she notices how strangely Odenigbo passes the car key to Amala, avoiding "any contact, any touch of skin, as if they were united by a common knowledge so monumental that they were determined not to be united by anything else" (223). Bothered by her observation, but unsure of what it means, she observes when Odenigbo's mother and Amala have left that she was not expecting to see them. Odenigbo's reply is simply "Yes", but his body language sparks Olanna's recognition of what has happened:

> He began to rearrange the newspapers, avoiding her eyes. And, slowly, shock spread over Olanna. She knew. She knew from the jerky movements he made, from the panic on his face, from the hasty way he was trying to look normal again, that something that should not have happened had happened. 'You touched Amala,' Olanna said. (224)

Olanna follows the trail of Odenigbo's body to his state of mind and the recognition of the event to which it is linked.

Olanna's *anagnorisis* here is a pivotal scene in the novel, resulting in a number of significant repercussions, both material and epistemological, marking a turning point in the narrative. The most immediate result is that Olanna leaves Odenigbo, uncertain if they will reconcile. Additionally, her relationship with Ugwu is strained, and when she learns that Amala is carrying Odenigbo's child—that she became pregnant after only one night with him, while Olanna herself, after months of trying, was unsuccessful—she sleeps with Richard, her sister's lover. Sex with Richard is a redeeming and rejuvenating experience for her, and it is not long before she begins to sleep with Odenigbo again and tells him of her affair with Richard. He is incredulous and, seeing this, Olanna has a sorrowful moment of recognition. "She sat up and realized that distrust would always lie between them, that disbelief would always be an option for them" (244). She recognises a fundamental change in their relationship: that even if they reunite, things have been permanently altered. And it is a recognition that is proved later in the novel when, during the war, Olanna begins to wonder whether Odenigbo has again cheated on her.

It is when Olanna, the morning after revealing her affair with Richard, learns from her neighbour that white people have killed four children in a bombing of a black Baptist church in the USA, that these ethical recognitions coalesce into a critical realization. Olanna's neighbour's grief makes her "feel helpless, brought up the urge to stretch her hand into the past and reverse history". Olanna,

> sat thinking about how a single act could reverberate over time and space and leave stains that could never be washed off. She thought about how ephemeral life was, about not choosing misery. She would move back to Odenigbo's house. (245)

Brought about by Edna's grief and her own reflections, the events and recognitions of the past weeks converge into the knowledge which Olanna here gains: the irrevocability of actions and their consequences, and the transitory nature of life. This is one of the main ethical thrusts of the novel, such that the importance of Edna's grief for Olanna's recognition foreshadows a similar role played by the civil war at a later moment, when the horrors of the conflict leads Kainene to realise a related point. The truth of this realization continues to play out in the last movements of part three. Unexpectedly, though, Olanna proposes that she and Odenigbo raise the child, which they do, and for a time it appears as if the web of relationships has returned, with a few changes, to its former equilibrium—until Kainene's discovery of Richard and Olanna's affair. Part three ends with Kainene and Olanna no longer speaking.

Intersecting with these relational recognitions, and building on *Purple Hibiscus*, is the relationship between belief systems. Before Olanna's recognition of Odenigbo's infidelity there is an important one by Ugwu: Odenigbo's mother has used witchcraft—bad medicine—to cause Odenigbo to cheat. Ugwu's suspicions begin with Odenigbo's mother's first visit, Amala in tow. Olanna, who has not met her before, greets them in a genial and friendly way only to be met by hostile accusations of not suckling at her mother's breasts, being called abnormal and being told to go back to her fellow witches and tell them that she did not find her son. Shocked,

> Olanna stared at her. Master's mother's voice rose [...] 'Did you hear me? Tell them that nobody's medicine will work on my son. He will not marry an abnormal woman, unless you kill me first. Only over my dead body!' Master's mother clapped her hands, then hooted and slapped her palm across her mouth so that the sound echoed. (97)

Olanna tries to placate her, but she only becomes louder, shouting out the door: "'Neighbours! There is a witch in my son's house! Neighbours!' Her voice was shrill'" (97). Stunned, Olanna leaves. Ugwu, present through this, is, of course, shocked himself. But he becomes afraid when Odenigbo's mother starts talking about going to the *dibia*, the witchdoctor, worrying if "Master's mother would tie up Olanna's womb or cripple her or, most frightening of all, kill her" (98). From that point, Ugwu is on the lookout for anything suspicious which might indicate the presence of medicine being used against either Odenigbo or Olanna.

He consequently begins to notice some strange occurrences, signs of bad medicine. Shortly after Odenigbo's mother's first visit a black cat appears in the back garden. When Odenigbo's mother visits again, the signs proliferate. Ugwu notices that she puts a mysterious powder into Odenigbo's food from a black packet, claiming it is a spice. He also spots her rubbing a lotion onto Amala, but "there was something wrong about the way Mama's hands were moving in circular motions, slowly, as if in consonance with some ritual" (216). And there is a strange swarming of flies in the kitchen that suddenly disappears. Beautifully illustrating the instability of knowledge gained through moments of recognition, Ugwu concludes that there is bad medicine at work and tries to warn Olanna and Odenigbo: Olanna after he sees the cat, and Odenigbo after seeing the flies. Both of them are dismissive of the idea of witchcraft and give rational explanations for the phenomena, causing Ugwu to doubt his recognition. That night, however, Odenigbo sexually betrays Olanna, and Ugwu is convinced that "Mama's medicine had done this" (216).

At first glance, the novel appears to present Ugwu's recognition of bad medicine, and the traditional belief system that it indicates, as something that is at best a psychological aid, at worst a hindrance. When Odenigbo comes to Olanna's flat after she was accused of being a witch, he explains his mother's actions as relics from an old world, unsuited to the new:

> Do you know what a small bush village [she lives in]? Of course she will feel threatened by an educated woman living with her son. Of course you have to be a witch. That is the only way she can understand it. The real tragedy of our postcolonial world is not that the majority of people had no say in whether or not they wanted this new world; rather, it is that the majority have not been given the tools to *negotiate* this new world. (101, emphasis in original)

Odenigbo's view of the insufficiency of the traditional understanding of the world, the only one the uneducated have available to them, recurs when Olanna relates to him that Ugwu believes his infidelity is due to bad medicine. Odenigbo comments, neglecting the fact that Ugwu suspected bad medicine at work prior to the infidelity, "I suppose it's the only way he can make sense of it" (253). Olanna concurs and points out that it is irrational since if the pregnancy was the result of the medicine then the child should have been a boy and not the girl that was disowned by both her mother and grandmother. Interestingly, though, when Odenigbo replies that it is "no more irrational than belief in a Christian God you cannot see", Olanna disagrees. Accustomed to half agreeing with him, she can no longer do so and responds, "I do believe [...] I believe in a good God" (253).

Ugwu's recognition of bad medicine at work remains unstable, then, discredited by the primary characters as a false recognition based on false reasoning. Given no more than psychological credence, it is considered a limitation, a marker of lacking the tools to navigate the postcolonial world. Odenigbo argues for precisely this during the war. As part of his "win the war effort" he travels to various villages, teaching the inhabitants about the conflict. After one such visit, "Master was standing, gesturing, talking about the last village he visited, how the people had sacrificed a goat at the shrine of *oyi* to keep the vandals [the Nigerians] away." When a friend ridicules it, Odenigbo replies, "No, no, you must never underestimate the psychological importance of such things. We never ask them to eat the goat instead" (284). The psychological effects of belief are given precedence, and are manipulated to further the ends of the war.

This psychological understanding is, however, complicated by two factors. On the one hand, and illustrating the importance of *paralogismos,* false reasoning, to recognitions in general (Cave 1988, 39–43), there is the fact that Ugwu's alleged false recognition of bad medicine at work was actually correct. While it is unlikely that the black cat and other signs noted by Ugwu had any truth to them (hence it is still false reasoning), it seems very probable that, considering her belief in witches and the powers of the *dibia,* Odenigbo's mother did indeed use traditional medicine to try and separate Olanna and Odenigbo. Ugwu's warnings were dismissed at Olanna and Odenigbo's own peril. To dismiss "bad medicine" so easily is to neglect that traditional medicine often has scientific veracity. In this case, one could understand the mysterious powder as an aphrodisiac, which, combined with strong drink and fragrant oils rubbed onto a woman, facilitated temptation.

The most suggestive use of traditional beliefs, though, is at the close of the novel. Kainene disappears and is never heard from again, and Olanna and Richard are shattered by the loss. Richard's thread of the narrative comes to a close with the recognition "that he would never see Kainene again and that his life would always be like a candlelit room; he would see things only in shadow, only in half glimpses" (430). Olanna, in desperation, consults a *dibia* who assures her that he can bring Kainene back. But, despite the sacrifice of a goat, Kainene does not appear. Olanna fears she did something wrong, at which Odenigbo assures her, "The war has ended but hunger has not, *nkem.* That *dibia* was just hungry for goat meat. You can't believe in that." Her reply is that she "'will believe in anything that will bring my sister home" (433). Yet Olanna's narrative thread, and the novel, ends on the same acknowledgement as Richard's, as she turns to the only belief that now gives her comfort:

'We come back again,' she said.
'What?'
'Our people say that we all reincarnate, don't they?' she said.
'*Uwa m, uwa ozo.* When I come back in my next life, Kainene will be my sister.' She had started to cry softly. Odenigbo took her in his arms. (433)

It is suggestive that having earlier realised her belief in a good, ostensibly Christian, God, Olanna turns for hope not to the Christian belief in the afterlife but rather to the Igbo belief in reincarnation—a belief that she had previously discredited (253). This moment affects the understanding within the novel of both Christianity and traditional belief. That Olanna turns to the Igbo belief in reincarnation for comfort, causes Odenigbo's psychological understanding of traditional religion to be extended to Christianity. Coupled with the ambiguity of Christianity that, as Daria Tunca (2013) has observed, results from the duplicity of the Catholic priests in the refugee camp (helping the refugees, but then being exposed as also sexually abusing vulnerable women) (62), Christianity, as was implied in *Purple Hibiscus*, is consequently left open to be read together with traditional religion as "elaborate forms of self-deception" (67). Simultaneously, however, while traditional beliefs do not entirely escape the framing of psychological credence, this moment also suggests that in negotiating the tragedies of the postcolonial world they may be more psychologically or emotionally effective, more productive, than Odenigbo or Olanna originally thought.

While the interactions between atheism, Christianity and traditionalism are thus suggestive, the main ethical thrust in the novel in terms of belief is the interaction between the Muslim north and the Christian east. One of the major fault lines in Nigeria, it corresponds largely with the tribal and geographic divisions along which the civil war occurred. The concern here is mainly essentialism, and links to the ethical challenge present in all remembrances of suffering to resist the pull towards hatred and revenge. In the first section of the novel, we are introduced to a branch of Olanna's extended family. Significantly poorer than her own, they live in Kano in northern Nigeria where their home provides a frequently needed refuge for Olanna. However, they are brutally murdered during the massacres (the scene of which is the main focus of Cooper's criticism of Adichie's representation of violence) and the shock leaves Olanna physically paralysed for some time. Present in the north when it happens, Olanna herself only survives because her ex-boyfriend, a Muslim Hausa, helps her to escape. Given this history, she is very surprised when, much later during the conflict, Odenigbo gets annoyed over her concern that Mohammed "must be so upset about all this [the war]"; he rebukes her for "saying that a bloody Muslim Hausa man is upset". Incredulously, she asks if he is joking, to which he replies, "Am I joking? How can you sound this way after seeing what they did in Kano? Can you imagine what must have happened to Arize [Olanna's cousin]? They raped pregnant women before they cut them up!" (Adichie 2007a, 191). Olanna is furious. "She could not believe he had brought Arize up like that, *cheapened Arize's memory in order to make a point* in a spurious argument" (191, emphasis mine). Although the narrative as a whole positions itself in favour of the secession as a response to the massacres and the memory of lost loved ones, this interchange between Olanna and Odenigbo cautions against blanket condemnation of social groups and the cheapening of the memory of the dead by enlisting them to unworthy ends—or, indeed, even more worthy ones, as will be seen in my discussion of Coetzee's *The Lives of Animals*.

Adichie's concern to resist and problematise essentialism and the instrumental use of the memory of the dead in this way can also be seen in her short story "A Private Experience" (Adichie 2009a). Only a dozen pages long, the story narrates an evening spent in Northen Nigeria by Chika, hiding in an abandoned shop. There is a riot in progress, and she is led to the safety of the shop by a woman, an onion seller in the market. We never learn her name, though we do learn of the completely different worlds that she and Chika inhabit. Chika is Igbo, Christian, rich and educated (training to be doctor), while the trader is Hausa, Muslim, poor and largely uneducated. Unknown to the two women, while they are speaking "Hausa Muslims are hacking down Igbo Christians with machetes, clubbing them with stones" (Adichie 2009a, 44). Yet despite their differences, the violence of the riot leads them to share a common anxiety about their family members from whom they are separated. And in the course of the evening they share a little of their lives with each other: the trader prays and cries for her daughter, and Chika examines the trader's nipples which are burning. Through a series of prolepses we learn that the cause of the violence was an Igbo accidentally standing on a Koran, and that Chika will never find her sister. As the evening, and the story, comes to an end, the narrator informs us that "later, Chika will read in *The Guardian* that 'the reactionary Hausa-speaking Muslims in the North have a history of violence against non-Muslims'". This totalizing description is immediately challenged as the narrator continues: "and in the middle of her grief [for her sister], she will stop to remember that she examined the nipples and experienced the gentleness of a woman who is Hausa and Muslim" (55). In the midst of representing grief, we see a resistance to the enlisting of the memories of lost loved ones to essentializing ends.

Adichie, then, makes the ethical move of rejecting essentialism, hatred and the instrumental use of the dead. She has also, however, presented a highly accurate account of the conflict. Richard Kearney argues that there are multiple ethical challenges that confront works of remembrance. On the one hand there is the requirement to remember accurately while, on the other, which we have already seen, the requirement not to succumb to hatred or a desire for revenge. When we add the consideration of the right of the artist to produce works of creative imagination, the difficulty of navigating a path becomes apparent (Kearney 1999, 18).[34] Adichie acknowledges these tensions when she comments that

> to write about a war, especially one central to the history of one's country, is to be constantly aware of a responsibility to something larger than art. While writing *Half of a Yellow Sun*, I enjoyed playing with minor things [....] Yet I did not play with the central events of that time. I could not let a character be changed by anything that had not actually happened. (Adichie 2007b, 11)

Adichie gives greatest weight, as perhaps she should, to the ethical requirement of accuracy. And indeed this bears up under scrutiny. The fall of the three most important towns for the characters—Nsukka, Port Harcourt, and Umuahia—are kept in their historical order; the speeches in the novel—most importantly three by the Biafran head of state Lieutenant-Colonel Ojukwu (the Declaration of the Republic of Biafra [161–162], the Ahiara Declaration [386] and his speech before leaving the country [407]) and Lieutenant-Colonel Efiong's announcement of Biafra's surrender (411–412)—are extracts from the actual speeches; and the Caritas refugee centre in Orlu, which becomes Kainene's personal cause and obsession and for which she, fatefully, goes cross-border trading, actually existed. It seems, in fact, that the largest event of the war which Adichie altered is when "the miracle of Abagana" occurs (332). In the novel it is after

---

[34] See also Kearney (2002a).

the fall of Port Harcourt, while in reality it was before. Adichie comments, accurately: "I'll hear from people who are displeased by certain things. But they won't be able to say that I lied. I'm sure people will be upset, but it will be ideological" (Mundow 2006, n.p.).

A further aspect of the ethics of remembering violence raised by Adichie, and one of her anticipated points of ideological disagreement, is the question of who can tell the story of Biafra. Throughout the novel we are introduced to another text: *The World was Silent when We Died* (henceforth 'The Book'), which relates information about the background to and the events of the Biafran war. Revealed in fragments recounting its writing, all of which, except one, are placed at the end of sections focalised by Richard, the reader is led to believe that Richard, Kainene's white English boyfriend, is the author. This is strengthened by the use of the anonymous 'he' to describe the writer in each fragment, Richard's expressed intentions of writing a book, and his invention of its title (Adichie 2007a, 374).[35] It is only at the very end of the novel, in a moment of epistemological inversion characteristic of recognition—in the sense of "an outcome that defies expectations yet appears in retrospect to be a *logical* outcome" (Cave 1988, 31, emphasis in original)—that the author of 'The Book' is named as Ugwu. And indeed, as Ngwira (2012) has shown in his analysis, the novel contains within it all the indications that this is the case, which in re-reading after the recognition come to the fore and show Ugwu as having been the author all along: his education provided by Odenigbo, his access to Odenigbo's books, his exposure to Odenigbo and his peers' debates about the history of Nigeria. Taken together with his experiences during the war, they establish Ugwu as the preferred witness for Biafra. The final revelation of Ugwu as the author of 'The Book', then, withdraws the "legitimacy to speak for Biafra" from Richard and grants it to Ugwu instead (Tunca 2014, 92).

It is this withdrawing of the 'The Book' from Richard that has been criticised as running counter to Adichie's resistance to essentialism. Cooper, for instance, contends that excluding Richard reinforces an essentialist view of culture (2008, 147). Richard is not, however, a straightforwardly sympathetic character whose exclusion is based solely on ethnic grounds. Through his relationship with Kainene, he is revealed, as Krish-

---

[35] For a detailed analysis of 'The Book's' fragments as a reflection on the process of writing, see Ngwira (2012).

nan (2012) shows, to be implicated in the discourse of exoticism. Having first come to Nigeria because of his interest in the bronze cast roped pots of ancient Igbo-Ukwu art, his love for Kainene and his love for the pots repeatedly slip into one another. Thus, a case in point is when he is speaking with Count Von Rosen:

> Richard opened his diary and showed the count first a photo of Kainene, taken by the pool with a cigarette between her lips, and then the photo of the roped pot. 'I fell in love with Igbo-Ukwu art and then fell in love with her,' he said. (Adichie 2007a, 310)

The slippage between Kainene and the pots, which recurs throughout the novel, shows how "Richard's desire for the pots is [...] displaced to his desire for Kainene, turning her into the object of exoticism and fetishistic desire, all the while implicating himself within that same relation" (Krishnan 2012, 31). That Richard is in a position of relative powerlessness in comparison to Kainene does not, as Zoe Norridge (2012) suggests, indicate that the slippage between Kainene and the pots is "more [a gesture] of reverence" (23). Indeed, Krishnan demonstrates that it is Richard's sense of self being "based on negation" that energises his quest of identity through exoticism (2012, 30).

Richard could be understood, then, as being excluded not because he is white, but, in part, because of his implication with exoticism. His search for a stable identity, however, takes him further an imbrication with this colonial discourse. He also desires "participation in the Biafran community" and, more than this, "makes an illicit claim for exclusive ownership of Biafranness" (Tunca 2014, 91). That this exclusivity is rejected by the novel should not be a surprise. However, it is in the more generalised questioning of Richard's identification with the "we" of Biafra (by Kainene and the American journalists [Adichie 2007a, 373, 374], to name two examples) that implies an ethnically based community, and makes Cooper's caution important. Although accurate, Tunca's response to the problem—that in the novel "identities [...] are not shaped against a blank historical canvas" and Richard cannot, therefore, claim identity with this "we" due to the colonial history in which he didn't share (on the part of the Nigerians) and can't so easily discard (on the part of the Europeans) (2014, 92)—fails to remove the implication of cultural essentialism.

This question is raised at the beginning of the novel, when Odenigbo and Ezeka debate whether a pan-Igbo identity existed prior to colonialism (Adichie 2007a, 20-21).[36] Odenigbo, in the words of Miss Adebayo, is "a hopeless tribalist" (21)—a tribalism that is contiguous with his essentializing of the Hausa criticised by Olanna, and discussed earlier. In addition to having Olanna and Miss Adebayo critique Odenigbo's essentialism, however, Adichie also acknowledges that Biafra, while majority Igbo, was also comprised of other minority ethnicities, who as the war worsened became scapegoats, accused of being saboteurs (314-315). This, as with Odenigbo's essentialism, is strongly resisted—this time by Kainene—when an Igbo woman spits on Dr Ingyan (from a non-Igbo minority). Kainene slaps her twice and shouts "We are all Biafrans! *Anyincha bu Biafra!*" (320). What this suggests is not only an awareness of the dangers of essentialism—and its past reality—but that Richard fails to belong, not because of ethnicity but because of his own investment in colonialist discourses; not as part of his cultural background, but as an active part of constructing his responses to the world, which is revealed most explicitly at the very end of the novel when he invokes racist discourses against Madu (430). The novel's final moment of recognition—where Richard, due his own weaknesses, is actively excluded rather than simply failing to belong—is focused on not being able to *tell* the story of Biafra, not because genuine participation in the Biafran community is prohibited a priori on the basis of his race, but because of his complicity with colonial discourse.

Adichie's narrative is, in all then, admirably faithful to the numerous ethical demands exerted on such a work, negotiating the challenges of essentialism while also maintaining historical accuracy. Richard Kearney argues further, however, that in a manner similar to the Greeks' remembrance of their heroes, so too "the horror of moral evil must be retrieved from oblivion by means of narrative memory" (1999, 28). Discussing the Holocaust, and particularly Lanzmann's critique of Spielberg's movie *Schindler's List*, Kearney details Lanzmann's argument (an argument that we will have reason to take up again in the next chapter) that the horror of the holocaust is "uncommunicable" and that to represent it in traditional narrative or cinematic form is to commit "the most serious transgression"

---

[36] See Appiah (1992), particularly "Topologies of Nativism", in which Appiah argues, in agreement with Ezeka, that colonialism produced a reification of African tradition along tribal lines.

(quoted in Kearney 1999, 28). Kearney responds that while Lanzmann's austere, non-representational approach is a very important part of remembering past violence, the shortcoming in positing it as the only ethical option is the neglect of the need for the

> reminiscence of suffering [...] to be *felt* [...] Historical horror requires to be served by an aesthetic [...] quite as powerful and moving as historical triumph—perhaps even *more* powerful if it is to compete for the attention of the public at large. (30, emphasis in original)

And it is in this regard that the romance narratives and their accompanying recognitions in *Half of a Yellow Sun* become particularly important.

We have already seen something of the interplay between the war and these romantic narratives, their effect of conveying the human scale and cost of the war. I want to return to that now, picking up the thread which I left at Kainene's understanding of Olanna's betrayal as unforgivable. In part four of the novel, well into the war, the sisters are eventually reconciled and begin to repair their relationship. At the start of this process, Kainene makes a crucial observation: "There are some things that are so unforgivable that they make other things easily forgivable" (Adichie 2007a, 347). While not a moment of recognition in itself, this comment comes after an extended exposure to the horrors of the war and Kainene reveals a newfound ethical knowledge, echoing Olanna's recognition of the irrevocability of actions and the transitory nature of life. The moment's significance is double, however, being also an instance of the mutual contamination of war and life. On the one hand, this is a scaling of the horror and cost of the war. An unforgivable betrayal of trust, the genesis and consequences of which have been portrayed in detail, is dwarfed to a forgivable size by the sheer atrocity of the war; a violation which the reader is more easily able to comprehend becomes the yardstick by which the war is measured.

On the other hand, however, this very scaling serves to reinforce the serious, irrevocable nature of Olanna's betrayal. This becomes apparent when we consider an important difference between Kainene's and Olanna's understanding of ethics—and particularly Olanna's infidelity with Richard. Immediately after sleeping with him, the narrator tells us that Olanna "felt filled with a sense of wellbeing, with something close to grace" (234). This is expanded for us as Olanna later thinks about her disclosure of her affair to Odenigbo:

> She should not have told him about Richard. Or she should have told him more: that she regretted betraying Kainene and him but did not regret the act itself. She should have said that it was not a crude revenge, or a score-keeping, but took on a redemptive significance for her. She should have said the selfishness had liberated her. (244)

There are two elements at play against each other here: Olanna's sense of duty, with her corresponding failure in it, to Kainene and Odenigbo, and her sense of duty to herself. It is the latter that governs her understanding of the event, outweighing the violation of trusts, even that of her sister. Only when Kainene discovers what occurred, and severs all communication with Olanna, does she come to the full sense of her betrayal. Kainene's response, though, is in synchrony with her understanding of ethics. Throughout the novel she places her responsibility to other people as a priority. It is precisely this that leads, in part, to her involvement with the refugee camp and to her fatal attempt to trade across enemy lines. That it takes something as horrendous as the civil war to make Olanna's betrayal forgivable reinforces how serious the offense was, making Kainene's statement an echo of Olanna's earlier recognition of the concatenating power of a single action.

The centrality of the war for this reconciliation between the sisters takes us to the final mutual contamination of war and everyday life: the affective impact of the characters' narratives. By the close of the novel the reader has followed the convolutions of the relationships between Kainene, Richard, Olanna and Odenigbo, witnessing the negotiation of the trauma of the war in and through their intimate, sexual interconnections (Norridge 2012). And for this reason, when Kainene goes missing it is one of the most moving losses of the narrative. The involvement that the narrative has invested in the web of relationships serves a larger purpose than the romance plots. To come back to Hawley's imagined critics, rather than being "too heavily laden with love stories and with comparatively little gore" (2008, 21), it is precisely the limited narrative perspective intertwined with the affective involvement and scaling effect of the web of relationships that makes *Half of a Yellow Sun* an effective, emotionally powerful, remembrance of the Nigeria-Biafra war. And it is here that the recognition is again caught up in the folding into each other of war and everyday life. The close link between the war and Kainene's gain in ethical knowledge effects a broadening of the recognition's predicate to include the war: it is the unchangeable, gruesome reality of the war that changes what is forgivable, and which leaves Olanna and Richard grieving the loss of Kainene. In this way the novel becomes a remembrance that manages to turn the war into a shaping force for the ethical recognition of the power of "a single act [to] reverberate over time and space and leave stains that could never be washed off" (Adichie 2007a, 245), and by the same move folds this recognition back onto the war such that the "single act" comes also to designate the war itself.

V

A number of points have emerged in this analysis of Adichie's two novels. In *Purple Hibiscus* I traced the ethical move that Kambili makes as she comes to the knowledge that her father's form of Catholicism is oppressive and intolerant. Although the novel presents an inculturated Catholicism as a viable, and desirable, ethical framework, I also noted that matters are not so clear-cut as a simple ethical rejection of a particular (colonial) form of Christianity. Kambili's father is indeed intolerant and abusive. Yet simultaneously, he is dearly loved by his daughter (though at the end she is ashamed to admit it) and is fearless in the use of his newspaper to fight for democracy in an authoritarian Nigeria. Moreover, the Catholicism which is rejected in the novel was crucial in educating Eugene and Ifeoma, making possible his resistance to the government as well as her further education in the academy and inculturated Catholicism. In addition to an ethical intervention in some of the debates around Christianity in Africa, there are therefore two ethical concerns that emerged. In the first instance, we can see Eugene as something of a tragic figure. His Catholicism, although rejected, is both ethically valuable and abhorrent, inspiring both his abuse and his political interventions. The movement to an inculturated Catholicism enacted in the novel is, as it were, the salvaging of that which is beneficial. This does not, however, result in the elimination of the layering of the ethical value of Eugene's colonial Catholicism. The two ethical judgements of Eugene are maintained in tension.

In *Half of a Yellow Sun* the ethical concern shifts. Approaching the remembrance of the Biafran war through the personal lives and crises of her characters, Adichie draws out the mutual contagion between the war and everyday life. Threading through the novel what might seem an ethical truism—the recognition of the irrevocability of action and consequences—it is given fresh poignancy through being folded into the narration of the war. The conflict injects the ethics of everyday life with a new significance through portraying the horrors that need to occur in order to make such a betrayal forgivable. This recognition, in turn, folds back into the representation of the war: that the war makes Olanna's betrayal forgivable creates a powerful sense of its cost and magnitude. And at the close of the novel we see the extent to which the "irrevocable act" of the war has irreversibly stained the lives of the characters. That a single act can radiate outwards to affect an entire history is deployed here more explicitly than in Ghosh, and with an important difference. In Ghosh's work, we see how a single choice is caught up in a complicated sequence of events; how Deeti's recognition of Kalua and her corresponding intervention on his behalf sets in motion their journey to the *Ibis*, where their presence (and their past) is crucial in the events that occur on board. In Adichie an additional layer is added: we see how a single act can reverberate over time and space, as well as the potential for a single moment to shape the meanings of actions beyond its immediate occurrence. In this case, Olanna's recognition shapes the understanding of both the war and the characters' everyday lives.

Despite the important divergences from Ghosh's work, in both context and form, the shape of the ethics that I traced there can also be seen in Adichie's work. Most prominently, the recognitions in the novel retain their significance for delineating its ethical sense. Though the predicates of the recognitions are different, bringing into play a new set of debates, and the relations among them differ from those in Ghosh, their usefulness as a lens through which to approach ethics in the novel remains. Woven into the play of recognitions, we can also note the continued importance of the emotions for ethics in Adichie's novels, both as a cause of recognitions and contributing to the ethics' effectiveness. There is, further, an element of the tragic shape of ethics that I delineated previously, most clearly seen in the figure of Eugene, a tragic combination of good and evil that Kambili responds to with her combination of love and terror. It is, however, the more nuanced ambiguity that I analysed in Ghosh's use of a common humanity that carries over most effectively. The instability of the idea of a common humanity in Ghosh, the un-erasable possibility of human relations turning to violence, is also seen in the ethically viable form of Catholicism in Adichie, hosting within itself the possibility of that which it rejects.

Adichie's novels, then, are primarily concerned with two of the three ethical themes that are the focus of this book: religion and the remembrance of violence—though the idea of a common humanity, as Dalley (2014) has noted, can be inferred from her focus on the materiality of the body as revealing a common ability to feel pain (133), as well from the possibility of forming connections across cultural and religious differences. More than this, the recognitions in Adichie's two novels give rise to a recalibrated sense of self, a recalibration that leaves the relation to the other more open than it was previously: Kambili does not in the end possess a comprehensive understanding of her grandfather, only the certainty of his value. In this openness to the difference of the other we can say that the humanism implied in these novels is comparable to what was observed in Ghosh. Caryl Phillips, to whom I now turn, engages all three ethical themes. As with Adichie, this shift of authors will entail a corresponding change in context. Importantly, turning to Caryl Phillips will enable me to further refine my approach to ethics in the novel through engaging with a different kind of writing: Ghosh and Adichie both write within a more traditional realist mode, while Phillips disturbs the generic norms of realism in a number of significant ways.

Chapter Three
The Failure of Recognition

> Through some atavistic mist, Martha peered back east, beyond Kansas, back beyond her motherhood, her teen years, her arrival in Virginia, to a smooth white beach where a trembling girl waited with two boys and a man. Standing off, a ship. Her journey had been a long one. But now the sun had set. Her course was run. *Father, why hast thou forsaken me?*
>
> (Phillips 2006, 73)

I

The author of ten novels to date, Phillips's oeuvre presents "a body of work rich in diverse settings, time periods, characters and styles" (Taylor 2009). Ranging across several centuries and straddling the continents of Africa, North America and Europe (sometimes in the same book, such as *Crossing the River*) Phillips's novels are populated by characters as diverse as a nineteenth century upper class woman travelling to the Caribbean, a nineteenth century black missionary in Liberia, American GI's in England during the Second World War, and an eighteenth century slaver Captain, to name but a few. Much of Phillips's work is also marked by polyphony, which has characterised in his oeuvre since his third novel, *Higher Ground* (1989), with the first two novels, *The Final Passage* (1985) and *A State of Independence* (1986), being narrated through one central character. Yet despite this impressive range and diversity there is, as Bénédicte Ledent (2002) observes, an "obvious thematic unity" (1), namely, the intersection of questions of identity, race, and migration and exile, each explored as aspects of the legacy of the Atlantic slave trade (Ledent 2002; Eckstein 2006).[37] As such, his works engage with the ethical themes under consideration, namely, remembrance of violence, the human, and

---

[37] Apart from being noted in critical studies of Philips' work, this thematic unity can also be traced in the comments of reviewers on a number of his novels. See for instance Walter (2003), Taylor (2009), and Boddy (2009).

religion. Of all his works published to date, *Cambridge* (1993)[38] and *Crossing the River* (2006)[39] will constitute the focus of this chapter as they present the most sustained and direct consideration of the slave trade and colonial settlement in the Caribbean and Africa, and engage with all three of the ethical themes under consideration.

Cambridge and *Crossing the River* are also notable for being among the most polyphonic of Phillips's works, consisting of multiple narratives in various voices from different ideological positions. Unmediated by an overarching narrator, the multiple narratives leave the reader to negotiate between them, a feature of the works that has often not been kindly reviewed (see Bewes [2006, 45]), though the criticism that has built up around his work has been more positive, appreciating the challenge it poses to readers. This unmediated polyphony contrasts with the more unified narratives that constitute the novels of Adichie and Ghosh that have been considered so far. Importantly, this fragmentation of narrative voice alters the functioning of recognition in relation to the novels' ethical sense. While moments of *anagnorisis* are at play in particular narratives, the ethical effect of the novels relies on the cumulative impact of the interaction between the narratives, and consequently it is more overtly dependent upon the reader than in previously considered texts. In other words, the recognition arises from the narrative form of the novels. In the works of Ghosh and Adichie the characters'/narrators' realizations and the ethical sense of the novel were coextensive. The connection between these aspects now becomes more oblique, though there is still a connection: the novels are carefully crafted to spark particular recognitions in the reader, and an ethical concern that is broached by the texts in this way is precisely the lack, or failure, of recognition in the characters' perceptions and understanding.

Unlike Phillips's later novel, *The Nature of Blood* (1997), in which the narrative threads are interwoven with little more than a line break to mark the alternations between them, in both of the texts considered here the narratives are clearly demarcated and are narrated, uninterrupted, in their entirety. Phillips's narrative strategy in *The Nature of Blood* serves to

---

[38] Originally published: London: Bloomsbury, 1991. All references are to the Vintage International edition.
[39] Originally published: London: Bloomsbury, 1993. All references are to the Vintage edition.

emphasise the thematic continuities between Nazi Germany's treatment of the Jewish people and sixteenth-century Venice's treatment of both Jewish and African peoples, constituting a poignant exploration of Europe's obsession with blood, that is, with issues of race and identity. In *Cambridge* and *Crossing the River*, however, the effect of the structure is to draw overt attention to the narratives' formal aspects, an attention that yields important results. Rarely narrated extra-diegetically, the narratives are constructed as pieces of autobiography or testament—letters, journals, and final testaments—and their style matches the period and form which they represent. This has been particularly noted in *Cambridge* (Eckstein 2006; O'Callaghan 1993). As we saw in Adichie's *Half of a Yellow Sun*, representing periods of trauma in the history of colonialism and its legacies evokes questions on the ethics of memory. What makes Phillips's two texts, particularly *Cambridge* on which I want to focus for now, interesting in this regard is their use of actual historical documents: the accuracy of style in each narrative fragment is reflective of the extensive citation of original documents from the period and genres represented. The result, as Evelyn O'Callaghan (1993) has put it, is a "sense of familiarity, of *déjà vu* which the informed reader experiences in *Cambridge*" (43).

O'Callaghan notes three main sources for Emily's journal, namely "writings by Monk Lewis, Lady Nugent, Mrs. Carmichael *et al*" (1993, 36), while for Cambridge's narrative she notes as the main source *Equiano's Travels* (38). Lars Eckstein's more comprehensive study, to which I will turn in a moment, uncovers a number of other source texts, which includes some historiographic works from the period in addition to the near exact replication in part three of an historical report of the murder of a Mr Brown by a slave Cambridge (presumably, Eckstein comments, "the very historical document that served as [Phillips's] initial inspiration for the novel" [2006, 92]). He adds to O'Callaghan's list of main sources for Emily's narrative Janet Shaw's *Journal of a Lady of Quality*, and a number of less cited travelogues by F.W.N. Bayley, Henry Nelson Coleridge, and J.B. Moreton (Eckstein 2006, 75–76); for Cambridge's narrative he adds James Albert Ukasaw Gronniosaw's *A Narrative of the Life of James Albert Gronniosaw*, Ottobah Cuguano's *Thought and Sentiments on the Evil of Slavery*, and Ignatio Sanchos' *Letters* (85). The report in part three is taken from Mrs. Flannigan's *Antigua and the Antiguans* (92). However, O'Callaghan's insights into the novel are not affected by the omission of these additional source texts. Eckstein's argument is dependent upon detailing the historical citations, which takes up a large part of his chapter on the novel, and includes a detailed Appendix that lists the source fragments for the entire text. For O'Callaghan (1993) what needs to be established is simply that "Phillips has gone to great pains to establish the historical 'authenticity' of his fiction" (39). The significance of this is twofold. On the one hand, *Cambridge* is able to reveal the web of links and contrasts among the "intersecting peripheries" of the time that Phillips represents: Cambridge, Emily and Christiania are all marginalised to differing extents by the racist patriarchal discourse that shapes their worlds (40). On the other hand, it draws our attention to the links between fictional and historical narratives, that is, to "the essentially 'fictional' nature of these texts, particularly in terms of the way conventional formal structures shape the manner in which the 'objective' narrator shapes and judges the 'facts'" (42). O'Callaghan's argument is that the novel exposes the fictional quality of history while simultaneously reminding us of the historical character of the story that is told. And in that capacity, it brings two marginal narratives into a productive proximity.

I will take up both of these insights—the limitations on Emily and Cambridge's discourse, and the productiveness of the proximity of their narratives—in my own analysis with some important differences. In the first instance, though, it should be noted that O'Callaghan's reading is more historical than ethical: as her title states she is concerned with "Historical Fiction and Fictional History". It is in Eckstein's analysis that we approach some of the ethical and political implications of Phillips's narrative strategy. At one point in her article O'Callaghan comments that "it is important to note that while the reading of *Cambridge* is a disconcertingly echoic experience [...] there is no sense of a stylistic patchwork. Each of its narratives is relatively consistent and suited to its presumed author" (1993, 39). This synthesis of numerous stylistically diverse fragments is the focus of Eckstein's analysis. In order to dissect more rigorously the method behind Phillips's success, he distinguishes between "montage" and "pastiche": "montage" is to be understood as the citation of fragments from earlier works, while "pastiche" is the sustained imitation of the style of the earlier works. Eckstein writes:

the novel is composed of numerous, in most cases slightly modified fragments of older texts (montage); at the same time, these fragments are supplemented and interconnected by passages which merely imitate the source-material stylistically while relying on Phillips's own imagination (pastiche). (2006, 73)

Eckstein proceeds by placing the various source texts alongside the passage which draws on them, enabling him to note the elements of montage as well as to analyse the technique of pastiche deployed in incorporating and connecting them into a coherent narrative. Eckstein's aim is to defend Phillips from charges of plagiarism by, firstly, demonstrating the "sheer craft and aesthetic brilliance of Phillips's montage technique", showing the novel to be an "imaginative performance belying any charge of dull repetition". Once established, in the manner adumbrated above, he turns, secondly, to consider the "mnemonic functionality and ideological complexity of Phillips's approach" (75). It is here that Eckstein locates the ethical and political implications of the novel.

Eckstein argues that through his use of montage, Phillips picks a careful path through the debates on the ethics of memory. As with Kearney—and, as will be seen in the final section of this chapter, Bewes—Eckstein draws on the debates surrounding the representation of the Holocaust, and notes three main positions. Two of them I have considered in relation to Adichie's *Half of a Yellow Sun*. On one side of the debate is the argument for the exclusive use of personal testimony and reports since narrative imposes a structure of meaning on otherwise meaningless suffering, and thus does an injustice to the memory of those who suffered. Opposed to this is the argument for the importance of fictional narrative construction precisely because of its shaping effects, that is, in order to personalise and make the effect of the horror on an individual consciousness *felt*, so as to guard against the Holocaust being reduced to impersonal reports and facts which are "too gigantic to be digested or comprehended as such" (100–103; see also Kearney 1999). We saw that Adichie, although accurate in the major historical details, came down on the side of making the horror felt through the skilful deployment of popular narrative form. Phillips's montage, Eckstein argues, manages to combine these two approaches. Drawing extensively on historical, personal testimonies and reports, Phillips fuses them into a cohesive, fictional whole. In comparison to

Adichie's inclusion in *Half of a Yellow Sun* of actual speeches and events from the Biafran war, Phillips's form and subject matter enable him to combine these two approaches to the ethics of memory to an extent that Adichie, most likely, did not intend to. The third approach Eckstein notes is a more strictly formal one: a matching of the narrative form to that which it represents. Citing Glissant's argument on the necessity for literature from the Antilles to disrupt linear time, Eckstein proposes that the intertextuality of *Cambridge* as such "embodies the 'explosion' of formal and temporal unity as Glissant describes it" (104). Beneath the smooth surface of the text, the source fragments leap backwards and forwards through time. Eckstein therefore argues that the novel successfully negotiates three different imperatives of the ethics of memory "without sacrificing any of them" (105).

There is also what Eckstein designates as a political aspect to the montage and pastiche in *Cambridge*. To draw this out he turns to recent theory that "expresses an increasing dichotomisation of the spheres of recollection into 'memory' and 'history'". Memory is understood as recollection that is lived and effective in the present for an individual or collection of individuals who "derive norms and values from it" and deploy it to "negotiate identity". History, on the other hand, has no immediate bearing on life lived in the present, "comprising all those manifestations of memory that are not linked up with any individual or collective agency" (108). The example here is the archive or library. Through extensively citing archival material, Eckstein suggests that Phillips is engaged in a work of revitalization, transforming history into memory (these two spheres are not, he notes, categorically opposed but are marked by slippages between them). Eckstein writes: "Throughout the novel, these older texts are resurrected into a communicative sphere of memory where they can be considered afresh in negotiating contemporary norms and values" (109). Phillips's techniques of montage and pastiche accomplish this revitalizing function through deploying "arresting narrative voices that encourage an *emotional* engagement rather than a merely intellectual one", an engagement in which readers must negotiate their "own position ideologically" "in relation to that of the ideal readers implied in the older narratives" (109). Eckstein's political reading of the novel is in this regard closely connected to his reading of Phillips's negotiation of the ethics of memory, and connects back to Kearney's argument for the importance of the emotions in negotiating memory and working to prevent the horrors of the past from being repeated.

Despite this success there is a possible ethical difficulty that arises from Phillips's method in *Cambridge*. If Emily and Cambridge's narratives are constructed from selected citations of earlier works, to what extent are they, as it were, set up by their author to represent specific ideological positions? In other words, is there a sense in which we could say that, due to the process of selective citation of older texts, Emily is the historical worst case scenario with the more ambivalent or positive aspects of the source texts being passed over and omitted? This feeds into a further difficulty that will emerge during my discussion of the discursive constraints that become evident in the characters' actions: to what extent is Emily responsible for her failure to recognise Cambridge's humanity? These concerns will be addressed in the course of the chapter, but it is important to note that it seems Phillips was not unaware of them. On the one hand, the citations of older texts cover a range of topics, from the more ideological (and offensive) characterizations of slaves, to the more mundane descriptions of the Antilles, the plantation houses, and the process of making sugar. While Emily (and Cambridge) are no doubt ideologically positioned by their author, this is not exclusively because of the selection of citations, which exceeds their ideological positioning. Nevertheless, what will be seen as making Emily a responsible agent is the inclusion of the extradiegetically narrated prologue and epilogue. The latter, importantly, shows an ethical *change* in Emily, effected through her (previously constrained) friendship with Stella, creating more depth in her character.

There is a sense, though, in which my reading of the novel renders these questions less crucial. My concern is to analyse, through the rubric of recognition, an ethical consideration in the novel that is more immediate than the ideological gap, according to Eckstein, from the implied reader that readers must negotiate. Eckstein notes it in passing. Adding to O'Callaghan's discussion of intersecting peripheries the observation that Emily and Cambridge share an acceptance of "aspects of the colonizer's discourse" (112; see also Ledent 2002), and pointing out that the novel hosts a dialogical ideological conflict between slave narratives and colonial travelogues, Eckstein writes:

> At no stage in the three parts of the novel do we come across an explicit expression, in all its sordid detail, of the sufferings of the African diaspora, yet this suffering is evoked *ex negativo*, as it were, in the pervasive racism of the British travelogues and histories. (112)

The ideological conflict between the narratives, "the massive discrepancies between their accounts and the dehumanizing perspective of the British travellers and historians", Eckstein argues, implies the literal conflict and suffering that resulted from slavery (122). While I do not contest that the immense suffering of slavery is implied in the novel (though expressions of this suffering are not entirely absent), it is my argument that Phillips presents the reader with a positive ethical recognition which is fundamental to both O'Callaghan's intersecting peripheries and Eckstein's ideological conflict and complicity: a recognition of a common humanity. As will be seen, it is the lack of any such recognition within Emily's and Cambridge's narratives, which, paralleled as they are and bookended by Emily's epilogue revealing traces of a partial recognition, that this is accomplished. As such, the positive recognition of the novel relies on the form of the novel, through the juxtaposition of the narratives, and is to an extent effective regardless of historical veracity, so long as Emily is believable, and for which the prologue and epilogue are crucial.

This failure of recognition relies on an additional feature of Phillips's use of narrative voice that has yet to be mentioned, and which marks a further difference from the work of Adichie and Ghosh. In an interview with Graham Swift (2009), Phillips comments about his use of the first-person narrator: "It seems to me, at this stage anyhow, that the first person gives me an intimate flexibility which I can't find in the third person" (16). Throughout the book I have been detailing how the novel form, namely its focus on particularity and the emotions, shapes its ethical engagements. These aspects will be further explored in Phillips's novels. What will also emerge, though, and what is intimated by Phillips's comment in this interview, is the role of narrative voice. I have noted that the ways in which each of the selected authors organise their texts, and that the consequent place of recognition within them, is varied. Yet there is also the fact that Phillips's narrators are mostly unreliable. An unreliable narrator, I suggest, is often characterised by a failure of knowledge, a lack of recognition of which the reader is aware. And what will emerge is that this unreliability, coupled with the narrative fragmentation, enables the most significant ethical difference between Phillips and Ghosh and Adichie: both *Cambridge* and *Crossing the River* narrate ethical *failure*. The works of Ghosh and Adichie, with significant differences between them, are organised around a positive gain in knowledge and, as such, they dramatise ethical success—gains in ethical knowledge, which correlate to the novels' ethical sense. Phillips, on the other hand, although his narratives are frequently narrated as autobiographical, refuses the move of a positive recognition, the overt correction of ignorance and youth, and dramatises instead its failure. I will return to these connections between narrative form and the ethical engagement that it allows further on. Now I turn to an analysis of *Cambridge* beginning with Emily, "one of the most skilfully created unreliable narrators in contemporary fiction" (quoted in O'Callaghan 1993, p.44).

II

As with *Higher Ground*, *Cambridge* is constituted by three main narratives. The longest is the journal of Emily Cartwright, the daughter of a plantation owner, which records the experiences of her journey to the West Indies to visit her father's plantation. While at the plantation, on a fictional island, she has several encounters with the eponymous Cambridge. Yet despite the disruptive nature of these moments to Emily's discourse they do not result in an alteration of Emily's understanding of (racial) difference. It is her relationship with Mr Brown, the manager of the plantation, which is more significant for this, and which also crystallises the role played by her emotions in bringing her to the partial recognition which she does, in the end, achieve. The second major narrative in the novel, and much shorter than Emily's, is the final testament of Cambridge before his execution for the murder of Mr Brown. This narrative can be read as serving as a corrective to Emily's overtly racist discourse, inverting a number of common stereotypes (Low 1998, 125). Yet it will be seen to be subject to its own limitations and racism. The third, and shortest of the three narratives, is a report providing a sensationalised (though ostensibly objective) account of the murder of Mr Brown by Cambridge. Peculiar to both *Cambridge* and *Crossing the River* among Phillips's polyphonic novels is the inclusion of a prologue and epilogue. In *Cambridge*, a text which is meticulously written in the style of the historical genres which it represents, it is significant that the prologue and epilogue are written in a modern, free style in which an extra-diegetic narrator first introduces us to Emily Cartwright in the prologue, and then in the epilogue relates the resulting changes to Emily due to her time on the island; both reveal aspects of her character that are elided in her journal.

As this synopsis indicates, the novel, which is named after the slave Cambridge and whom we therefore expect to occupy most of our attention, subverts our expectation in being dominated by the voice and perspective of Emily. The structure of the novel in this way enacts the historical marginality of Cambridge, and when we hear his voice in his last testament it is mediated and shaped by the colonial discourses that he has internalised through the process of learning to write. This determination by colonial discourse of what is claimed as authentic speech is ubiquitous in the novel—in the narratives of both Cambridge and Emily—and prevents the disruptive effects of Emily's encounters with Cambridge from culminating in recognition. As Timothy Bewes (2006) observes, Phillips's text effects the "systematic evacuation of every discursive position that might claim freedom from implication in colonialism" (46). Nevertheless, there are significant resonances between the lives of Emily and Cambridge. That these are resonances rather than strict parallels is important. European women's experiences of patriarchy and marginality in society should not be equated with the violence (both physical and discursive) that characterised slavery—a point which Phillips rightly emphasises in an interview (Jaggi 1994, 27). A number of critics have still argued for several important similarities and resonances which show what we have seen Evelyn O'Callaghan call, in the words of *The Empire Writes Back*, "intersecting peripheries" (see also Ledent 2002, pp.100–106). Despite Emily remaining unaware of them until the very end, the presence of these resonances gives the moments at which their lives intersect a particular poignancy, emphasizing the very lack of recognition within them. Crucial to Emily's failure to see the similarities between herself and Cambridge, and the prevention of her interactions with him from giving rise to recognition, is her unreliability as a narrator. It is her dislocation from herself, her unrecognised racism and gullibility, which make her unreliable and also ensure that by the time she first speaks to Cambridge her perspective has become entrenched in the pervading racist ideology of the plantations.

In the prologue, Emily, aboard the ship that is to take her to the West Indies, remembers back to the time when her father brought news of his decision that she travel to his plantation and upon her return marry Thomas Lockwood, "a fifty-year-old widower with three children" who is "ably provided for" (Phillips 1993, 3). Unable to express her feelings about the arrangement, she locks eyes with her father and "listened as her voice unspooled in silence". Not able to speak her mind, the narrator gives us her thoughts in narrated monologue and we learn that she wishes her father understood her desire for more than "years of cold fleshiness made intimate only by the occasional brushing of lips against cheek". But all that she sees in his eyes is a "determination to insure his own future" (4)— likely because the wealth of her future husband will help to secure him in the "heavy-pocketed" lifestyle to which we soon learn he has become accustomed (7). The resonances with the observations of slavery that follow, in addition to the position of powerlessness, can be seen in the description of the arrangement as "daughters sacrificed to strangers" and the "rude mechanics of horse trading" (3, 4). Emily's understanding of her journey to the West Indies is therefore as a flight from a society that restricts and marginalises her sex, symbolised synecdochically through the practise of fastening women "into backboards, corsets and stays to improve [their] posture" (4).

Bénédicte Ledent, in the only book-length study on Phillips's work at present,[40] argues that Emily's introduction in this way as critical and fleeing the marginalization of women in English society initially positions her as a reliable narrator, which the opening pages of her journal reinforce (2002, 84). In those opening pages we learn of Emily's scientific intentions to keep a record of her observations during her travels in order to "better recount for the use of my father what pains and pleasures are endured by those whose labour enables him to continue to indulge himself" (Phillips 1993, 7). Critical of the practise of absentee landlords drawing wealth from their plantations without ever visiting them, her hope is that her "adventuring will encourage Father to accept the increasingly

---

[40] It is an insightful study, though I agree with Bewes's argument that its overarching attempt to argue for an essential "Caribbeanness" that characterises Phillips's works is problematic (2006, 50–53). I will return to Bewes's wider argument—which presents a different understanding of ethics in literature to my own—in the final section of this chapter.

common, though abstract, English belief in the iniquity of slavery" (8). These ambitions, coupled with the uncontroversial factual descriptions of the nautical aspects of her journey, Ledent argues, "inspires the reader with confidence" in her perspective (2002, 84). While this is so, the traces of what will soon undermine her reliability are already present in this opening, namely, the degree to which her perspective is determined by the discourses of her home country. She reflects the (gendered) norms of courtesy in being appalled at the Captain's treatment of her and her companion Isabella, norms which will play an important role in some of her initial judgements of slaves upon her arrival in the Caribbean. But most revealingly, she couches her objection to her father's absenteeism in the following terms: "There is, I suspect, small virtue in leaving one's creatures to the delegated dominion of some overseer or manager" (Phillips 1993, 7). Her designation of slaves as "one's creatures" reveals a crack of dehumanizing racism in her abolitionist façade. Rather than showing, as Ledent suggests, "a critical but balanced view of absentee landlords" (Ledent 2002, 84), this criticism of her father is the first hint that her lament over the "many persons scattered throughout our kingdom who inwardly cling to their old prejudices" foreshadows the revelation of her own prejudice (Phillips 1993, 8), when she herself begins to defend slavery.[41]

An aspiration to scientific objectivity can, nevertheless, be observed here in the meticulous cataloguing of her observations. It is an important motif throughout her journal and constitutes one of the main axes around which her unreliability accrues. These first fissures in her objectivity widen upon her arrival in the West Indies. The alien newness of the island is, from her first sight of it, related to the Old World from which she has departed. The shoots of the "infamous sugar cane" "billowed in the wind like fields of green barley", and later en route to the plantation house the fields which are "neatly dressed as though preparing for turnip husbandry as practised in England" are separated by hedges which, in their thorniness, "resemble our hawthorn" (18, 23). While, for Ledent, it is usual for a newcomer to a region to relate what they see back to what is familiar, Emily's descriptions could, she suggests, be "read as an attempt to 'make order out of chaos', an epitome of Europe's standardisation, then appropriation of the planet" (2002, 85). What is more significant in Emi-

---

[41] See also Gail Low (1998) who makes a similar observation.

ly's descriptions is the disclosure of the (not unexpected) shaping of her understanding of the Caribbean by her European perspective. This is evidenced in Emily's occasional deployment of images from classical antiquity: the house is "at the end of this Arcadian grove", the slaves perform "Sisyphean labours", and they sing "Bacchanalian songs" (Phillips 1993, 27, 77, 87). Peter Hulme (1992) argues that this is a common aspect of the discursive construction of the Caribbean, a means by which European colonialists smoothed, in Ledent's words, the "transition from the Old world to the New" (2002, 86; cf Pratt [2008]).

That Emily's encounter with the strangeness of the Caribbean is negotiated through the categories of Europe in this way is not unusual. What undermines it more radically is her lack of self-awareness and her gullibility. While still on board the ship, Emily has her first recorded encounter with an African slave: the pilot who comes aboard to guide them into port. Emily records: "It caused me a little discomfit to hear our captain immediately baptize the pilot with the title, *nigger*, but the pilot seemed somewhat resigned to his appellation" (Phillips 1993, 17). This is consistent with her earlier view of opposition to the slave trade. She revealingly proceeds to note that the sailors "were to a man generally less polished than the negro" (18). Seemingly a passing explanation of the sailors' respect for the man, it references her earlier adherence to the norms of European dress and behaviour and becomes particularly pertinent when the lack of an approximation to these norms begins to expose the racist ideology that she has, unbeknown to her, held all along.

Upon reaching the land, Emily is therefore repulsed by what she sees. "I [...] noted that the negro men wore thin-clothed apparel which left scarce anything to the imagination, and that their women wandered hither and thither barely stirring to cover their bodies". Although she envies the greater comfort such scant attire brings in the intense heat, she is disgusted by the lack of "concern for conventional morality" (21), a phrase which again exposes her eurocentrism. In addition to considering the slaves immoral, and contrasted to the "noble English horses" that pull the carriage, we quickly learn that the curiosity exhibited for her arrival is a "savage curiosity" (22). What is most striking, particularly for the short time of the journey from the docks to her father's plantation, is that she mistakes for a "parcel of monkeys" some African children, naked and "parading around in a feral manner to which they were not only accustomed, but in which they felt comfortable" (23–24). Interestingly this is one of Phillip's citations of an older text, in this case Janet Schaw's *Journal of a Lady of Quality* (Eckstein 2006, 245). In a remarkably short time, slaves have gone from suffering the appellation of "nigger" to being immoral, savage, and contentedly animalistic.

The ease with which she views the slaves as immoral savages goes some way to explaining the readiness with which she a moment later uncritically accepts the racist ideology of her escort from the docks, the plantation's book-keeper. After her misrecognition of the children, Emily tells us that "I expressed my general concern at the blackness of the native people", which elicits a response from her companion that she describes as being "corrected" and "instructed". The authoritative ascription which Emily grants her companion's "short but edifying lecture" indicates her complete acceptance of what she is told. And so she learns that the slaves are not native to the island any more than the Europeans are, with the important difference that while slaves were "imported from Africa to help ease our labour problem", Europeans "are here on a civilising and economic mission". As for what happened to the native people, she is told that they "were discovered to be too troublesome and unused to European ways and had to be dispatched". This euphemism elides the genocide that is being discussed, shaping it into an ideologically acceptable form. Its justification illustrates the argument that the hierarchical division between human and animal authorises violence: the Carib Indians were ferocious, bearing more "semblance to the wild irrationality of the lion than the passionate intensity of a man"; "their powers of reasoning" were underdeveloped; and they were cannibals, demonstrating an "implacable opposition to correction" (Phillips 1993, 24). In short, in an echo of the argument seen in *The Hungry Tide*, they were sub-human and thus, in colonial terms, could be legitimately eliminated.[42]

---

[42] See Hulme (1992, 13–87) for an excellent, detailed analysis of the ways in which the native peoples of the Caribbean were discursively constructed, first as savage, and subsequently as either Arawak (characterised as peaceful or docile) or Carib (characterised as cannibals) according to the degree of resistance displayed towards the Europeans' presence. The book-keeper's "unused to European ways" can be seen to stand in for "unwilling to be subjected to European control", with the savage, cannibalistic description of the Caribs functioning as the definition of such "unsuited" peoples, and working as a justification for their extermination.

Accepting this, Emily reports that "having been corrected on the count of the native peoples, I was now instructed on the question of colour" (25). The continued repetition of "correction"—its reference switching between Emily's seemingly scholarly acceptance of it as opposed to the native's unreasoning opposition to it—distances Emily, perhaps unconsciously, from the "cannibals" that she has been hearing about, reinforcing her sense of racial superiority. Additionally, it is suggestive that Emily is writing this section of her journal "on land" (18), that is, after this journey to the plantation, and her recollection and understanding of events is shaped by those events themselves, not to mention her encounter with Mr Brown at the dinner table. It is not implausible, then, that this unconscious reinforcement of racial superiority and distancing from the "dispatched" natives contains the shadow of Emily's own vulnerability and unease which she feels at the end of the section when she is writing. There is here another possible resonance between herself and the "others" of Europe. As for what she learns in her instruction on colour, it is that "there are many shades of black [....] the lighter the shade of black, the nearer to salvation and acceptability was the negro". And that this is so "should be clear to even the most egalitarian observer" (25). Again, we observe that she readily accepts this as fact.

What begins to be revealed is how the combination of Emily's lack of self-presence, her racism and naive gullibility is the primary factors undermining her aspirations to objectivity. Correspondingly, this marks the beginning of her immersion in and acceptance of an intensely racist discourse. However, the traces of scientific aspiration remain throughout her journey to the plantation and the rest of her journal: her referencing of sources, her meticulous summaries of what she considers authoritative explanations, the recurrence of phrases such as and similar to "it should be clear", as in the ubiquitous "I have been led to believe" (67). All of these discursive markers abound in her journal, yet, as Ledent (2002) notes, her discourse has the effect of "expos[ing] her rather than the objects of her research" (86). Timothy Bewes (2006) sums this up when he comments, "Emily is an aspiring writer and lecturer [...] But what we read in her journal are the outpourings of a stilted, derivative, and ideologically unreflective writer, inhabiting the literary discourse of a hegemonic, culturally dominant Europe" (4). It is unsurprising then, given the ease of her shift in perspective at the beginning of her time in the Caribbean, that the rest of

Emily's journal tracks the process through which she begins to "warm to the racism of plantation life" (Low 1998, 124). While the exposure of her racism and naivety is quite sudden, her shift towards supporting the institution of slavery is more gradual, though it proceeds through the same combination of racism and naivety, that is her unreliability, which I have detailed here and to which I will return.

Pivotal for her transition to supporting slavery is her relationship to the plantation manager Mr Brown. While still en route to the plantation, Emily enquires of her companion about the manager that she expects to find there, a Mr Wilson. The book-keeper is unwilling to give a clear answer and Emily holds her peace. Upon arriving at the Great House she hears of a Mr Brown, and meets him later at dinner that evening. It is an upsetting experience for her. Mr Brown fails to accord with her expectations of manners, his announcing of himself and shaking Emily's hand marking "the onset and the conclusion of this man's civility" (Phillips 1993, 30): he dismisses her enquiry after Mr Wilson with "mocking laughter", and makes no objection when the enigmatic "black wench" Christiania briefly interrupts their meal to whisper in his ear with a smirk (31). Christiania is important, and will be considered in turn. At this point, though, Emily is not pleased with Mr Brown, and is still ignorant of the fate of Mr Wilson, which she remains for a few more weeks since after dinner she falls seriously ill and only sees Mr Brown again once she has recovered.

Emily's next encounter with him does nothing to shift him out of her negative opinion. Taking a tour of the grounds with Stella, the slave who is filing the role of her personal servant, she comes across Mr Brown whipping a slave, "a black Hercules of a brute who far outweighed and outspanned him" (41), and who is later introduced as Cambridge. While Emily thinks that slaves, as they are mortal and accordingly make errors, need to be whipped (another startling revelation of her racist disposition), it is something that must be done in a "judicious" manner and not with "vindictive malice". It is precisely such a vindictive whipping that she considers herself to observe the "villain" Mr Brown applying to Cambridge (41). Emily's opinion of him during these two encounters is quite clear from her chosen adjectives. Describing the whipping, in addition to calling him a villain she describes him as a "coarse man" and a "fool" (41, 42). In relating the earlier dinner, she writes that he is wont to "cackle rudely and attack his meat", that he is an "arrogant man" whose "ignorance knows no boundaries", and whom she is persuaded "must go" (31). It is remarkable then, and an instance of, ironically, her own ignorance and gullibility, how swiftly and thoroughly this opinion is inverted.

Shortly after witnessing the whipping, Emily entertains her first guests at the Great House of the plantation: Mr McDonald, the doctor that tended her during her illness, and his friend Mr Rogers, a minister. During the visit, the form of Emily's conversation with the book-keeper is repeated: she largely accepts the views of these two men as authoritative and consequently shifts her perspective closer to the position from which she begins to defend slavery. At one point in the afternoon Mr Rogers accidentally mentions the fact that Mr Wilson is no longer resident on the island. The men are unwilling to say any more and Emily remains ignorant of the reason for Mr Wilson's absence. Shortly after her guests have left, however, Mr Brown surprisingly requests that Emily join him for dinner (57). She does not consider what might suddenly motivate Mr Brown to engage with her—only regretting her assent to the proposal—but it is suggestive that he does so shortly after Emily's exposure to those outside of his direct purview.

Initially the topic of discussion is Christiania, who Emily is disturbed to realise is joining them at dinner. When she challenges Mr Brown on it, he is again dismissive, commenting that once she had spent more time there she "might come to understand that everything is not as in England" (58). Angered by this, she calms herself and takes advantage of the "little momentum" of Mr Brown talking to enquire after the injudicious whipping she witnessed. Her record of his response is significant. Against expectations he provides an explanation, informing her of a perpetual fear of "insurrection" by the slaves, with the result that "discipline" is the "chief and governing principle on every estate". Cambridge, as the main cause of trouble, must be subjected to the whip. She is even more surprised, when "he apologised, yes, he apologised for any discomfort caused by my witnessing of his behaviour" (59). This interchange marks the beginning of the shift in her attitude towards Mr Brown, her surprise registering a consideration that her earlier assessment of his character was perhaps mistaken, a misrecognition.

Proceeding from the dinner, there is a more sustained engagement between Emily and Mr Brown, and it soon becomes habitual for them to "engage in a few pleasantries" (61–62). It is during one of these that he explains the absence of Mr Wilson: "Apparently this man had been stealing from the estate and has fled to another island [....] apart from the petty thieving, the chief complaint against Mr Wilson was that he was not sufficiently aware of the imminent threat of a slave revolt" (62). Emily remains uncertain as to whether Wilson was forced to leave or did so of his own accord, but she nevertheless uncritically accepts Brown's account of events. Indeed, she has no evidence to the contrary: the book-keeper, doctor and minister have all been reticent with their knowledge. And so, with Brown's "initial resentment" towards Emily apparently fading—that is, her opinion of him slowly warming—she accepts what he tells her (62). His designation has tellingly shifted from being a rude and arrogant man to being a skilful manager of the plantation despite "all his surliness" (63).

Mr Brown will climb still higher in Emily's esteem after what is to be their major confrontation. Emily arrives one afternoon lunch and "yet again found Mr Brown's strange and haughty black woman, Christiania". Promptly ordering her to leave as she is "not accustomed to eating [...] in the company of slaves" (73), Christiania is uncompliant and so Emily repeats her command. When she still refuses to leave, citing Mr Brown's permission to remain, the attending slaves are unwilling to forcefully remove her from the table due to their fear of her occult *Obeah.* Emily finally flees to her "bed-chamber", she writes, "where I concealed both my tear-stained face and my impotent rage" (74). This is Emily's first direct experience of powerlessness. Suspecting that Christiania is Brown's mistress, she interrogates Stella on the possibility and is met only with a stony silence. Needing to respond to the situation in some way, Emily resolves to confront Mr Brown himself. She ventures into the fields in the heat of the day to do so, and the resulting scene is significant. The focus is the confrontational climax between her and Mr Brown. Demanding that Christiania no longer sit at the table with them, she plays her "last card": "Mr Brown, if you do not display more consideration for my position, immediately upon my return I shall have you replaced" (77–78). The threat is effective, resulting in a complete change of Mr Brown's behaviour towards Emily, though she will utterly mistake the cause. This passage is also revealing in Emily's reaction to the slave Fox. Instructed by Mr Brown to return Emily to the house, "the nigger laid his black hands upon my body, at which I screamed and felt my stomach turn in revulsion, at which its contents emptied upon the ground" (78). Here we see not only the visceral character of her racism, which is relatively easily provoked, but that the interpellation "nigger"—which caused her "a little discomfort" when used of the pilot aboard the ship (17)—surfaces after an entire journal where slaves have been meticulously referred to as either "blacks" or "negroes". The term is quickly submerged once more, however, but it is only a week later that Emily formulates her desire to conduct a lecture tour and write a pamphlet which will defend the slave trade. She is convinced that abolitionists only decry slavery because they "do not comprehend the base condition of the negro" (86), implying, since she had previously supported the emancipation of slaves, that she had until then also failed to comprehend the slave's true condition.

After this confrontation, Emily quickly notices the change in Mr Brown's behaviour, and we see the staggering misrecognition of his motives: "This past week has marked a profound change in the heart and soul of Mr Brown. *I can only assume that his gentler aspect has made an appearance as a result of guilt*, but whatever it is that has provoked this miraculous improvement [...] I am truly grateful" (82, my emphasis). This is a remarkable moment, conveying Emily's characteristic certainty that she understands the internal workings of the people she observes and with whom she interacts (an ethically problematic position as has already been seen in earlier chapters, and which is later disrupted). That she "can only assume" that it is due to "guilt" that Mr Brown has changed his behaviour—rather than a calculation on his part to retain his position of power—is a vivid moment of naivety. That he is indeed motivated by less noble ends, and not "a profound change" of "heart and soul", is revealed later when he deserts Emily after impregnating her. For Emily at this point, however, the interpretation of Mr Brown's change as revealing a "gentler aspect" completes the shift in her view that had begun with Mr Brown's apology for his whipping of Cambridge. The position that Emily occupies at this point of the narrative is the inverse of what she occupied aboard the ship. Having come to believe that slavery should be continued, the previously villainous Mr Brown has now been elevated to the level of a friend and an "instructor" in plantation matters, including slavery (85). Later, he will become her lover and she will feel "pure, undistilled, happiness at [her] good fortune to have discovered a man such as Arnold [Mr Brown] in the tropical backwater of the Americas" (118). It is only after this that Emily has her main interactions with Cambridge, and the racism and gullibility that have led to her misrecognition of Mr Brown and the acceptance of his, McDonald's and Roger's racism, ensures that the possible recognitions within these various engagements never occur.

It is important to note that although these possible recognitions are prevented from arising due to the discourse which Emily inhabits, she is nevertheless responsible for this failure. I have traced in detail the path that Emily travels to reach this point and it should be clear that she is aware of an ideological alternative: she understands her position in opposition to one that she has rejected. Despite the fact that it is her own naivety and willingness to trust as authoritative the men on the plantation that has led her to change her mind, she has nevertheless come to her own position within the discourse that she has adopted. She is, however, not "fully" responsible in the classical Enlightenment sense. She has indeed made a choice of her own volition, which has ethical repercussions. Yet we can also see that her autonomy is circumscribed by her circumstances, and that she is not a self-aware subject. She is, in short, an instance of the subject for which I argued in the introduction: vulnerable to the vagaries of circumstances, required to make the best choice available to her. That she has made the wrong one becomes clear in the epilogue where we observe her recognition of this error. For now, it is important to bear in mind that the power of discourse to foreclose recognitions, which we are about to consider, reveals Emily as a responsible agent caught in the vulnerability of goodness.

In addition to Emily's first encounter with Cambridge when she witnesses Mr Brown whipping him, there are two further recorded instances of their meeting. The key moment is when Cambridge is asked to guard Emily's room against Christiania (89–93). Mr Brown is away from the plantation for several days, during which time Emily "began to discern nocturnal scratching noises". When she eventually finds the courage to investigate she discovers "the arrogant black wench, Christiania", "scratching in the dirt" and "uttering sinister sounds" (89). It is assumed that she is working her Obeah, a "dark practise" that was "brought by the negroes from Africa, where open and devoted worship of the devil is still encouraged" (89–90). The fear that Emily here and elsewhere in the novel experiences due to Christiania's actions (she likens it to that which she felt while aboard the ship, when after Isabella's death "I feared that I should soon be reunited with my dead companion" [89]) marks an important difference from the disruption caused by Cambridge. At present, what is salient is that the slaves have been forbidden by Mr Brown from interfering with Christiania, with the result that the book-keeper, who oversees the estate in Mr Brown's absence, is sent for. His solution to the problem is to post a sentry outside Emily's bedroom in case, she tells us, of "any intrusive assaults, or magical manifestations". Emily agrees since the arrangement will "render some support to [her] failing spirit" (92). The slave who is posted as sentry is Cambridge.

It is when Emily peeks through her door to see her "negro sentinel" that she learns who he is. The brief interaction that follows is worth citing at length.

> My dark sentry looked up at me, and I noted that I appeared to have disturbed him in the most unlikely act of studying the Bible. I asked if this was his common form of recreation, to which he replied in highly fanciful English, that indeed it was. You might imagine my surprise when he then broached the conversational lead and enquired after my family origins, and my opinions pertaining to slavery. I properly declined to share these with him, instead counter-quizzing with enquiries as to the origins of his knowledge. At this a broad grin spread over his face, as though I had fallen into some trap of his setting. Indeed, so disturbing was the negro's confident gleam, that I quickly closed in the door, for I feared this negro was truly ignorant of the correct degree of deference that a lady might reasonably expect from a base slave. (92–93)

We see here Emily's response to a slave who, as Low puts it, is "lettered, articulate, educated, and a Christian, the antithesis of Emily's sons of Ham" (1998, 125). Her initial response is surprise and curiosity, which transmutes into fear. The understanding of slaves that she has developed through her journal up until this point can be discerned in her description of the scene. It is "unlikely" for them to read the bible, indeed to read at all; it is startling for a slave to take the "conversational lead", and improper to share certain details of her life with them. In short, she neither expects nor desires any true engagement or dialogue. Cambridge refuses to accept this role. Not only does he take initiative in the conversation, which Emily finds surprising and refuses to answer, but this turns to fear when he refuses to reply to her in turn. It is primarily Cambridge's "confident gleam", however, that disturbs her: his refusal to relate to her as an inferior, objectified being. Forced, as Ledent puts it, to respond to Cambridge as a subject (2002, 90), Emily retreats both physically and intellectually, and unconvincingly imposes her racist discourse upon the situation. She designates a man who is clearly educated enough to elicit her inquiry into "the origins of his knowledge" as "ignorant", and supports it by claiming as sensible the "deference" that she "reasonably" expects "from a base slave". On the one hand though, this self-assured claim of being on the side of reason is, ironically, at odds with the entire situation, which Ledent observes exposes her "carefully concealed irrationality" (90). Emily writes that the mysterious nocturnal sounds made her afraid that "some strange beast might be waiting for an opportunity to assault and devour me body and soul" (Phillips 1993, 89). Additionally, she is soothed by the knowledge that there will be a sentry to guard against any physical as well as "magical manifestations" (92). In a situation thus marked with irrational fear (irrational, that is, within her own Enlightenment framework), Emily nevertheless asserts the reasonableness of her fear of Cambridge. On the other hand, if it were reasonable for a slave to show deference in a manner that reflects his "base" state, then Cambridge's refusal to act as an inferior creature—that is, his confidence—might be a demonstration of ignorance and disrespect. But it is precisely this understanding of slavery and of himself which he *knowingly* contests: his evident education marks his refusal of the role of "a base slave" as being founded on knowledge and not as a display of ignorance. Although Emily does not consciously recognise this contestation, it registers in her fear. Her immersion in the ideology of the plantation has foreclosed the possibility that Cambridge's confidence could be anything other than sinister— "some trap of his setting"—and so she flees from it, contradicting the evidence of the situation and her own actions within it, by designating Cambridge as ignorant and dangerous. In this way she forecloses any possible recognition that might have arisen from the commonality between them.

It is necessary, however, for Emily to explain away the counterevidence to her assumption of Cambridge's inferiority. As such, his fluency in

English is described as "highly fanciful". This derogation of skills and behaviours that fail to conform to Emily's idea of slaves is a common feature of her journal, as Ledent has observed (2002, 87). Cambridge's fluency, which in his own narrative he describes as superior to Mr Brown's (Phillips 1993, 161) (and is therefore likely close to Emily's own), is later characterised by Emily as a "lunatic precision in his dealings with our English words" (120), though there is more at work than simple derogation at that point. This pattern is also evidenced in her disgust when witnessing a slave woman bathing, even though she knows that the woman is dirty due to her labours (101–102), and in her characterizing of the loyalty of slaves as "the animal fidelity of the dog" (54). This last is particularly important as it will return, in a transformed form, in the epilogue. That Emily uses the word "lunatic" to describe Cambridge's handling of the English language is not accidental, exhibiting as it does a continuation of her initial response to Cambridge's confidence.

The characterization of "lunatic" occurs after Cambridge has appeared before Mr Brown on a charge of theft. Emily and Mr Brown have just returned from a romantic evening when the matter is brought to Mr Brown's attention. Emily is a witness to the proceedings (constituting her second and final encounter with Cambridge, though she does not speak with him directly), during which he answers Mr Brown's questions rationally and in his "polite English", exhibiting "the manner and speech of one familiar with conventions of the bar" (112). When matters are not progressing quickly, Mr Brown is persuaded by Emily (we learn later [128]) to "suspend judgement" of the case, leaving the situation unresolved. Suggestively, Emily is not engaging with Cambridge directly and her characterization of him during the hearing correspondingly lacks the fear that was a part of their earlier conversation. Yet in the time subsequent to Cambridge's impromptu hearing, Emily becomes physically intimate with Mr Brown. Nearly two weeks later, she urges him to come to a decision over Cambridge:

> The curious behaviour of this over-confident, Bible-reading slave demanded immediate attention. I confessed to Arnold that to my observation this bondsman had about his gaze an unsound quality. Furthermore, I insisted that he seemed determined to adopt a lunatic precision in his dealings with our English words, as

though the black imagined himself to be a part of our white race. (120)

Cambridge's speech has shifted from being disparaged as "fanciful", through being described as "polite", to now bearing the mark of madness. Once again, Cambridge's confidence is central to Emily's fear. As she has now had greater exposure to Cambridge's evident education, and the contestation of his inferiority is correspondingly stronger, she is no longer able to classify it as ignorance. Rather, she has come to recognise the claim that he is making: that he is equal to them (which in his own narrative is also thought of as being part of the "white race": "Truly I was now an Englishman, albeit a little smudgy of complexion!" [147]). Emily also now recognises that Cambridge's fluency in English is extensive, as more than a slave's "highly fanciful" attempt at imitation: it is part of his claim to equality, to "be a part of our white race". As Ledent notes, "Cambridge's mastery of English jeopardises racial boundaries" (2002, 90). It is not possible, however, for her racist ideology to acknowledge such a claim as anything other than madness, and so we see again how her discourse circumscribes the disruption that Cambridge effects. It is "as though the black imagined", the phrasing implying that this is a ludicrous idea. The inferiority of darker people is considered established, and thus to claim equality and to contest that inferiority is to demonstrate "an unsound quality".

Key to understanding this argument that knowledge is shaped and limited by discourse is Foucault's (1972) well known watershed study, *The Archaeology of Knowledge*. It will be useful to take a brief detour through his argument before returning to Emily. In his study, Foucault begins by setting out to investigate the validity of the categories by which we commonly understand and categorise statements. What is it that makes, for instance, the discourse of Psychiatry a unified discourse? Working systematically through the commonly held reasons, Foucault eliminates each one: there is no common object, no common speaker, and so on. The unity of a discourse, Foucault argues, rests not in these elements within the discourse but rather in their rules of formation, the rules according to which the statements must be made: "[If] there really is a unity, it does not lie in the visible, horizontal coherence of the elements formed; it resides, well anterior to their formation, in the system that makes possible and governs that formation" (80). This "system of formation" refers to the relations between societal elements (such as, for Psychiatry, the laboratory and the hospital, to name only two) that must be activated for the statements within the discourse to be made. It designates

> a complex group of relations that function as a rule: it lays down what must be related, in a particular discursive practice, for such and such an enunciation to be made, for such and such a concept to be used, for such and such a strategy to be organised. (82)

These rules of formation form the coherence that Foucault terms a "discursive formation". Proceeding to analyse the idea of the statement, Foucault again systematically eliminates common definitions which equate statements with grammar or logic. He argues instead that a statement is an enunciative function that "has a bearing on a group of signs" and which require certain relations to be in place (129), that is, they require a discursive formation. He concludes:

> We shall call discourse a group of statements in so far as they belong to the same discursive formation [...] it is made up of a limited number of statements for which a group of conditions of existence can be defined. (131)

These conditions of possibility, the rules according to and by which statements are made, Foucault goes on to "propose to call *archive*" (145). This is not an archive in the sense that Eckstein uses it, as referring to a library, a store of texts. The archive for Foucault "is *the general system of the formation and transformation of statements*" (146, emphasis in original). The archive is the rules which enable us to speak, while simultaneously limiting what it is possible to say: it is the "principle of rarification", the reason why "on the basis of grammar and of the wealth of vocabulary available at a given period, there are, in total, relatively few things that are said" (134). Having developed this understanding of the archive, "the first law of what can be said" (145), Foucault is able to define what is involved in an archaeology of knowledge: "Archaeology describes discourses as practices specified in the element of the archive" (148); it is an approach to discourse that is concerned not with the elements within a discourse, or the biography or intentions of the speakers of a discourse, but with the material conditions and relations that both limit and enable statements to emerge. It must be emphasised, though, that the archive is not static: discourses change and evolve. Foucault uses the term "historical a priori" to describe it (143): the archive is a condition of possibility, it is an a priori; it is also subject to change, it has a history.

What is pertinent from this is that what is said by any one person at any one time is dependent upon what they are able to say, an ability which is decided not by their intentions but by their social context. An important instance of this can be found in Peter Hulme's careful analysis of Christopher Columbus' journal of his first voyage to the Americas, which I referred to earlier. There are, Hulme argues, two discourses at work in Columbus' journal, at first co-existing relatively peacefully, but later vying for interpretive mastery: "there is what might be called a discourse of Oriental civilization and a discourse of savagery" (1992, 21). Both discourses have a common referent, gold, which is the main object and purpose of the voyage. In the first discourse, "gold" is accompanied by the key terms "'Cathay', 'Grand Khan', 'intelligent soldiers', 'large buildings', 'merchant ships'"; in the latter it is accompanied by "'savagery', 'monstrosity', 'anthropophagy' [cannibalism]" (20–21). Although Columbus never believed that he had failed to arrive in the Far East, and the discourse of Oriental civilization is initially dominant in the journal, there is a crucial moment at which the discourse of savagery attains the upper hand.

Upon arriving in the Americas, Columbus heads in a south-westerly direction thinking that it will eventually take him towards the "great Khan". When he comes upon Cuba, he is faced with a choice: The Cuban coastline runs north-west to south-east; he can go no further south-west and must turn either north or south, each direction corresponding to one of the interpretative discourses. What follows next "marks the site of a discursive conflict". Turning north-west, the obvious choice "if he were seeking the Grand Khan's cities" due to his latitudinal position (30), he sails north-westerly along the coast of Cuba for two days before turning about and heading south-east instead. The change in direction marks the shift from the Oriental discourse to the discourse of savagery, from one discourse of white supremacy to another. Hulme's reading of this section of the journal is detailed, covering the faulty quadrant reading (three times Columbus gets a reading of 41° rather than the 21° of his true position), the dispatch of an embassy inland, and the exaggerated weather report. Each event serves as a justification for the change in direction, masking the unconscious shift of interpretative discourses (22–34). What is important is the way in which the record of this crucial episode in the history of the Caribbean shows the traces of the shaping force of discourse. These two discourses, each with their own, but intertwined, political context in Europe at the time (34–39), provide the possible ways in which the Caribbean can be understood, as either Oriental or savage. The primacy of the discourse of savagery has, as I noted, moulded the understanding, naming and categorizing of the New World. And we have seen Emily shift discourses, coming to accept and function within this racist discourse of white superiority. Consequently, Cambridge's claim of equality is refused as false, and his assertion of it is designated as unsound.

Cambridge is not categorised as completely mad, however. He has only an unsound "quality" (Phillips 1993, 120). Part of the reason for this, as Ledent suggests, is that Cambridge's disruption of Emily's racism is graspable: he reads the bible, speaks English, and exhibits familiarity with legal conventions. In short, while his manner and appearance are contrary to Emily's assumptions regarding Africans, Cambridge does not articulate anything that is contrary to her idea of civilization and reason. She is unable to accept it because he is African, not because of what he does. It is only the combination of the two terms—civilised and African—which her discourse is unable to allow. Christiania on the other hand, while exhibiting confidence (she is regularly denigrated by Emily as "arrogant" and "haughty" [73, 89, 120]), is very unlike Cambridge. While Cambridge speaks civilly, Christiania looses "invective", "hurling abuse like some sooty witch from *Macbeth*" (75), and utters "sinister sounds" (89), making "noises as if she were communing with the devil himself" (91). Where Cambridge's spirituality is recognizable, Christiania's alleged Obeah (Cambridge denies the claim) is unknown and terrifies Emily, exposing her own irrational, dark self (Ledent 2002, 90–91). Christiania thus slips entirely beneath the surface of comprehensibility for Emily, becoming unreadable and as a result is characterised as "crazy" (Phillips 1993, 89).[43]

---

[43] It is worth noting that Cambridge considers Christiania mad as well (163–164). The difference is that Cambridge is aware of the trauma Christiania has suffered, and has witnessed her steady deterioration. Emily is simply faced with behaviour that is unreadable, which when added to the allegation of

Christiania's name, linking her to Christianity, only serves to sharpen her unreadability, marking everything which she is not.

In this way the disturbing presence of both Cambridge and Christiania is contained by the racist discourse which Emily has accepted and affirmed, never leading to a shift in her understanding, to recognition. It is not insignificant that at the time of her interactions with Cambridge (and, to a certain extent, Christiania), Emily is relatively content with life. Before the close of the novel she will come to a transforming recognition—the main predicate of which is Stella—but, similarly to the recognition of Kalua by Deeti in Ghosh's *Sea of Poppies*, it is only through emotional distress that this breaching of an entrenched social boundary occurs. There are two catalysts for this, the return of Mr Wilson and Emily's pregnancy. Occurring in the epilogue, this recognition is only present in its traces. Even after occurring, therefore, the lack of its presence only serves to emphasise the lack that I have been tracking in Emily's journal, and which we will likewise see in Cambridge's final testament. As such, the functioning of recognition is almost the inverse of what we observed in *Sea of Poppies*. Although in both instances the ethical effect is to affirm a common humanity, in Ghosh this commonality is the positive predicate of the recognition which functions as the novel's climatic *peripeteia*; here the commonality is only marginally confirmed in the narrative (it is, indeed, overlooked by a number of critics), leaving it primarily to the reader to affirm, in response to its absence in the main narratives.

One similarity between the narratives of Emily and Cambridge is how each is peripheral to the other. Although Cambridge plays a significant part in Emily's narrative, his importance is tethered to his role in her

---

Obeah transforms Christiania for her into a lunatic witch. Whether Christiania is actually involved in Obeah remains in doubt throughout the novel as Cambridge denies it, although he recognises that her "undeniably spiritual nature was absorbed in an entirely different direction" (159). The possibility cannot, then, be ruled out that Cambridge is in denial and that, in addition to the trauma of abuse Christiania has suffered, her ventures into "zones of illogicality" are in part related to her Obeah (164). They would of course have their own logic for Christiania, but would be unreadable for Cambridge since he has completely internalised English civilisation and its rationalism. Indeed, he tellingly describes Christiania's eating dirt as "paganism" (164), though this designation could, given the rest of Cambridge's narrative, plausibly stand in for his understanding of something like "inhuman" or "savage".

primary concerns: to her comfort on the plantation and her relationship with Mr Brown. He does not constitute a sustained focus. For his part, Cambridge explicitly states: "The English woman did not concern me" (164). His narrative is his final testament, and is concerned to recount for us the story of his life and how it is that he came to kill Mr Brown. We thus learn that as a young man, Olumide (who would finally be renamed Cambridge) was captured and sold into slavery. He was transported to the Americas, where he was bought by an Englishman, was renamed Thomas, and again transported, this time to England. Spending nearly a decade in England, he learns the language, converts to Christianity, and marries an Englishwoman. It is his conversion that enables him to write his testament, as a part of the conversion process was receiving an education. Upon completion of his training he is again renamed, this time as David Henderson. When his owner passes away he travels the country with his wife, preaching against the slave trade (doing what Emily only aspires to do, but for the other side). His wife soon dies in childbirth and shortly after he buys passage back to Africa where he intends to work as a missionary. However, upon arriving at the coast he is taken as a slave by the captain of the ship, resold, and comes to be at Emily's father's plantation in the West Indies, where he is renamed Cambridge.

Cambridge's education as a Christian marks his entire narrative, demonstrating his acceptance of the discourse of civilization and progress, which depends upon the existence of Africa as savage and uncivilised. So we read that he learns to write in the "blessed English language" (142), and that his "uncivilised African demeanour began to fall from [his] person" (144). That there is a significant amount of ideological conditioning in his embracing of English civilization is indicated when he comments that "already Africa spoke only to me of a barbarity I had fortunately *fled*" (143, my emphasis). This imputation of his own agency to being taken as a slave is later reiterated when he designates himself as an Englishman, defining himself against Africa which "spoke to me only of a history I had cast aside" (147). It is only when he is again taken as a slave that the full extent to which he has internalised the values of English civilization, and justified his enslavement to himself, become apparent. Bemoaning his situation, he writes: "That I, a virtual Englishman, was to be treated as base African cargo, caused me such hurtful pain as I was barely able to endure" (156). The implication is that even though he speaks out against slavery, denouncing it as evil, he is nevertheless partly constituted by the discourse of civilization and therefore conveys, as Ledent puts it, a sense in which he considers himself "an exception to an otherwise acceptable treatment" (2002, 98).

In addition to the savagery and inferiority of Africa, part of the discourse of Christian civilization that Cambridge has imbibed with his education is a severe patriarchy: the prejudices of a society that, as Emily puts it, "despise my sex" (Phillips 1993, 113). We see this in his reaction to Christiania's worsening condition, which eventually leads to her scratching in the dirt beneath Emily's window. Becoming mentally unstable through the sexual and emotional abuses that she has suffered as a slave, not least at the hands of Mr Brown who rapes her, Christiania (whom Cambridge has taken as his wife) begins to deteriorate further after Emily's arrival, and "began now openly to mock at my Christian beliefs and to scream out for her long-lost mother". Her condition causes Cambridge both sorrow and anger: "for, as is well known, a Christian man possesses his wife, and the dutiful wife must obey her Christian husband" (163). The telling phrase "as is well known" occurs in both Emily and Cambridge's accounts, where it indicates an acceptance of the status quo (Ledent 2002, 97). It is his concern for Christiania that brings Cambridge to resist Mr Brown, and which leads to the confrontation during which he kills him. His stated intention for that confrontation is clear: "That he must cease his tormenting of my *wife* would be the main thrust of my message" (Phillips 1993, 168). He draws strength for his challenge to Mr Brown by understanding it as "couched in terms of a holy crusade" and it is in the next sentence that he dismisses Emily as irrelevant. We see then that in the same way that Cambridge has only secondary significance for her, Emily is of concern to him only insofar as her presence causes a worsening of Christiania's condition (164). He thus (correctly) assumes that she is near to powerless, and uncritically accepts the patriarchal organization of the plantation. For this reason, Ledent rightly argues that Cambridge and Emily "inversely participate in the oppression of each other" (2002, 102): Emily through her acceptance of racism and defence of the slavery; Cambridge through his acceptance of patriarchy.

Both Cambridge and Emily have the possibility of an authentic recognition of the common humanity of the other foreclosed by the discourses through which they interpret and understand the world. Despite the similarities between them—the resonances of powerlessness and marginality, of being governed, as it were, by the wills of white men—the possible disruption that each could be to the other's understanding never achieves recognition as it does with the characters I have considered in the works of Ghosh and Adichie. Ironically, Emily and Cambridge have similar views on the savagery of Africans, differing mainly in degree and in their understanding of the cure—slavery versus education. This gives Cambridge's narrative a tragic structure to it, which rests in his acceptance of European civilization. It is his education that enables him to resist Mr Brown, to gain the respect of the other slaves, and to work against slavery while still in England. Nevertheless, as I have noted, his acceptance of the discourses of civilization results in his justifying his own initial slavery to himself, and feeling that his second enslavement is unjust, not primarily because it is enslavement but due to his identity as a virtual Englishman, with a "superior *English* mind, inferior only to the Christian goodness in [his] heart" (Phillips 1993, 155, emphasis in original). In short, his acceptance of the discourse of progress and civilization, while enabling him to challenge slavery, simultaneously undercuts that resistance and can be seen to ultimately legitimise it. It is precisely this discourse that served as slavery's alibi, something which is evidenced in Emily's narrative where it forms a crucial part of her justification of the practice (85–86). Cambridge's resistance to the system is therefore simultaneously a reinforcement of it; his resistance of his subjection is founded upon its justification. This tragic double bind in which Cambridge finds himself has distinct similarities to that outlined by David Scott, which I discussed in the introduction: the use of Enlightenment terms to critique it. It is because of this tragic tension that Low suggests that Cambridge's final fear may "not only be [...] the despair of a Christian man who commits a murder, but may also be the despair of a man who is 'truly frightened' by the prospect that all he holds dear may be a sham" (1998, 126).

While Cambridge and Emily both fail in this way to recognise the similarities between them, Emily's ethical position does not remain static as Cambridge's does. Caryl Phillips comments in an interview: "The supreme irony in *Cambridge* is that the black man becomes the character you're supposed to like the least, because [Emily] grows, he shrinks" (Jaggi 1994, 27). Crucial for Emily's growth is the crisis with which her journal closes. The catalyst, as I have said, is Mr Wilson returning to the island, who in Emily's words, "has thrown himself upon my mercy" (Phillips 1993, 123). Meeting with him, she hears a different account of his departure from the island to what she received from Mr Brown. Asserting that he was "banished by Mr Brown at gunpoint" (124), he presses upon her that "through a perverse stubbornness Mr Brown was mis-managing and abusing the property of my family, and that had Mr Wilson not been in fear of his life he would never have abandoned the estate" (125). When she counters that she had been "reliably informed that he had been dismissed for theft"—her source of course being none other than Mr Brown—Mr Wilson "threw back his head and roared with laughter" (125). Insisting on the ludicrous nature of the charge, Mr Wilson's version of events confuses and distresses Emily. Whether his testimony is true or not is irrelevant, though it is shown later to be true. Its importance rests in it being the first counter-evidence to Emily's understanding of affairs that she is unable to simply dismiss: it is presented by an educated, white gentleman. As such, it throws into disarray her carefully mapped intellectual progression, as she has thought of it, which was heavily dependent upon the understanding and opinions of others. Her distress is, however, more than just intellectual confusion and doubt: her sexual relationship with Mr Brown is based upon the same foundation which is here called into question. The misery of her crisis is, therefore, intensified when she discovers that she is pregnant and that Mr Brown has abandoned her, which further confirms Mr Wilson's testimony. For the first time in the novel, Emily has real doubt about what she has so confidently assumed to know, and this is distressing. At the close of the journal entry in which she relates this, she begins to speculate, seemingly with her usual confidence, about the kind of person that settles in the Caribbean. But she then, for the first time, stops herself: "I do not know. How can I know? I have so much still to learn" (127).

This Socratic admission of ignorance by itself does not result in a change of how Emily understands racial difference. Her next and final journal entry records the death of Brown at the hands of Cambridge and is shaped by her sorrow at that event, the "injuries that are daily afflicted upon mankind, let alone my poor soul" (127–128). Throughout the experience of her knowledge being thrown into question, of her emotional distress as a result of her pregnancy, Mr Brown's abandonment of her, and his murder, she still maintains her racist views:

O lucky Isabella that she never lived to see these shores, never lived to witness the treachery of the negro that some would set free to wreak havoc upon our persons. Their lying subservience, their sly pilfering, their murderous violence, mark them out as very like the Irish [...]. (129)

Although reflecting her emotional state at Brown's death, her racism here is congruous with its earlier manifestations. At the journal's end Emily's understanding is largely unchanged. It is only in the epilogue that we learn how these tumultuous experiences eventually result in an alteration of her perspective. That the journal closes with a comparison between Isabella and Stella is, in view of this, salient since many of the traces of Emily's coming recognition involve Stella, who at this point is only a "sad black imitation" of Isabella (129), but will become much more important.

The epilogue, narrated by the same modern, extra-diegetic narrator of the prologue, tells us of Emily's condition roughly nine months later. She is living in a rundown cottage, and has delivered her child stillborn. There are only three people present: the doctor Mr McDonald, Stella, and Emily herself. Throughout Emily's journal Stella has been seen to be a faithful attendant, genuinely fond of her; Emily has, however, refused to reciprocate the affection. A case in point transpires not long after Emily's arrival at the plantation. She records that Stella "asked me if I might address her as *Aunt* Stella". What the reader understands as an overture of friendship and companionship, Emily views as an example "of the looseness of negro morals", exemplified in "how easily they appropriate titles which in our world have a deep and proper meaning". She therefore refuses the request, writing that "her Aunts Mabel and Victoria bore no relation, physical or otherwise, to this ebony matriarch" (36). While Emily does not reciprocate the friendship, she nevertheless finds comfort in Stella's faithful attendance. After confronting Mr Brown in the fields, Emily awakens and writes,

> I was pleased to see the loyal Stella hover over me with concern writ large and bold across her sooty face. How far she has come in matching the loyalty of the dearly departed Isabella! Although

sadly lacking the natural advantages of my former companion [...] my sable companion has virtue still. (78)

There are a number of moments in Emily's journal when this pleasure at Stella's loyalty is evident. Yet despite this, Emily continues to demarcate and enforce what she perceives as inherent racial boundaries. Throughout, Stella remains fond of Emily such that Cambridge notes in passing, towards the end of his narrative, her tearful state when "Mr Brown had taken no interest in her beloved Miss Emily once the details of the latter's condition had been discovered by the physician" (167). Emily's opinion of Stella as but a poor imitation of Isabella persists until the end of her journal. It is particularly striking, then, how much concern Emily evidences for her in the epilogue. She has just lost her baby, yet it is Stella's pain at the loss, Stella who "had hoped for something they might share", that occupies most of her mind to the point that she "dreamed of something that she might give Stella to replace that which had been lost" (178). Dramatised by the narrative focus turning repeatedly to Stella in the epilogue's opening pages, this concern, together with Emily's reflection that for Stella "a terrible ordeal was reaching its conclusion" and her designation as Emily's "grief-stricken companion" (177, 178), all signify that something has changed.

One aspect of the change is the continuation of the doubt we saw at the close of the journal. In the nine months since then, the slaves have been emancipated and life on the island has changed considerably as a result. Talking about the effects of emancipation and his plans for returning to England, Mr McDonald says, "I take it you're not an emancipationist" (179). His assumption is not unreasonable, given the previous influence of his views over Emily's. Yet she replies unexpectedly. Where previously, she thought that slaves, if freed, would "wreak havoc upon our persons", she now replies, "You may take it that I am not sure of what I am" (179). More hesitant to posit an opinion than she was before (though there is also the possible reason that she does not want to reveal her thoughts to McDonald), we can see the internalisation of the doubt she earlier experienced. No longer confined to a specific object of knowledge—Mr Brown—her uncertainty has become more epistemic, something that could already be observed when she interrupted her habitually certain thoughts after visiting Mr Wilson. That she has become less ignorant and naive is most consciously marked when she reflects back on her relationship with Mr Brown:

> Love, love, love. You see, I'm not such a bad woman am I? Except love for him ran only a short distance. To the point where he was losing control. And freedom. She knew this now. And then it was turned off. And forgotten. A mistake. She fell over like a foal. (182)

The gullible naivety that was seen in her relationship with Mr Brown has here been replaced by the knowledge that for him love "ran only a short distance" and could be "turned off" when things spiralled out of control: it was not the unexpected, amazing discovery that she had thought. This error is also recognised as having been a stage of growth, as a stumbling that is part of a foal learning to walk.

There is more at work, though, than a progression out of naivety. Immediately following this reflection on her relationship with Mr Brown, Emily "thought warmly of Stella. Without doubt their greatest virtue was their unswerving loyalty" (182). The emotional bond that has formed between Emily and Stella, evidenced here and in the opening of the epilogue, is crucial. The close connection between Emily's recollection of falling over like a foal and her warm thoughts of Stella suggests that, for Emily's part, this bond flourished when she was vulnerable. That Emily goes onto speak of loyalty suggests that it formed particularly due to Stella's continued faithfulness. Emily is repeating here, with a correction, her earlier mention of the slaves' "unswerving loyalty". I noted above how the slaves' loyalty was denigrated by Emily as "the animal fidelity of the dog" (54). Here, not only is Stella a "companion", someone of whom Emily thinks "warmly", but her loyalty, which had given Emily comfort and pleasure before, is now taken as representative of her race as "their greatest virtue" (182). This is a *moral* designation that, despite the remaining racial essentialism evidenced by the general pronoun "their", is quite distinct from the inherent, amoral loyalty of dogs,[44] and as such is distinct from Emily's earlier understanding of Africans as immoral savages. This is a complete

---

[44] While, as we have seen in earlier chapters, the idea of the animal as the limit of ethics has been questioned, for Emily it is a clear boundary and thus at play here.

change in Emily's understanding, serving as evidence that a positive gain in knowledge, namely the recognition of the humanity of the slaves, of their distinctly moral qualities, occurred at some point in the previous nine months.

There are further traces of this recognition, throughout the epilogue. In her final journal entry, she writes that Isabella had told her, "I must never allow myself to grow old in a country that is unkind to me". Isabella had been referring to England, and Emily at that point suggests that she is in the West Indies due to Isabella's "urgings", which led her to leave England and, ultimately, to her catastrophic situation (129). This is reinscribed in the epilogue: "Do not (Isabella had reminded her) grow old in a place that is unkind to you. They were kind, they journeyed up the hill and brought her food" (182). Kindness is therefore ascribed to the former slaves, confirming that the recognition is not limited to Stella alone. There is, importantly, also a significant change in her self-understanding in relation to the slaves. During the night after the stillbirth which the epilogue narrates, Emily says a prayer, "dedicating the prayer to those, like herself, whose only journeys were uprootings" (180). During one of her earlier observations of the slaves on the plantation she had noted "the rootlessness of these people who have been torn from their native soil" (71). That "those, like herself" might refer to the slaves, to a feature which they have in common with her, stands in vivid contrast with her earlier views of racial superiority and difference.

In view of such a dramatic change in Emily, it is interesting that throughout the epilogue this recognition is neither recounted nor recollected. There are only these traces, the changes that we observe in her. It is, nonetheless, possible to infer what served as the catalysts for this change. There is, to begin with, the complete reversal of her situation. Of itself, I noted, a change in material circumstances would not lead to a change of mind: it was seen that in the midst of the turmoil, Emily maintained her racist views. It is for this reason that the bond between Emily and Stella is important: not only is it a manifestation of the change in Emily's understanding, but it also seems to be one of the main causes. Emily's situation at the close of her journal is one of acute emotional pain, and, I suggest, the bond between the two women was able to form due to the intense doubt and distress that Mr Wilson's return caused for Emily's racist position. The reversal of Emily's circumstances, therefore, played the crucial role of creating the possibility for the connection between her and Stella to flourish. That their relationship was the main cause of the recognition explains the emotional connection and Emily's correlative concern. After all, the friendship with Stella, being contrary to Emily's racist ideology, was neither acknowledged nor could be held in tandem with it. Additionally, this understanding of the recognition concurs with the closing sentences of the epilogue. Mourning the loss of her child, desiring death but knowing that she must live on, "that, in all likelihood, she would have to witness the dying of the sun come dusk", Emily's source of comfort is thinking of Stella: "She remembered. Journeying up the hill to Hawthorn Cottage. With her friend. Stella. Dear Stella" (184).

There is definite growth in Emily's narrative in *Cambridge*, which adds an important depth to her character, and shows her as responsible for her earlier, racist position. That is to say, her surpassing of her ethical failure (and ideological position) reveals her (circumscribed) responsibility for it. This is a significant development that suggests some similarities with Adichie's *Purple Hibiscus*. For one, instrumental in both novels is the forming of relationships that were previously avoided—in Kambili's case with her grandfather. The characters also learning through their emotional assessment of their situation is a pattern similar to what we saw in *Sea of Poppies* between Deeti and Kalua. Deeti's recognition of Kalua as a fellow human being, as equal with her, is brought about through her emotional response.[45] Stumbling across Kalua being humiliated and violated, his experience resonates powerfully with her own rape on her wedding

---

[45] It tends to be a particular kind of emotion that is effective for causing the recognition. Emily feels fear of both Cambridge and Christiania, but this does not result in any change to her understanding. Although this would likely be context specific, it is possible to speculate that this is due to what the different emotions communicate. As Nussbaum (2001) argues, fear correlates to danger: something which we value is threatened. The natural response to fear is thus defensive, as indeed we saw with Emily. It follows that what is required for emotions to catalyse recognition is a more positive affirmation of the value of something previously un- or undervalued, rather than the threatening of something already valued. This seems to be the case with Emily. Her fear of Cambridge and Christiania results in her designating them as mad, but the positive bond with Stella, which introduces something new of value, results in recognition. An exception to this would be when fear highlights to oneself a discrepancy between what one feels one should not fear, and what one in reality does.

night. Unexpectedly for Deeti, Kalua shifts through this resonance from being viewed as a shadowy member of a lower caste, to being like her. In each of these scenarios, purely intellectual disruptions alone are insufficient: it is the emotional distress of being unmoored and the bond that forms between Emily and Stella that enables her recognition of a common, equal humanity with the slaves.

As I suggested at the beginning of this chapter, though, it is that which separates Phillips's work from Adichie's and Ghosh's that is more significant. As has been seen, the main text of *Cambridge* is marked by a distinct lack of recognition despite possible moments for one. Although the reader, due to the juxtaposition of the narratives, can recognise similarities between them, Emily and Cambridge themselves are constrained by their discourses. Instead of recognizing their commonalities and the equal humanity that underpins them, they inversely participate in the oppression of each other. Even in the (marginal) epilogue, where we can see that Emily has dramatically changed, recognition is still conspicuously absent. The effect is precisely to sharpen the lack of recognition that has gone before and, through Emily's painful success, to emphasise her and Cambridge's failure which has constituted the majority of the narrative. Phillips can therefore be seen to represent in *Cambridge* ethical failure: a failure that in part arises from the constraining effects of discourse and which, I suggest, has been effectively conveyed through the use of unreliable narrators.

The close connection that I have detailed between Emily's unreliability as a narrator and her failure to recognise Cambridge as an equal human being warrants some further consideration. James Phelan, in his study on the ethics of character narration discussed in the introduction, presents a comprehensive taxonomy of unreliable narration. He argues for three axes of unreliability: "Narrators", he writes, "perform three main roles—reporting, interpreting, and evaluating [...] They may, therefore, deviate [...] in one or more of these roles simultaneously, sequentially, or intermittently" (2005, 50). The axes of unreliability correspond to these narrator functions: "unreliable reporting occurs along the axis of characters, facts, and events; unreliable reading (or interpreting) occurs along the axis of knowledge and perception; and unreliable regarding (or evaluating) occurs along the axis of ethics and evaluation" (50). Phelan proceeds to argue for a further distinction along each of these axes: either the narrator's words need be rejected and a more satisfactory account constructed by the reader, or the narrator's words need to be supplemented (50–51). In other words, the narrator is either unreliable in the sense of reporting (knowingly or not) something that is false and misleading the reader, or they are unreliable in that what they tell us is true, but incomplete. In combining these aspects Phelan creates his taxonomy of six kinds of unreliability: "misreporting, misreading, misevaluating—or what I will call misregarding", each of which, except the first, correlates to when the narrator is incorrect and their words are rejected; and "underreporting, underreading, and underregarding" (51), each of which, except the first, corresponds to when the narrator is correct, but their words need to be supplemented (50–51).

Phelan's discussion in which he develops this taxonomy is concerned with the ethics of Kazuo Ishiguro's *Remains of the Day*, which I considered in the introduction. His discussion is useful here, however, as it enables a more accurate grasp of the kind of unreliability presented by Emily and Cambridge. Both of them are largely reliable along the axis of facts and events. When Emily tells us that Stella requested that she be called Aunt Stella, there is no doubt that this occurred. Similarly, with Cambridge, when he is retaken as a slave there is no doubt that this happened, nor that the Captain stole his money. It is along the axes of interpretation and evaluation that both Emily and Cambridge are distinctly unreliable. Emily's evaluation of Stella's request is a case of misregarding due to a mistaken value system: the reader knows that Stella is trying to be friendly, while Emily evaluates it as a bastardization of proper English categories. And so also Cambridge, in objecting to his re-enslavement on the basis that he is a virtual Englishman, similarly displays a mistaken value system. My attention has mainly been occupied by Emily's pervasive misreading. One of the most overt examples is her interpretation of Mr Brown's change of behaviour as reflecting "a profound change in the heart and soul of Mr Brown" which she can "only assume" is because of "guilt" (Phillips 1993, 82). While, as Phelan points out, misreading can result from a misregarding—which is possibly the case, as I noted before, with some of Cambridge's assessments of Christiania whom he rigidly interprets through the lens of a European, rational Christianity and so denies the possibility that she is a practitioner of Obeah—Emily's misreading arises from her dislocation from herself which allows her naive gullibility and unacknowledged racism to masquerade as objectivity. As a result, the story depicts her increasing acceptance of the ideology of the plantation.

What emerges, then, is that unreliable narrators such as Emily and Cambridge are particularly suited to exploring ethical failure in a nuanced way. Unreliable narrators dramatise a failure of knowledge (one is tempted, in cases of misreporting, underreading and underregarding, to say misrecognition) along the axes I have noted, and such failure can often be an ethical one: not only overtly as in cases of misregarding, but also more implicitly in misreading. This is what we have seen with Emily and Cambridge and their failure of recognition. However, through fragmenting the narrative voice, Phillips has further managed to capitalise on this feature of the unreliable narrator. Refusing the representation of a positive recognition, even in the epilogue, Phillips has succeeded in crystallizing the focus of *Cambridge* on ethical failure in a manner that contrasts with a novel like *Purple Hibiscus*, where the focus is less on the error than on the process of growing out of it.

It is, finally, necessary to briefly consider part three of the novel—the official report of the murder—which returns us to the epilogue and asks why Phillips relates the traces of Emily's recognition in the language of a modern, far more reliable, narrator. In an interview with Caryl Phillips, Graham Swift (2009) picks up on this and quizzes Phillips on the "sense of a language that can talk about things suddenly bursting through Emily's own language in which she can't" (16). Swift turns this towards Phillips's own sense of being a writer, but the statement can still be seen to broach this question. Swift's own suggestion that we hear a modern narrator in the epilogue because Emily cannot speak about such things is appealing: it seems to fit with the unreliability of her earlier narration and, after all, she does not expressly reveal her new perspective—it is recounted for us. This is challenged, however, by a large portion of the epilogue being narrated monologue: Emily is seen to be aware of her new perspective and, as I have shown, she is aware of it as maturation: she is no longer a tottering foal, no longer immature.

Instead, what seems to be a likely answer concerns the third narrative, and brings us back to the historical, intertextual details that I discussed earlier. Following Paul Sharrad's discussion of the novel, Ledent comments that the third narrative in *Cambridge* is the "most likely to survive in real life" (quoted in Ledent 2002, pp.102–103). What Ledent and Sharrad suggest is that the kind of grossly exaggerated and biased report represented by the third narrative, which is almost an exact duplication of an actual report, is the most likely record of a story like Cambridge's to have survived. Consequently, it would shape our understanding of history. It "thus raises the issue of what is eventually included into history" (103), and casts Phillips's intervention as involving more than a recuperation of historical texts into memory, bringing his work into proximity with Ghosh's interest in excavating forgotten and suppressed histories. Emily's and Cambridge's narratives would come to be understood as important parts of the story which the historical record of the report elides. As the extensive citing of historical travelogues and slave testimonies demonstrates, however, the texts represented by Emily and Cambridge's narratives do survive (though perhaps not as frequently as the kind represented by part three since they are published and disseminated less frequently). The significance of Emily's prologue and epilogue is that they fall entirely beyond this purview of archival history, and it is precisely as such that they work to add a further (fictional) layer to the historically unspoken in the narrative. They respond to those gaps in and connections between the narratives which emerge due to their proximity. It is this distinct quality which is marked by the use of the modern narrator.

III

The third narrative in *Cambridge* functions as the main historical moment around which Phillips's technique of pastiche and montage recuperates archival texts for the purposes of memory, and, negotiating the ethics of memory, marks an intervention into the question of the historical record itself, which is supplemented by the modern narrator of the prologue and epilogue. *Crossing the River* functions according to a similar structure. Eckstein notes that two of the four parts that constitute *Crossing the River* deploy techniques of pastiche and montage. Part one, "The Pagan Coast", draws on "letters by repatriated African-American slaves" which are collected in Bell I. Wiley's *Slaves No More: Letters from Liberia, 1833–1869* (2006, 113). Hamilton's journal that is part three, "Crossing the River", "quotes verbatim from the *Journal of a Slave Trader* by John Newton" (114). Eckstein's purpose in noting this is to show that Phillips's ethical and political project as he has outlined it is not restricted to *Cambridge*, but rather characterises much of his oeuvre. What I find of particular interest, though, is the way in which quoting verbatim from the journal of Newton sets up part three as the historical anchor, as it were, of the novel. It will be seen that in distinction to the earlier novel, Phillips constructs a more intricate web of contrasts and similarities, with a slightly different effect. While there is an extension of Phillips's engagement with the ethical questions of history and memory, the manner of engaging these undergoes some salient alterations.

One of the more overt differences from the earlier novel is the use of section titles. The journal of Hamilton, for instance, is marked as pivotal not only by being a direct citation of an historical text—of which only an informed reader would be aware—but by sharing the title of the novel (though this has also been differently interpreted and will be returned to). Further, whereas *Cambridge* has a unity of character and location with a fragmentation of perspective, the narratives that constitute *Crossing the River* are more diverse, being made up of characters that never meet and are spread across three centuries. Set in the late nineteenth century, part one, "The Pagan Coast", alternates between the letters of Nash Williams to his former master Edward Williams, and Edward's own search for Nash in Liberia when the letters cease to be sent. Part two, "West", is also set in the nineteenth century and tells the story of Martha Randolph's escape from her slave owners and her flight to the west. Jumping a hundred years back into the previous century, part three is the journal of the slave trader Hamilton, while part four, "Somewhere in England", transpires during the second World War and is made up of fragments from the journal of Joyce, an Englishwoman who falls in love with Travis, an African-American GI stationed in England. Such a diverse range of characters is united, on the one hand, in that they are all part of the African diaspora. On the other hand, and more immediately, they are all connected through the voice of the prologue and epilogue, the "guilty father" who, "for two hundred and fifty years" has listened to the "many-tongued chorus" of that diaspora (Phillips 2006, 236–237).

A further divergence between the two novels is located in their chronology. In *Cambridge,* as Eckstein points out, there is a covert disruption of chronological time by the source texts beneath the surface of otherwise chronologically sequential narratives. This disruption enters the narratives themselves in *Crossing the River.* Not only does their ordering disrupt temporal linearity, but the only narrative that progresses internally in a linear fashion is Hamiton's journal: a strict chronology which is significant in its contrast to the other narratives. It is notable that Pichler (2011), apparently independently of Eckstein's earlier study, interprets this disruption of chronology through the same theoretical frame deployed by Eckstein for his reading of Phillips's use of source texts. Where *Cambridge* could be described as effecting the recuperation of historical texts for the purposes of memory (as can *Crossing the River*, considering the citation of source material), Pichler argues that the disruption of narrative chronology in *Crossing the River* dramatises the difference between history and memory. History relates to the past through trying to construct the details and connections between discreet moments, creating a comprehensive vision of what has gone before; memory, as it were, is more selective, retaining "from the past only what still lives or is capable of living in the consciousness of the groups keeping the memory alive" (quoted in Pichler 2011, 2). That is, it relates to the past through the present, as that which retains significance for the present, and as such is characterised by the disruption of linear time. This is dramatised particularly in Martha's narrative through the combination of different voices and tenses. Martha's present circumstances are narrated in the past tense by an extra-diegetic narrator, while her memories are narrated in the present tense by herself as an intra-diegetic narrator. The effect is to make the memories more immediate than the present, demonstrating something of the working of memory (see also Low [1998, 136]).

The common ethical preoccupations with history and memory that can be noted across the two novels are therefore explored more overtly in the later one through these more surface features of narrative voice and structure. Significantly, the narrators in *Crossing the River* also tend to be more reliable than both Emily and Cambridge. While a negotiation of characters' misreading and misregarding is required, such as with Nash William's assessment of his position in Liberia in his early letters and Joyce's blindness to the politics of race in the United States and Britain, the misreading is not as comprehensive or pervasive as in *Cambridge*. Most significantly, Martha's narrative is reliable, which contrasts importantly with the unreliability of the narrative to which it is closely connected: Hamilton's journal (which will be seen, together with

Martha's narrative, to constitute the ethical and interpretative core of the novel). What will emerge is that while the unreliable, multiple narratives of *Cambridge* emphasise ethical failure and correspondingly shape the novel's ethical sense, the increased reliability in *Crossing the River* is important for its more positive ethical stance. A number of critics, following Phillips's own comments on the novel (Davison 2009, 21), have noted that *Crossing the River* conveys a positive link between the characters, an "affirmative connection" (Low 1998, 123). My examination of the novel will concur with this, though what I draw out is the importance to this of ethical failure: it is the interplay of Martha's reliable narrative and Hamilton's unreliable one—closely connected to the "guilty father" and linked to the narratives of Nash and Travis—that conveys this positive affirmation. This is not, contra Low and Ledent, an ironic or paradoxical story of origins, of a betrayal that produces an affirmative diaspora. Nor does it only signal "a common origin" in Africa which is the "only connection between the disparate narratives" (Goyal 2003, 17). Rather, the ethical failure it represents is, as will be seen, far more pervasive. The concern with a lack of recognition, with the ethical failure of not recognizing the equal humanity of the slaves is thus important in this later novel as well: it functions as a critical, enabling (and simultaneously undermining) counterpoint to the positive affirmation.

The figure of the guilty father, so critical to the ethical sense of the novel, is first introduced in the prologue, which narrates for us the "shameful intercourse" of selling his three children: "My Nash. My Martha. My Travis" (Phillips 2006, 1). The opening paragraph is marked by the intertwining of voices that will be more fully dramatised in the novel. Interrupting the father's narrative is an italicised voice narrating the purchasing of the three children from the perspective of the slave trader. We are told: "We watched a while. And then approached. *Approached by a quiet fellow.* The children only. I jettisoned them at this point, where the tributary stumbles and swims out in all directions to meet the sea. *Bought 2 strong man-boys, and a proud girl*" (1). Only when the reader gets to Hamilton's journal in part three do we have the source of these italicised lines confirmed. The result is that from the first (and to the last), the African father's voice is inexorably intertwined with that of the slave trader, linked by the "shameful intercourse"—the phrase "intercourse" conveying the intimacy of mutual exchange and communication while also denoting its original meaning of trade or commerce. As a result, Hamilton's journal cannot be read without the interpretative overlay of this shame, a conjunction that is only more poignant since the journal is written in the mode of an emotionless, meticulous recording of a trade journey.

The first intertwining of voices intimated in the prologue, "The Pagan Coast" is concerned, as Low puts it, with an "exploration of the relationship between masters and slaves as a form of kinship" (1998, 132). We are first introduced to Edward Williams, "the son of a wealthy tobacco planter" who as a young man inherited the estate, "and with it the sum total of three hundred slaves" (Phillips 2006, 13). Sharing his father's aversion to slavery, he begins to educate his slaves, becomes involved with the American Colonization Society, and starts to "repatriate" his former slaves to Liberia (8). From the outset, Edward is presented by the extra-diegetic narrator as benevolent, as someone who departs from the norm by taking "the unusual initiative" of educating his slaves (13). As with Emily in *Cambridge*, though, it quickly becomes apparent that his stated objectives are deceptive. Edward's racism is not only implicit in his acceptance of the discourse of civilizing Africa prevalent at the time, but also overtly when, for instance, he describes Nash possessively as "the most successful of his Christian Blacks" (14). Although later possessives of this sort could be ascribed to pride in one whom Edward considers a protégé, here Nash is only one of many "Christian Blacks" who are "his". More undermining of his benevolent self-representations are his motives and ambivalence. Edward finds slavery distasteful, yet continues to enjoy the immense financial benefits it provides. Additionally, we observe that Edward is interested in educating and repatriating his slaves only as a solution to a social problem. In short, as Low puts it, "Edward is far from the benevolent and disinterested philanthropist that he makes himself out to be" (1998, 133).

In these early sections of the narrative, there are also hints of Edward's homosexual relationships with his slaves, which is only fully revealed later. We are told that Edward's wife, who "sadly [...] was no more" (Phillips 2006, 14)—we only learn later that she committed suicide—would have been "gravely suspicious of the motives which lay behind his projected expedition" to seek out Nash (12), who has disappeared in Liberia, and that she had "slowly come to tolerate the strange behavior and desires of her husband" (14), a comment which seems to refer to his philanthropy but is made ambiguous due to the doubt raised by the surrounding references. For instance, when Edward receives news that Nash is putting his health in danger by working in the rain, he "secretly" pens a plea that he not continue to do so. The narrator cites for us "a portion" of the letter that contained "words of wisdom", which seem relatively banal (10). However, the narrator notes that "this letter was uncovered by Edward's wife, Amelia, and not conveyed" (11). Why Edward's wife would have been suspicious of his motives in seeking out Nash, or what else in the letter caused her to destroy it, is not stated, and only later do we come to know that the reason is his sexual relationship with Nash. At this point in the narrative, however, we know only that Edward (and the ostensibly objective narrator) is concerned with presenting a particular portrait of himself as fitting the nineteenth century ideal of a gentleman. Although Edward is not as he is presented to be, it is not possible to discount the bond between him and Nash. He does, after all, defy all advice and undertake a perilous journey to find him. There is still a degree of self-interest: he goes "not simply to discover the truth surrounding his Nash, but in order to confirm that his life's work, and more importantly his own life, had been of some worth" (14). Nevertheless, his concern for Nash is real, and the journey of self-discovery is crucial to the conclusion of the section.

While Edward is significant, most of the space in "The Pagan Coast" is taken up by the five letters that Nash writes to Edward from Liberia. Low notes that Nash is "reared in the image of his master", and as such shares his racism (1998, 133). Addressing him as his "Beloved Benefactor" and his "Dear Father" (Phillips 2006, 17, 23), Nash can be seen at first to share Edward's conviction of the need to civilise and evangelise the "heathens" (19). Accordingly, in his first letter he writes in gratitude to Edward who was "kind enough to take me, a foolish child, from my parents and bring me up in your own dwelling as something more akin to son than servant". The resonance here with Cambridge's gratitude at being taken as a slave is striking. Nash continues: "Had I been permitted simply to run about, I would today be dwelling in the same robes of ignorance which drape the shoulders of my fellow blacks" (21). Nash views Liberia as "the star in the East for the free coloured man. It is truly our home". It is a place where "we may sit under the palm tree and enjoy the same privileges as our white bretheren in America" (18). That this is false and that Liberia, at least in Monrovia, is marked by the same racism and white privilege as America is later revealed by Edward's arrival. Nash nevertheless calls Liberia a paradise to the end, though his reasons for this, as well as his opinion of the "garb of ignorance" Edward delivered him from, will alter significantly.

Five years after his first letter, in the third of the series that constitutes his part of the narrative, we begin to see Nash's understanding of the world shift. Writing about the belief among the locals that sudden death is due to bewitching, Nash describes a practice of consulting "the grand devil man of the village" to ascertain who "bewitched the person that died". He writes:

> This person will then be fed some poison in order to dispatch him for his wrongful deed. This appears to me not an entirely unjust method of administering justice, and one from which we of the so-called civilised world might learn something valuable. (31)

Nash's language here intimates his confusion. The criminal is identified and executed by the "devil man", a description congruent with European judgements of traditional African religion at the time. Yet this is immediately inverted by Nash calling the practice just, and one from which America and Europe could learn. A new assessment of traditional practises is beginning to emerge amidst the familiar judgements and interpretations of them. What is crucial is the questioning indicated by Nash's prefacing of the "civilized world" with "so-called". This uncertainty as to America and Europe holding the title of "civilized" will become central to his last letters. Similarly important in this letter—and indeed in all the others—is Nash's pain at Edward's lack of reply, which he reads as rejection. At this point he is still able to de-emphasise the hurt, suggesting self-deprecatingly that his letters are "unworthy of response" (29). This soon passes, and in his next letter he writes, "Why your heart remains hard against me is a mystery which has caused me emotions of great distress" (38).

Nash Williams' final letter is the most severe. Written while Edward is at sea in response to Nash's previous letter "making it plain that he had no desire ever to hear again from his former master, and informing him that his own communications would now cease" (8), it emphasises his pain at Edward's rejection and makes explicit his rejection in turn of Edward's view of Africa and Africans. Having taken three wives, Nash is living "the life of an African". He declares that Liberia is the "finest country for the colored man" because of the freedom it offers:

> We, the colored man, have been oppressed long enough. We need to contend for our rights, stand our ground, and feel the love of liberty that can never be found in your America. Far from corrupting my soul, the Commonwealth of Liberia has provided me with the opportunity to open my eyes and cast off the garb of ignorance which has encompassed me all too securely the whole course of my life. (61–62)

We see here the complete inversion of Nash's conception of the "garb of ignorance". In contrast to his first letter, his tutelage under Edward and at college in Virginia did not liberate him from ignorance but rather wrapped him more securely in it, a condition which Liberia provided the opportunity to cast off. Also unlike his previous discarding of ignorance, his agency is here retained: Liberia only provided the opportunity, Nash was responsible for grasping it. There are two points about which he has gained enlightenment, and consequently repudiated Edward's view. First, is the recognition that there is no liberty for "the colored man" in America: the "your" both distances Nash from America and implies that it belongs to white people, in so far as Africans are denied an equal place. He also, however, repudiates the ostensible purpose for being sent to Liberia in the first place. He writes that the "school is no more, and shall never again occupy a position of authority in any settlement of which I am a part", going on to assert the futility of the missionary enterprise: "The truth is, our religion, in its purist and least diluted form, can never take root in this country" (62). Although he still considers himself a Christian, he feels that he is "bound to an African existence". Nash must therefore "suspend my faith and [...] choose to live the life of an African" since Christianity has no place in Africa (62). This is a view that is problematised by Adichie. It is no surprise, however, that in the opening of the letter Nash expresses his concern that Edward will think him "corrupted [...] into this heathen whom you barely recognize" (61). In contrast to Goyal's (2003) claim that Nash shows "no substantive emotional, moral, or psychological development" (19), we can see that he in fact evidences a significant reversal in outlook.

Nash's criticism of America and the purpose behind his journey to Liberia makes it all the more striking that he is so intensely distraught at Edward's seeming rejection of him. In his penultimate letter, he exclaims, "Why have you forsaken me?" (Phillips 2006, 42). The full significance of this will be picked up later, but at this point it is clear that Nash's letters convey his increasing pain at the separation and silence between the two of them, steadily building to this despairing question and his final rejection of Edward. His bitterness, as noted earlier, is explained by the revelation in Edward's narrative of the sexual nature of their relationship (55-56), which, coupled with Nash's inability to share his past life with his African wives (42), bestows an immense significance on Edward for his emotional life. The sexual nature of the relationship only emerges late in Nash's narrative, in his final letter: "I find the process [of writing to Edward] humiliating, and I fail to see what hurt I ever inflicted upon you that could justify such a cruel abandonment of your past intimate, namely myself" (60). Low interprets the relationship as one of paedophilia, since Edward confesses to craving the "unconditional love of a child" (55). It is not clear, though, that this is the case. Edward tells us that he lavished "an excess of affection upon a new retainer" only once Nash had left (56), suggesting that what he craves is sheer devotion and obedience such as we see evidenced in Nash's early letters. Regardless of the question of age, it is clear that such devotion is the result of an abuse of the power differential between Edward and Nash that, coupled with the role which Edward plays as Nash's surrogate father, casts the relationship as "an abuse and perversion of that kinship" (Low 1998, 135).[46]

It is poignant, then, that at the close of this section of the novel, Edward and his life's work—the validity of which he had set out to ascertain—is not only rejected by Nash, but by the extra-diegetic narrator. After Nash's death, Edward arrives at his final settlement with another former slave, Madison, as a guide, and is shocked by what he finds. The settlement is a small village made up of a "litter of brown cones", that is, a collection of huts which Edward views as "straw grass hovel[s]" (Phillips

---

[46] This is, of course, an abuse in addition to that of slavery itself.

2006, 68–69). Unable to "disguise his true feelings of disgust" (69), he cannot bring himself to enter Nash's final home. He turns to Madison for help: "But Madison had about his person an air of nonchalance. And then it struck Edward with a terrible force. He was alone. He had been abandoned" (69). This is a powerful moment of recognition. He realises the failure of his ideals, and it rattles him. He tries to sing a hymn to calm himself, but, silenced "despite his ridiculous attempt to assert his religious and cultural sovereignty" (Boutros 2012, 181), the words fail to form. The narrator continues:

> Still, Edward continued to *sing* his hymn. The natives looked on and wondered what evil spirits had populated this poor man's soul and dragged him down to such a level of abasement. Their hearts began to swell with the pity that one feels for a fellow being who has lost both his way and his sense of purpose. This strange old white man. Madison turned away. (Phillips 2006, 69, emphasis in original)

In these final lines, the focalization shifts. Having closely narrated Edward's perspective until this point, the narrator suddenly switches to that of "the natives". It is a narrative move that echoes (for the second time in this book) Achebe's ending of *Things Fall Apart*. Except that it does not reveal the violence of colonial discourse. Instead, it shows a recognition by the villagers of a common existence, a commonality refused by Edward, even as it simultaneously serves to reject him. In his final letter, which Madison delivered personally, Nash rejected Edward and his purposes. At this point, Madison refuses to ally himself with Edward's inability to accept and understand what he sees. Then, in the shift of focalization, the narrator also abandons Edward, conveying the Africans' pity for Edward's despair, emphasizing the failure of his sense of purpose, and that, like Nash, he is alone.

This combination of recognitions works to dramatise and support the African father's argument that "There are no paths in water. No signposts. There is no return" (2). Nash tries to return, first as a missionary and then as one living "an African life". Although he has some marginal success, his painful longing for Edward shows that he is never at ease, and is always unable to belong fully. In this way, then, the first narrative introduces the main thematic of longing for kinship, for meaningful affective connections, and reiterates the guilty father's perspective on the diaspora. That this first part contains the perspective of both a slave owner and a former slave is important as this pairing is continued and developed in the next two narratives. Despite the structural similarity in this pairing to that of Martha and Hamilton, it highlights some differences. Hamilton's narrative will pick up the duplicitous attitude to slavery held by both Edward and his father. Yet while Edward progresses through guilt to arrive at a significant recognition, such a moment is absent from Hamilton's section. In contrast, Martha's narrative has a greater continuity with Nash, responding to his early glossing of his separation from his family as beneficial, problematizing it and dramatizing the "enduring pain" of the loss of kinship (Low 1998, 135).

The present time of Martha's narrative, narrated in the past tense, is less immediate than her memories, narrated in the present tense. Through them we learn the details of how her family was split up, her escape from slavery, and her new life in Dodge. She enjoys a decade of contentment with a new husband, but when he is murdered she needs to flee again. She joins a group of pioneers heading west but is too old to complete the journey and is left in Denver, where she passes her final hours, freezing to death in spite of the paltry aid of an anonymous white woman.

Despite the happiness that Martha finds with her new husband, her narrative centers on the pain of the repeated breaking of affective ties. Low argues that the trauma of the splitting of her original family organises Martha's entire life and thus also the narrative. Her "connection with [her family], her desire for them" is transformative (1998, 135), with the result that all "of Martha's journeys are also journeys in search of family, and journeys that create and perform kinship ties", causing Martha's story to represent "is a diaspora of connectedness via the pain of original loss" (136). Although perhaps more immediately traumatic than the guilty father's pain, Martha's quest for connection is not, according to Low, marred by betrayal and is consequently "a more uplifting example of what is possible" (135), a positive instance of affirmative connections, including, Abigail Ward (2011) argues, the forging of an (albeit ambiguous) connection with the white woman providing her with shelter (52).

Martha, longing for her daughter as she passes her final moments, dreams that "she had travelled on west to California, clutching her bundle of clothing. Once there she was met by Eliza Mae, who was now a tall, sturdy colored woman of some social standing" (Phillips 2006, 2). But things are not as they should be. Her daughter is going by her former mistress's name, Cleo, reflecting the destructive effect of slavery on kinship relations, how it infiltrates the unconscious (Ledent 2002, 128). More significantly, in the dream it was soon "time for Martha to leave, but her daughter simply forbade her mother to return east." Weeping in response, Martha has an important moment of recognition: "She would not be going any place. She would never again head east. To Kansas. To Virginia. Or to beyond. She had a westward soul which had found its natural-born home in the bosom of her daughter" (Phillips 2006, 94). "Beyond" Virginia, of course, lies Africa. What is implied by the failure of Nash's return to Africa is here reiterated more overtly: there is no return, "She would never again head east". The "natural born home" of her soul—which though "natural" has also to be "found", a description that supports Low's and Ledent's reading of the performative, earned nature of kinship in the novel—lies to the west, in "the bosom of her daughter". That is, in the future, in the "new trees" of which the father speaks in the prologue (2).

For Low, Martha presents the "central theme of *Crossing the River*. Her reason is its privileged position in the novel. Not only does Martha's story lie "at the novel's heart" (1998, 136), but she also remembers the "shameful intercourse" on the beach. When Martha first begins to remember her past, we read:

> Through some atavistic mist, Martha peered back east, beyond Kansas, back beyond her motherhood, her teen years, her arrival in Virginia, to a smooth white beach where a trembling girl waited with two boys and a man. Standing off, a ship. Her journey had been a long one. But now the sun had set. Her course was run. *Father, why hast thou forsaken me?* (Phillips 2006, 73, emphasis in original)

Although the phrasing suggests that she was born in Africa, the "trembling girl" is not her—at least not literally so. In Denver after the

Civil War, Martha here reaches back more than a century, remembering the ancestral "shameful intercourse" of the father selling his children, an event which, we learn through Hamilton's narrative, occurred on the 19th May, 1753 (124). That the trembling girl is not Martha is in one sense irrelevant: the betrayal by the father of his children has a synecdochal relationship with the slave trade and the African diaspora which it initiated. There is therefore a sense in which the trembling girl is indeed Martha, and every other African woman sold as or descended from a slave. Nevertheless, Martha here echoes the guilty father. For in addition to remembering the shameful intercourse, she also hears the same chorus: "Voices from the past. Some she recognized. Some she did not. But, nevertheless, she listened" (79). Centrally placed, and linked in this way to the presiding voice of the father, Martha's positive difference from him becomes, for Low, central to the novel's meaning, to the sense of affirmative connections (1998, 136).

This is correct, so far as it goes. What has been neglected by critics, however, are the connections between Martha's narrative and that of Hamilton, and the effect of this on the novel's ethical impact. Her connection with Hamilton is twofold: one direct and one indirect. On the one hand, she remembers the "ship standing off" from the beach where the trembling girl waits; yet, less directly, her connection with the guilty father also links her to Hamilton. The result is that rather than Martha holding the "heart" of the novel, as Low suggests, the center is instead held by two closely linked, contrary narratives: Martha and Hamilton together, joined by a common memory, constitute the second, and most important, narrative pairing in the novel.

Hamilton's narrative, which I noted above "quotes verbatim from the *Journal of a Slave Trader* by John Newton" (Eckstein 2006, 114), is distinct from the other narratives in the novel in a number of aspects. Meticulously recording the details of Hamilton's trading journey along the west coast of Africa, it is strictly chronological and written in a matter-of-fact tone of "commercial detachment" (Phillips 2006, 119), vividly illustrated in Hamilton's record of his response to an attempted rebellion by his newly taken slaves: "Surprised 4 attempting to get off their irons [...] Put 2 in irons and delicately in the thumbscrews to encourage them to a full confession of those principally concerned. In the evening put 5 more in neck yokes" (114). Hamilton's emotionless account of torturing two slaves by slowly crushing their thumbs in thumbscrews is chilling, and indicative of a complete lack of empathy, and the lack of a recognition of the humanity of the slaves that enables it. This is present throughout the narrative and is a striking feature, particularly in comparison to the pathos of the previous two. It is often noted that this portrayal is complicated by the insertion into the journal of two personal letters addressed to his wife, which reveal his longing for her and possible family.[47] While this conflict between his work on the ship and his emotional life does indicate the "ambivalent nature of colonial interaction" in which Hamiton is not at ease (Boutros 2012, 184), the letters nevertheless show minimal thought for the slaves, with them surfacing only in relation to complaints about noise and his quest to find his father's final resting place; with regard to latter, he confesses to "deep feelings of revulsion" towards the slaves (Phillips 2006, 119). In short, there is no ambiguity in the absence of recognition of the slaves' humanity.

Hamilton's part in *Crossing the River* has been variously understood by critics, though it has not held a position of much priority in many analyses and in some cases, such as in Pichler, is omitted entirely. However, Ledent brings a few important aspects to light. Her overall reading of the novel is concerned with the literal and metaphorical crossing of rivers in each narrative, the latter referring to "the mental borders that need to be crossed again and again in order to meet others" (2002, 110). She focuses on how Phillips explores the relations between individuals and in so doing problematises essentialisms, the binary of oppressor/oppressed, temporal chronology, and an essentialised or romanticised idea of the diaspora. Within these terms, Hamilton's significance for Ledent is twofold: narrating the purchasing of slaves, he is both the preeminent example of people who are "unable to leave their thick-skinned self-centeredness" (122), and is the mechanism through which Phillips destabilises any romantic notion of the African diaspora.

He is also important for Ledent due to the connections to the father of the prologue and epilogue, which I suggested earlier caused an ineradicable haunting of each by the other. The result is a sense of diaspora as a community held together by an experience of guilt and

---

[47] See for example Ward (2007), Ward (2011, 53–54), and Boutros (2012, 183–184).

shame, as well as pain and survival: "the family love that binds father and children originally derives from an act of treason" (126). I will return to this claim about origins, akin to Low's insight that Martha's "diaspora of connectedness" is founded upon the "pain of original loss" (Low 1998, 136). Ledent's interest in it, though, is the way in which it displays Phillips's "heterodoxy and nuance" by refusing a "romantic view of the continent [of Africa] and the dispersal of its people [...] The diaspora he depicts is marked from its very origins by paradox" (Ledent 2002, 126). It is the guilt of the father that creates the "group" of those in exile—a group that Ledent (and Low) consider Phillips to treat heterodoxically by including the character of Joyce, whom I will consider below.

That Hamilton is a partner in this originary shameful intercourse of the prologue, the founding violation of the African diaspora, Ledent argues, causes the title of the section, "Crossing the River", to be ironic. In contrast to the other narratives, the title suggests "a cross-cultural dynamics" while the narrative portrays cultural stasis and closed mindedness (111). More specifically, in a novel concerned with the crossing of rivers "whether real or metaphorical" (110), "the title hardly goes beyond its original concrete meaning [....] no doubt", she adds, "to suggest the lack of imagination of the man who unwittingly initiated the passages illustrated in the other sections" (111). For Ledent, Hamilton stands in contrast to the fluidity, non-essentialism and disrupted temporality of the diasporic community which he initiated, registering as the example of a failure to cross the divisions between individuals.

Low's analysis largely compliments Ledent's, though she is more concerned with its relation to the theme of kinship. For Low, Hamilton returns us to the master's side of the story of slavery, reminding us of the "'real' history" (1998, 137). Like Ledent, Low sees Hamilton as standing in contrast to the other narratives, though they differ in where they locate the irony. While for Ledent it rests mainly in the misnomer of the title, for Low it is in the presence of Hamilton's letters to his wife. The letters reveal a longing for affection and family that is completely expunged from the journal, and which he brutally denies to his slaves. As Low comments, in view of his longing for his wife "the irony of his enforced break up of slaves' families and kinsfolk is lost on him" (137; see also Ward 2007, 26).

Although insightful, I suggest that Ledent and Low do not go far enough in their analyses of Hamilton. Taking their arguments together, they present Hamilton's connection to the guilty father, holding a position of ironic contrast. However, for both of them Hamilton is secondary: a negative image of the exemplary narrative of Martha (for Low) or Joyce (for Ledent) in their demonstration of affective connection and kinship. The full impact of the novel's exploration of diaspora is diluted by this move. There are a number of connections between Hamilton and the other narratives that Low and Ledent do not consider and which lead me to suggest that Hamilton should rather be read in conjunction with Martha as constituting the interpretative core of the novel. I have already noted two points in support of Hamilton's pivotal role: the historical citation in the section's composition and the citation of the novel's title, which, while ironic, also situates it in the novel's interpretative heart (see also Ward [2011, 52–53]).

The question of citation is, however, more extensive and critical than this. In the first instance, Hamilton is connected by citation not only to Martha and the guilty father, but to Nash and Edward as well. Both Hamilton and Edward are duplicitous in their view of slavery as against their religious beliefs while simultaneously enjoying the financial profit it brings. Most significantly, though, what the reader discovers in the narrative of Hamilton is the origin of a specific sequence of citations. I noted that the father quotes Hamilton's account of purchasing his three children. During the exchange he tells us, "I could feel their eyes upon me. Wondering, *why?*" (Phillips 2006, 2). Suggestively, the children's thoughts are italicised in the same way as Hamilton's. Not this time a citation by the father, but rather the first in a chain of iterations set in motion by the father and Hamilton's combined action. Taken up in Nash's expression of despair at being abandoned by his "father" Edward, the "Why?" is expanded to "Why have you forsaken me?" (42). It is again cited and expanded by Martha in the opening paragraph of her narrative: "*Father, why hast though forsaken me?*" (73). Each reiteration is slightly different, the chain of citation progressing to its fullest in Martha's narrative. Occurring at the height of abandonment and the suffering of the trauma and injustice of slavery, each citation is, I suggest, precisely a citation of this trauma, a present reiteration of the first, despairing question.

These citations are themselves a quotation of the words of Jesus Christ on the cross: "'Eloi, Eloi, lama sabachthani', which is, being interpreted, My God, my God, why hast thou forsaken me?" (Mark 15:34,

KJV). The similarities are striking. Linguistically, the use of the older form "why hast thou" forges a strong connection. Beyond this, Nash and Martha both die shortly after uttering these words, which in Christian theology is the supreme instance of despair, separation, and abandonment, as well as the mechanism of salvation. It is particularly notable that the fullest citation and development of these words of Jesus and the children is uttered by Martha, whose narrative is not only the most overtly marked by the trauma of loss, but also by the refusal of the possibility of returning east. She suggestively substitutes Jesus's "My God" with "Father", and the resurrection redemption that usually accompanies these words in Christian theology is absent in Martha, who in contrast "felt the sadness of not possessing a faith that could reassure her that, having served her apportioned span, she would now be ushered to a place of reunion" (89). As a result, the separation from and abandonment by the father, signaled by the chain of citation, is most concentrated in Martha's narrative. Martha is, then, the final link in the chain, holding the center of the novel together with Hamilton, who along with the father's citation of him in his narratives initiates the chain of iteration that Martha completes.

This is a series of connections that is more significant than Goyal's designation of "textual echoes" suggests (2003, 17). Goyal argues that there is a lack of agency and development in the novel's black characters that, together with the juxtaposition of the narratives, "displace[s] the black descendants of the diaspora" and "reinstates the white Western subject at [its] heart" (20, 22). The claim that underpins this is that there is "no evident hierarchy" among the sections (20). The chain of citations I have mapped, however, demonstrates the opposite. Rather than simply treating the white characters with a problematic "evenhandedness" which places them at the "heart of the African diaspora" (21), the iterations of the despairing cry reveal an order, with Hamilton's narrative, in contrasting tension with Martha's, situated as the emotionless and recognition-lacking instigator of the trauma of slavery. Although Goyal is correct in noting "complicity and symmetry" between Hamilton and the father (19), the failure of recognition in Hamilton and the chain of citation contradict his claim that Phillips "refuses to distinguish between the two" (18–19).

A further result, however, is that this lack of recognition of the slaves' humanity becomes determinative of the novel's ethics, its affirmation, in the same way as in *Cambridge*. Low and Ledent are correct in noting the optimism of *Crossing the River*. Nevertheless, the positive affirmation is haunted by an ethical failure that is not simply a point of contrast, or origin, but is inextricable from the structure of the novel. Each section iterates the question of "*why?*" first asked on the beach, demonstrating that the betrayal and despair, Hamiton's brutal failure of recognition, is present alongside each attempt at a meaningful human connection and affirmation. The redemptive possibilities of the diaspora perpetually contain within them their own undoing, their condition of both possibility and impossibility, and are consequently more unstable and tenuous than Low and Ledent suggest.

Nevertheless, I am in agreement with Goyal on the problematic character of much of the criticism on Joyce, which often includes her as a kind of slave (2003, 19). This is where the structuring of the novel around Hamilton's failure of recognition through the chain of iteration becomes particularly productive, enabling a reading that makes sense of Joyce without generalizing the African diaspora to humanity as a whole: Joyce has no direct citation. An iterative chain that signals belonging to the African diaspora is, unsurprisingly, absent in the narrative of a white, twentieth-century Englishwoman. It is not completely without warrant, though, that Ledent and Low consider Joyce as included in the diaspora. It is in part because of her incorporation that Ledent considers Phillips's treatment of the diaspora as heterodox, and why Low argues "the utopic vision of the last pages of the novel is inclusive, for Joyce who is English and white is included as one of the many sons and daughters of the diasporan community" (1998, 139). Low and Ledent both refer to the moment in the epilogue when the father reports: "A many-tongued chorus continues to swell. And I hope that amongst these survivors' voices I might occasionally hear those of my own children. My Nash. My Martha. My Travis. My daughter. Joyce" (Phillips 2006, 237). Despite the conspicuous absence of the possessive "my" for Joyce, she is nevertheless claimed here as a child. If what I have suggested about the chain of citations and its impact on the ethical sense of the novel is correct, then this designation of Joyce as a daughter needs to be accounted for.

Low and Ledent locate their reasons for the inclusion of Joyce by noting salient similarities between her experiences as recorded in her diary and those of Martha and Nash (which are similarly temporally disjointed). Thus Low argues:

> Joyce's loneliness, her failed marriage with the miner Len, her embittered confrontations with a mother that did not want her, her betrayal by first [sic] lover Herbert, and her desire for someone to love are in many ways permutations of the essential matrix of love, desire, and yearning that runs through the narratives. (1998, 138)

On one level this cannot be refuted. Joyce's narrative does show us a life of exclusion and difficulty, of loneliness and longing, poignantly summarised in her emotional meeting of Travis on the station platform when he briefly returns from the front to marry her: "And then he reached out and pulled me towards him. I couldn't believe it. He's come back to me. He really wanted me. That day, crying on the platform, safe in Travis's arms" (Phillips 2006, 226). As Low notes, Joyce is also an outsider in the village, excluded. The diary entry describing the GI's arrival "registers the soldiers' marginality as much as hers" (1998, 138). It is only with Travis that her loneliness and exclusion is briefly assuaged.

This argument is taken a step further by Ledent. She argues that despite "obvious differences, Joyce can also be regarded as a slave of sorts, especially if, as she suspects, Len only married her to secure a shop assistant for his store". Like Martha and Nash, she needs "to fight to be allowed to read and is treated like a child" (2002, 129). Further, Joyce is affected by the fracturing of the family caused by slavery, for when Greer is born she "is forced by social pressure inspired by racism to put up her son for adoption" (127). More positively, for Ledent she is the character that stands in contrast to Hamilton's closed-mindedness: "It takes exceptionally open-minded people like Joyce to go against the grain of human meanness. Not only is she big-hearted, but she is also prejudice free" (122). Her conclusion, therefore, is that Joyce is included in the diasporic community as a matter of "emotional correctness" (134) while for Low it is similarly due to a commonality of emotional experience.

The difficulty with this argument is that it confuses characterization with what we might call qualification. The loneliness and exclusion that Joyce experiences is surely not limited to her among all white English(wo)men, and it would seem strange indeed to extend the idea of the African diaspora so as to include all who experience "permutations of the essential matrix of love, desire, and yearning" (Low 1998, 138). Rather than a matter of qualification in this way, I suggest that Joyce's experiences are a matter of characterization. It is precisely because she is an outsider, blind to racial differences and politics, lonely and hurt, that the love between her and Travis is able to flourish. If she had been assimilated with the other villagers in her outlook—with those whom, Len confidently asserts, consider her to be "a traitor to [her] own kind [....] no better than a common slut" for loving Travis (Phillips 2006, 217)—then she would never have married him, nor given birth to Greer. And it is in her union with Travis that I think we find the reason for her inclusion in the diaspora. Ledent's observation about the similarities between her and her "siblings" in losing her son Greer is more to the point here (2002, 129). It is not, however, a reason for her to belong to the diaspora as a matter of emotional correctness. Rather, she loses her child because she already belongs to the diaspora through marrying Travis and having a son with him, and is consequently subjected to something of the diasporan experience as dramatised in the previous narrative. She is, as it were, the father's daughter-in-law.

It is not completely surprising then that despite the lack of a direct citation of the suffering and abandonment of the diaspora in her narrative, there is a second-hand report of it in Travis's. As with Nash and Martha, it occurs shortly before he dies. Joyce has just received the telegram informing her of Travis' death in Italy.

> The telegram didn't say much. I had to try to imagine it. To die at first light on the Italian coast. Fear. Mud. Shivering cold. Noise. Silence louder than any noise. Mortar fire. A bullet. A young man screaming in pain, *shouting out for mercy to a God he no longer believed existed.* His flesh ripped open by hot, flying metal. A man with blood flowing like red wine from his open veins. In a strange country. Among a people he hardly knew. (Phillips 2006, 229, my emphasis)

The imagined cry for mercy to a God he does not believe in resonates with the cries of despair that we saw with Nash and Martha, as well their loss of faith. That this is not the same sort of cry that would be uttered by his fellow soldiers is suggested by the lack of familiarity with those among whom he dies. Shortly after the GI's arrival in the village, one of the officers tells Joyce that "a lot of these boys are not used to us treating them as equals" (145): due to institutionalised legacy of slavery still active in the United States at the time—the iteration of Hamilton's lack of recognition—Travis hardly knew the white soldiers with whom he was serving.

Low is correct in noting that both the section and the novel end on a positive note. Greer seeking out his biological mother as an adult "ends the cycle of pain, separation, and betrayal that echo through each of the four[48] main narratives" (1998, 138). Greer is, notably, the only one apart from Joyce to survive, which brings us to the survival that the father speaks of in the epilogue. Reemphasizing the positive aspect of the prologue, the father lists a number of voices that he hears in addition to that of Nash, Martha, Travis and Joyce, some of whom live difficult lives—a drug addict, a prostitute—but some of whom are more positive figures of resistance: "Brothers and Friends. I am Toussaint L'Ouverture, my name is perhaps known to you" (Phillips 2006, 236). As Ledent notes, these other voices allow "past and present, famous, infamous and anonymous children of the African diaspora to make themselves heard" (2002, 117). All of these children, but particularly the father's own, are "survivors' voices", who although having being sold, are "loved" (Phillips 2006, 237).

I have noted, though, that this positive ending to the novel is haunted by the absence of recognition that holds the center of and organises the novel's narrative structure. The penultimate sentence cites Hamilton again: "*Bought 2 strong man-boys, and a proud girl. But they arrived on the far bank of the river, loved*" (237). The "but" would position the affirmative connection between the father and his lost children as the privileged of the two sentences, as presenting, quite literally, the last word. Yet this is resisted by the centrality of Hamilton's narrative. Contrastingly holding the center with Martha, who iterates the impossibility of returning east, the novel's positive affirmation becomes

---

[48] I assume that Low is referring to the pain and loss experienced by the slaves in Hamilton's narrative, rather than Hamilton's own yearning for his wife and hoped for children.

marked by loss, by an inescapable fusion of ethical failure and success: a connection between Africa and its diaspora that is marked by separation and the impossibility of return; a love that is not only founded on betrayal, as Ledent and Low argue, but marked by the continuous reiteration of it. Martha and Hamilton's union in the guilty father and connection to Travis, Joyce and Nash through the chain of citations and narrative pairings, organises the novel around the stark absence of the recognition of human connection in Hamilton's journal and gives rise to this ethical complexity, showing *Crossing the River* as dramatizing the impact of a failure of recognition.

IV

In both *Cambridge* and *Crossing the River* the functioning of recognition in the novel's ethical sense has been seen to be on a more structural level, shaped by the careful structuring of the novels, rather than placed primarily within the characters' progression. These texts, therefore, contrast quite significantly to the works of Ghosh and Adichie. There is, nevertheless, a similarity in the predicates of these recognitions. Shaped as they are by the thematic content of the novels, the predicates show a concern with all three of the ethical themes discussed in this book. Two are of most concern to Phillips: the idea of the human, and the remembrance of violence.

For the latter, we have seen Phillips trace a path through the ethical tensions that were raised by Adichie's engagement with the Biafran war. Integrating fragments of historical witness into an emotionally powerful fiction, Phillips, like Ghosh, is involved in a work of excavating lost or suppressed histories while simultaneously fulfilling both of the ethical demands that accompany the task: the need for accuracy and the need for the horror to be felt. Phillips's structuring of *Cambridge* further exposed the gaps inherent within the historical record, bringing to light the significance of the imagination for addressing this, which was particularly seen through the combination of a modern unrestricted narrator and the controlled voices of Emily and Cambridge. The most complex and nuanced of the engagements with this theme seen in book so far, *Cambridge* and to a lesser extent *Crossing the River* are exemplary engagements with a violent past.

Phillips's engagement with the idea of the human is also particularly notable. *Cambridge* in particular dramatised an ethical subject that is dislocated from itself, circumscribed in its autonomy, and shaped by its emotional responses to circumstances. The primary ethical sense of both novels, namely the failure to recognise an equal humanity, is in this way carefully qualified. The humanity that the novels present as common across such a diverse range of narratives is deeply shaped by the discursive worlds in which they exist. As in the work of Ghosh, change only comes at a price, through pain and emotional distress. This nevertheless shows again the efficacy of the emotions for sparking intellectual recognitions. What sets Phillips's conception of the human apart from Ghosh's, however, is the question of self awareness. Through the use of unreliable narrators, Phillips's characters are seen as disjointed from themselves, and therefore rendered ethically vulnerable to their circumstances. This understanding of the ethical subject resonates with what we saw in the analysis of Ishiguro's *The Remains of the Day* in the introduction, and radically undermines the idea of a self-aware, autonomous subject with a will that is ethically invulnerable to outside influences.

The incorporation of religion into the narratives follows a similar pattern to what was observed with Ghosh. Forming a constitutive part of the discursive world in which his characters exist, religion is not engaged as a possible ethical framework as it is in Adichie. Instead, it is implicitly critiqued. Shown to be implicated with the project of colonialism, central to the discourse of civilization in which Nash, Emily and Cambridge find themselves, Phillps' work presents the clearest instance of the challenge posed by religion in the present. That is to say, Phillips's critique of religion as complicit with colonialism and ultimately leaving the characters desolate, can be understood as precisely the legacy with which Adichie engages in *Purple Hibiscus*, as we saw in the previous chapter. Across these two authors' works, there is a sharpening of the ethical difficulty of negotiating this particular legacy of colonialism.

The difficulty of ethical impurity is most closely attached to the central element of the novels' ethical sense: an equal humanity. Most of the characters' senses of self are articulated in a discourse that they wish to resist. Nash and Cambridge are both in epistemic situations similar to postcolonial theory, deploying the resources of the Enlightenment in resistance to it. Although Nash manages a degree of change and, we might say, escape that is beyond Cambridge, we saw that his loneliness and desolation indicate the impossibility of truly escaping his immersion in the discourse of colonialism. In *Crossing the River*, this tragic shape of ethics is particularly marked. The more positive ethical sense is structurally and thematically intertwined with the betrayal and ethical failure that is its condition of possibility. There is no affirmation of a common humanity, without the possibility that it will be denied and violated. In Ghosh's terms, there is always the possibility that the silence between individuals will be bridged by violence.

Before bringing this discussion to a close, it is necessary to spend some time on the reading of the novels that Timothy Bewes presents, and particularly the understanding of the ethics of literature that underpins it. While we have seen a certain amount of concurrance among critics that have written on these two novels by Caryl Phillips, the work of Bewes, whose analysis I have noted several times in passing, runs counter to this. In his article, "Shame, Ventriloquy, and the Problem of the Cliché in Caryl Phillips", Bewes argues that Phillips's novels do not provide "corrective narratives, telling a previously untold or mistold story about the past" but are rather an "almost pure example of the *pathos* of literary failure". This "failure" is inextricable, for Bewes, from the text's materiality, or contemporaneity, to which the "difficulties and 'infelicities'" of Phillips's work—namely ventriloquy and cliché—draw our attention (2006, 35). What emerges, Bewes argues, is that the novels are "caught up in a drama of literary possibility that is riveted to their contemporaneity" (36). The broader argument, to which I will turn in a moment and which is more fully developed in his more recent book *The Event of Postcolonial Shame* (2011), is that this "drama of literary possibility" is the negotiation of an inescapable tension within literature, namely the "incommensurability" of the ethical demand to speak with the aesthetic impossibility of speaking adequately (2006, 37), an incommensurability that, he argues, is an event of shame and marks the materiality of (postcolonial) literature more widely.

In his article (which is replicated in the book), Bewes's analysis of Caryl Phillips's work in these terms focuses primarily on *Cambridge* and *Crossing the River*. Due to the ubiquity of ventriloquy and cliché in these novels, there is, Bewes suggests, no "authentic" voice present within them—neither that of the characters, nor of the author—and as a result *Cambridge* and *Crossing the River* undermine the possibility of speaking adequately or authentically in the very moment of speaking. As Bewes puts it, in Phillips the "paradox" of "the aesthetic impossibility of speaking" and "the ethical impossibility of not speaking" "finds a 'voice' that is faithful to these impossibilities *as such*" (55). He therefore begins by noting that in Phillips's work, especially those "dealing with slavery", there

> is an almost complete absence of authorial commentary and third-person narration. Not only are his stories told entirely through the words and reflections of his characters; those characters are themselves, for reasons that are never specified, incapable of speaking 'authentically', on their own account or in their own voices. (43)

It is primarily the second sentence that is crucial for his argument. Noting that Phillips has "often been praised" for his characters' "authenticity of voice", Bewes goes on to suggest that in actual fact, "many of [Emily's] passages, especially those dealing with the physical appearance of the Negroes, read more like a satire of colonial speech". Further, her writing is "derivative" and "ideologically unreflective [...] inhabiting the literary discourse of a hegemonic, culturally dominant Europe", and is correspondingly riddled with clichés (44). For Bewes, the result is to make Phillips an "upsetting writer" because the "endless pages of derivative prose penned by his characters" are unmediated by any narrator and are thus coextensive with the novel itself (45).

Ledent's reading of Phillips's work is for Bewes "the most prominent illustration" of the tendency to attempt to avoid this (45), "to prize Phillips away from his characters by introducing a succession of secondary sources between his and their texts" (56). This, he argues, neglects the materiality of the text itself. Specifically, he suggests critics are missing that "Phillips's ability to 'ventriloquize' his characters" is neither a matter of achieving "authenticity of voice", nor of "speaking on behalf of anyone" (46):

> The purpose of what has been called 'ventriloquism' in Phillips's text is rather the systematic evacuation of every discursive posi-

tion that might claim freedom from implication in colonialism
[....] What we get [...] is the ubiquity of ventriloquy—voice precisely as ventriloquy. (46–47)

There is no authenticity of voice. Emily's discourse is derivative and clichéd, as is Cambridge's, with the consequence that Emily's denigration of Cambridge's English as showing a "lunatic precision" applies "identically" to her own discourse as well (48). In briefly extending this argument to include *Crossing the River*, Bewes argues that the voice of the guilty father of the prologue and epilogue does not exhibit "any pretense at realism; the voice [...] is disembodied, ventriloquized". Further, and most importantly, the novel "offers a structure in which, seemingly, each of the children sold into slavery in the opening pages will successively speak his or her experience, but in fact none of them does". For Bewes they are all, to some degree or another, mediated, with Nash's discourse coming closest to Cambridge's as "a discourse of pure imitation" (49). As such, Bewes argues that both of these novels respond to the ethical demand to speak precisely by dramatizing, in the very event of speaking, its impossibility.

What is crucial to his argument, and what runs into several difficulties, is that Emily and Cambridge's voices are not representative, that as characters they do not speak "on their own account or in their own voices" (43). If the characters in *Cambridge* and *Crossing the River* are not ventriloquized in the manner that Bewes suggests, then the novels lose their paradoxical quality which is crucial for his theoretical argument. As should be clear from what I have discussed above, the first difficulty is posed by the work of Eckstein. Published in the same year as Bewes's article (though O'Callaghan's, less extensive, article was published notably earlier, in 1993), it nevertheless remains unmentioned in the later book version of Bewes's argument. In his reading of *Cambridge*, there is one passage from Emily's journal that Bewes cites as an example of how "the level of overstatement in her narrative is so spectacular that many of her passages, especially those dealing with the physical appearance of the Negroes, read more like a satire of colonial speech than an attempt to achieve 'authenticity of voice'". The passage is, for Bewes, "a model of contrived racial and stylistic offensiveness" (44). What this fails to take into account, however, is that many of these passages of "contrived racial and stylistic

CHAPTER THREE: THE FAILURE OF RECOGNITION 199

offensiveness" are citations. Although the one example that Bewes provides (and he does not give much more support than this, in either the article or the book) is not amongst those that Eckstein's research has shown to be a citation, another possible example that could be described in Bewes's terms, and is a citation, is the following:

> Just after turning off the *island road* [...] a number of pigs bolted into view, and after them a small parcel of monkeys. This took me by surprise, and I must have jumped [...] However, on resettling my position, I discovered that what I had taken for monkeys were nothing other than negro children, naked as they were born, parading in a feral manner to which they were not only accustomed, but in which they felt comfortable. (Phillips 1993, 24)

What this shows is that while there is one sense in which the passage cited by Bewes is indeed "contrived", namely, what Eckstein terms pastiche, the sustained imitation of the style of the earlier works, they are, unfortunately, neither excessive nor pieces of satire. Bewes's example passage is carefully formed by Phillips to be consistent with the racially offensive passages that he has incorporated into the novel.

In the course of my argument, however, I have noted that there is another way in which we might say that Emily is contrived and this precisely due to Phillips's method of pastiche and montage: while accurately constructed in terms of voice, Emily (and to a certain extent Cambridge) is created by this process to represent a specific ideological position. I suggested, though, that Phillips is not ignorant of this difficulty and that it increases the importance of the novel's prologue and epilogue, which add depth to Emily's character, marking the shift in her ethical and ideological position. This reveals a peculiarity that these two sections, in which we gain access to Emily's thoughts through the extra-diegetic narrator, are omitted from Bewes's argument. Indeed, it is slightly ironic, considering Bewes's emphasis on the materiality of the text, that without taking the novel's structure into account he asserts that Phillips refuses "to signpost his intentions or to offer moral or political judgements, *even implicit ones*, on his characters" (2006, 45, my emphasis). Yet I have shown that Phillips does precisely this through the careful structuring of his works: the contrasting of Emily's and Cambridge's narratives in *Cambridge*, coupled with the impact of the prologue and epilogue, are precisely how Phillips conveys his moral and political judgements, how the novel transmits its ethical sense.

A final possibility for how we could understand Bewes's argument that Emily and Cambridge are "contrived" is that, if we assume Bewes accepts the novel as historically accurate and representative, he might be suggesting that, because Emily and Cambridge are writing in a particular *form*, they are bound to those form's conventions. This reference to form could be inferred from (in addition to the wider argument) Bewes's comment that "what Emily calls the 'lunatic precision' of Cambridge's use of English [....] applies identically to her own use and to that of the novel as a whole; to Phillips's use, to my own in this article; to literary language as such" (48). However, in his discussion of the passage that he cites, this is not what Bewes has in sight, for it is precisely the content of Emily's journal (the racial offensiveness, which is not dependent upon the form) with which he is primarily concerned.[49]

It seems that Bewes's argument for understanding Phillips's ventriloquy and cliché in *Cambridge* as non-representative fails to be convincing. The characters are not ventriloquized in the way he suggests, nor does Phillips proceed toward "becoming-imperceptible" (Bewes 2006, 49). His all too brief consideration of *Crossing the River*, which argues that none of the three children speak in their own voices, is similarly unpersuasive. For Bewes, Nash's English is imitative "of the discourse of nineteenth-century British literary English"—though we do not know if he had any other English with which to write, having been raised and educated by Edward—and Travis's story is told through Joyce—though as became clear in my discussion it is rather that Joyce's story, in which she speaks for herself, is included because of her love for Travis. Martha's story, meanwhile, is mediated "in a combination of third-person narration and free-indirect speech", a point which, on the one hand, is peculiar as it im-

---

[49] There is the added possibility that Bewes is referring to the fact, which I have pointed out above, that what is available for Emily to say is constrained by her historical moment, her archive in the Foucauldian sense. Yet if this is what he means, then the argument is generalised to the event of speech itself, broadening it to far beyond literature, in addition to omitting the fact that each iteration of discourse is done with a difference and does not negate choice (and thus some authenticity), neither within a particular ideological position nor—as we saw with Emily—between different ones.

plies that first-person narration is the only way to give "voice" authentically, despite the fact that free-indirect speech is an incorporation of direct speech into the narrator's own. On the other hand, this point is simply incorrect, omitting the prevalence of first-person narration in Martha's section. Further, Bewes does not consider whether Hamilton speaks "authentically"—a character that, as we have seen, is important beyond simply removing "any notion of asymmetrical guilt from the colonial project" (49). Bewes's reading of Phillips is therefore flawed.

More generally, though, what is problematic in Bewes's approach is that he posits the relationship between ethics and aesthetics as one of failure: that there is an incommensurability between the ethical demand to speak and the aesthetic impossibility of speaking adequately, which he suggests should be understood as an event of shame. While his characterization of an incommensurability between aesthetics and ethics as shame could be questioned on its own terms,[50] it is more productive to understand the relationship between ethics and aesthetics as more positive. As we have seen, Richard Kearney argues that in considering the Holocaust, which is a central example for Bewes, the ethical obligation with which we are faced is simply that it be remembered. Among theorists that reject the more overtly narrative modes of doing so (such as Spielberg's *Schindler's List*) due to the imposition of a narrative meaning and coherence (which is for Bewes an aspect of the aesthetic failure of literature), it is unadorned testimony that is the most ethical way to remember. Kearney's response is worth citing as some length.

> In reply [...] I would be inclined to say that even the most extreme form of what [Langer] calls 'anguished' or 'humiliated' memories, where the witnesses express deep anxiety about the lack of common ground between the reality they suffered and the words they are now trying to use, is still a form of narrative memory [...] For we are only able to experience the futility and failure of survivors' narratives because they are *trying*, however impossibly, *to narrate* the unnarratable [....] A story in ruins, granted, but a story nonetheless. (2002b, 196)

---

[50] See, for instance, Levinas (2003), and especially Derrida (2002) where incommensurability is the experience of justice, rather than shame.

This is, to a certain extent, quite similar to Bewes's argument: that every attempt to represent the trauma of the Holocaust (or slavery) is bound to fail (which, referring to two specific historical traumas, is nevertheless different from Bewes's wider argument that narrative *per se* is always bound to ethical failure). Yet there is a very significant, if subtle, difference. For Kearney, narrative (in a broad sense) is the *only* way in which to remember (see also Kearney [1999]). The relationship between ethics and aesthetics is thus more positive, allowing for the possibility that narrative does not always fail: that, although in some instances narrative is insufficient, it is not inextricably bound to failure. Further, and more importantly, it also allows for a consideration of other ethical responsibilities in addition to that of mimesis. For Bewes, the ethical demand on literature is oddly *singular*—to represent adequately. Yet, as I have argued, literature can do more than this, including meet the need for past violence (of the Holocaust, slavery, civil war, or whatever it might be), to be *felt*, an ethical requirement that literature is able to fulfil, and which I (as well as Eckstein) have argued Phillips's work accomplishes. Additionally, Bewes also neglects an important difference between the ethical remembrance of the Holocaust and that of slavery: for slavery is caught in the difficulties of history in a way that the Holocaust is not, with a number of witnesses still living. In remembering slavery, there are larger historical gaps, silences, and conformities to colonial discourses which it is important to interrogate and explore, as Ledent and others have noted Phillips attempting to do, and the ethics of which I have argued should be understood primarily through its revelation of the failure of recognition.

The relationship between ethics and aesthetics (which is sometimes a tension), rather than being an event of shame, is therefore a basis for a multifaceted ethical criticism, for which I have been arguing throughout this book, focused primarily on the importance of recognition in the novel. What has been seen, in my consideration of Phillips, is that while his work narrates, in contrast to Ghosh and Adichie, ethical failure, this failure can still be understood in terms of recognition. I turn now to the work of Zadie Smith, whose work, while less fragmented than Phillips's, shifts the focus back to the question of the human, exploring the importance of beauty for reflecting on our mortality.

Chapter Four
The Beauty of the Mortal Human

> Though her hands were imprecise blurs, paint heaped on paint and roiled with the brush, the rest of her skin had been expertly rendered in all its variety—chalky whites and lively pinks, the underlying blue of her veins and the ever present human hint of yellow, intimation of what is to come.
>
> (Smith 2005, 443)

I

Zadie Smith is a novelist whose work resists clear classification within common critical taxonomies. Successfully analysed as simultaneously modern, postmodern, and postcolonial (in a single text, in this case *On Beauty: A novel* [Paproth 2008; Anjaria 2008]), she can additionally, like the previous authors, be considered a writer of world literature, having won multiple international literary awards and having her novels translated into over 20 languages (British Council 2016b). This diversity of critical engagement with and celebration of Smith's work reflects the range of concerns negotiated within her novels: from identity and ethnicity to colonial legacies and aesthetics, to name only a few. Turning to consider Zadie Smith in the concluding chapter of this study thus allows me to shift the analysis from texts that are more overtly postcolonial in orientation to one that relates to the postcolonial somewhat more uneasily (Anjaria 2008, 31). *On Beauty: A Novel* (2005),[51] Smith's third novel and the focus of this chapter, has, as a result of its different engagement with postcolonialism, an additional shift of emphasis in the three ethical themes considered throughout this book. Most notably, it is the first of the selected texts in which the ethics of remembering violence drops from sight; Religion, similarly, is de-emphasised. The most interesting shift, however, is the novel's engagement with the question of the human. While Ghosh, Adichie and Phillips were seen to present the recognition of a common humanity—albeit a humanity far removed from the ideal of the

---

[51] Henceforth referred to as *On Beauty*.

Enlightenment subject—as crucial for ethical engagement, Smith is more concerned with a particular aspect of human experience: beauty. Taking the postcolonial critique of aesthetics (that representation is never politically or ethically neutral) as a given, she explores the impact of a strict anti-aestheticism (represented by the main protagonist, Professor of Art History Howard Belsey) on the everyday lives of a family, with the result that her engagement with the idea of the human is, so to speak, more qualitative. Beauty and art are, as will be seen, more important to human flourishing than Howard Belsey's theoretical position allows for, and Smith presents a case for the role of art in revealing the beauty of our everyday, mortal lives. In so doing, she also explores beauty as a catalyst for recognition, developing this in conjunction with the role of powerful emotional responses that has been observed in the other texts.

On Beauty follows the lives of the Belseys, a mixed race family, in the fictional American town of Wellington, a wealthy, majority white, town adjacent to a university at which Howard is a lecturer in art history. From the beginning, in its introduction of the family of Monty Kipps—another professor in art history at Wellington University and Howard's arch-rival—it is a consciously intertextual novel, drawing on several named source texts. Three are identified in the "acknowledgements": E.M. Forster's *Howards End* (2000), Elaine Scarry's *On Beauty and Being Just* (1999), and Simon Schama's *Rembrandt's Eyes* (2000). Two additional texts have been noted by Susan Alice Fischer (2008): Zora Neal Hurston's *Their Eyes Were Watching God* and *Tell My Horse*. As this suggests, *On Beauty* is a text that rewards investigation into its correspondences to and differences from these other works, on both the level of plot and theme. At the novel's release, however, initial reviews gave mixed assessments of its intertextual citations. For some, the correlation to Forster's *Howards End* does not go beyond pilfering a couple of scenes and characters. Robert Alter (2005) comments, "It is hard to see how [the parallels between *On Beauty* and *Howards End*] add a significant dimension of meaning [...] Smith's unsubtle imitation of Forster remains puzzling, superfluous, and perhaps a little precious" (29). He takes the same view of Smith's use of Elaine Scarry's *On Beauty and Being Just*. Scarry's work itself is for Alter a "mechanical effort", whose title is borrowed by the novel for "reasons that are hardly compelling" (29). Similarly, David Heim (2006), in his review, relegates intertextual echoes to comic effect: "The Forster parallels are mostly a humorous tease—what, the novel makes us wonder, will 'Howard's end' be?" (39).

While Alter and Heim are not alone in their dismissive view (see also Kemp [2005]), they are in the minority. A more common criticism is that Smith's use of Forster, while effective, nevertheless stifles her plot and characters. So we see Paproth (2008), discussing the scene when Carlene Kipps persuades Kiki Belsey to travel with her to Amhesrt, argue that "this scene, if not for the link to Forster, is completely unnecessary" and out of character for both individuals (23).[52] Paproth does acknowledge, however, that "the allusions throughout the novel reward the intertextual critic" (23), an acknowledgement which has come to characterise the body of critical work that has coalesced around the work, and which forms the foundation of a more nuanced reading like Ann Marie Adams's, in which she argues that Smith's detailed engagement with Scarry prevents her from approximating the work of Forster (2011, 394). Nevertheless, the degree to which Smith is undertaking a conceptual engagement with the three authors named in her acknowledgements still rewards further investigation—particularly her use of *Rembrandt's Eyes*, a text which has been almost completely neglected in the criticism. While it will be seen that the work's ethical sense still emerges through its recognitions, like the "theoretical or philosophical essays" which the form of its title cites (Lanone 2007, 189)—giving the topic of investigation but with the qualifier in the subtitle that it will be undertaken in novelistic form—it weaves these different sources together, clarifying and broadening the predicates of the central recognitions in the novel. The full impact of these recognitions are most clearly elicited in dialogue with the intertexts, which will consequently take much of my attention.

II

That connection is important in *Howards End* is succinctly introduced to the reader by the novel's epigraph, "only connect". The first stage of Forster's narrative, in a move mimicked by Smith and proclaimed in the almost identical opening lines, brings two very different families together. The Schlegels—"clever, cultured and idealistic" whose "surname inevita-

---

52 For more vitriolic criticism see Martin (2005), Mason (2005) Deresiewicz (2005) and Gray (2006).

bly evokes Romantic literature and philosophy, by association with the famous German brothers Friederich and Wilhelm von Schlegel"—and the Wilcox family—who "in contrast belong to the prosperous commercial bourgeoisie" (Lodge 2000, vxi). One family embodies what the narrative presents as the good life of pursuing beauty and meaningful relationships, while the other embodies the life of capitalism and commerce. Thus, the narrative opens with Helen Schlegel having responded to an invitation from the Wilcoxes and spending some time with them at their home Howards End. She falls in love with the son Paul, but quickly realises their incompatibility: The Wilcox family's existence, in contrast to the Schlegel sisters', is superficial, a wall with nothing of substance supporting it. Later, while discussing the incident with her sister, Helen comments, "I felt for a moment that the whole Wilcox family was a fraud, just a wall of newspapers and motor-cars and golf-clubs, and that if it fell I should find nothing behind it but panic and emptiness" (Forster 2000, 22). Helen and Paul's brief romance causes Paul's "wall" to "detonate", as Margaret puts it later in the novel (88), exposing the emptiness behind it—an emptiness that stands in contradistinction to what the Schlegel sisters dub the "real life" of "personal relations" (23).

As this intimates, the contact between these two families sets up a series of binaries that shape their relationships, of which this distinction between the depth of personal relations and the superficiality of commercial capability is but the first. Discussing correspondences between *Howards End* and *On Beauty*, Ulka Anjaria references Bjorken-Nyberg's catalogue of binaries in Forster's novel: "male/female, prose/passion, the middle class/ the masses, rural/urban and English/German" (quoted in Anjaria 2008, p.39). *On Beauty* similarly posits a series of opposites through a proximate situation: Jerome Belsey falls in love with Victoria Kipps, but the relationship, he soon realises, is not to be. The title and epigraph to the first section of the novel— "Kipps and Belsey", "We refuse to be each other"—enforces, even before the intertextual echoes, this distinction between the two families. Howard Belsey and Monty Kipps are long standing academic opponents, and whereas in Forster's novel the difference between the families only surfaces through the course of the narrative, in Smith's it exists prior to Jerome's stay with the Kippses. The incompatibility, or difference, between the two families is not, then, the same in the two novels. The Wilcoxes and the Schlegels are different in that one family lives the outer life of action and possessions, and the other lives the inner liberal life of meaningful relations and the pursuit of beauty. In *On Beauty*, however, Smith shifts the focus. The main schism running through the novel is that which makes Howard Belsey and Monty Kipps academic opponents who may "sometimes [share] a stage—but never an opinion" (Smith 2005, 29), that is, radically different understandings of beauty. Both are professors of art history; both are specialists on Rembrandt. Monty Kipps, however, is a conservative who holds that Rembrandt is a genius, that "Art [is] a gift from God, blessing only a handful of masters" (44); Howard Belsey, meanwhile, holds that "Art is a Western Myth" and rejects "the quasi-mystical notion of genius", presenting, rather, a Rembrandt who is a conformist (155). As a result, the binaries found in Smith's novel are also different, relating more to questions of beauty: "white/black, thin/fat, Mozart/hip-hop, Rembrandt/Haitian art, and beautiful/ugly" (Anjaria 2008, 38). Smith's differance from Forster in her first intertextual reference, then, works to introduce the novel's central concern: how to understand beauty.

With *On Beauty* following in *Howards End*'s narrative footprints by setting up the division between the two families in this way, the question arises of whether there is an attempt to bring the two families together. While Forster's novel presents the Schegels' way of living as superior to the Wilcoxes, they are shown to both have value and, indeed, to be interdependent. Where Margaret Schlegel excels, the Wilcoxes are weak; where Margaret is weak, the Wilcoxes excel (Forster 2000, 88). It is primarily through the marriage of Henry and Margaret that Forster endeavours to bring about the reconciliation, though many readers and critics find it unpersuasive (Lodge 2000, xx–xxi). There is no such reconciliatory relation in *On Beauty* between Monty and Howard's different views on beauty and Rembrandt. Both academics are, albeit to differing degrees, concerned with the ethics surrounding beauty. For Howard, beauty or, more generally, aesthetics is "a rarefied language of exclusion" (Smith 2005, 155), and Monty's lectures on Rembrandt have the "clear intention of antagonizing and alienating various minority groups" in the university community (328). Monty, on the other hand, asserts that in his writing he will be "employing [his] knowledge *as well as* [his] moral sense" (328, emphasis in original). Both of their views are thus informed by ethics. Both are brought to the same moral level by the end of the novel: each is exposed as having been involved in an affair with one of their students. Thus, while Smith imitates Forster in the manner in which she sets up the central theme of her novel, beyond this ethical levelling she effects no final reconciliation between the two academics. Rather, it is Kiki Belsey and Carlene Kipps, the wives of the professors, who "provide an alternate vision which moves beyond the ideological stalemate that these two men present" (Fischer 2007, 288), and in particular Howard's relationship with Kiki and his family—all of whom will be crucial for his final recognitions.

A further conceptual engagement that Smith makes with Forster is that of home and inheritance. The question of home in *Howards End*, which is not simply a material abode but also spiritual, raises the question of inheritance. Although Smith shifts what is inherited from a house to a Hyppolite painting, she nevertheless implicitly reflects on the question of home. Relatively early on in *Howards End* it comes to light that the Schlegels are going to have to leave Wickham Place, their home since birth, in a couple of years. Margaret is not initially perturbed by their need to move, but when the time has nearly arrived it is a different matter. While Margaret is reflecting on the layering of memory in the house, the narrator interjects and makes explicit the importance of a home for beauty:

> The feudal ownership of land did bring dignity, whereas the modern ownership of movables is reducing us again to a nomadic horde. We are reverting to the civilization of the luggage, and historians of the future will note how the middle classes accreted possessions without taking root in the earth, and may find in this the secret of their imaginative poverty. The Schlegels were certainly poorer for the loss of Wickham Place. (Forster 2000, 128)

To lose one's house is impoverishing, though not financially so. It is the imagination, which is closely connected in *Howards End* with beauty, that becomes poorer. In Smith's novel, while it is true that "a house stands at the centre" of the narrative (Fischer 2008, 108), the significance of houses shifts, and we do not see the same quest for a physical home. Rather, houses come to signify money: Carlene Kipps, missing her London home, comments that in her American house there is "nothing [...] except money, jangling" (Smith 2005, 91). Similarly, Kiki's house, bequeathed to her grandmother by "a benevolent white doctor with whom she had worked closely for twenty years", had the effect of making them "middle class" (17), and Howard's love of the place and youthful impatience to move in is primarily for reasons of employment at a good university. That houses tend to signify money in *On Beauty* is salient considering the link forged in *Howards End* between a home and beauty, bringing to the forefront in *On Beauty* a concern that is pervasive in *Howards End*: the relationship between money and beauty. I will return to this in a moment.

The manner in which Carlene leaves Kiki the painting is almost identical to the way in which Ruth leaves Howards End to Margaret in Forster's text. Both are bequeathed through a handwritten pencil note; both notes are disregarded by the family and destroyed. Further, the reason for the bequest of the painting is also similar. Howards End holds more meaning for Ruth than it does for her family, and this is why she desires that Margaret inherit it; for her, it is not just a house but a spiritual inheritance. The reason why Carlene leaves her Hyppolite painting to Kiki is akin to this. The language of the note on the back of the painting bequeathing it to Kiki could very well be used to refer to Ruth's leaving of Howards End to Margaret. It reads, in part: "It needs to be loved by someone like you" (430). The transformation of the inheritance from a house into a painting, while maintaining the aspect of spiritual inheritance, is an implicit recognition of mobility in that the painting can be transported. Consequently, it works to undermine Forster's claim that mobility harms the appreciation of beauty, even as it raises the question of where one locates home in a mobile, postcolonial word. It is only when Howard is separated from Kiki because of his infidelity that he recognises that his home is in the beauty of the interpersonal relationships he has been neglecting, thus recuperating, with a difference, Forster's emphasis on connection.

One of the more extended contrasts between Smith and Forster, however, is in the relationship between poverty and beauty intimated by the changing significance of houses. Forster explores this theme primarily through the character of Leonard Bast, presenting, for the most part, what could be termed an exclusionary view. Ann Marie Adams comments,

> Forster knew that the beauty of art was and is one of the integral features that separates culture from Culture, and he presented

this admittedly discriminatory element as a fundamental part of his liberal aesthetic. Art, Forster contends, is still a good thing, even if it is not intended for all. (2011, 390-391)

In engaging with this perspective, Smith creates two primary correlations in *On Beauty*, but also a third, more oblique one in the form of the Haitians. Where Forster's reflections seem to suggest that beauty is indeed limited by access to money, Smith disagrees, although extreme poverty seems still to be able to severely restrict one's appreciation of it.

In *Howards End*, Leonard Bast is a member of the lower-middle class, a bank clerk by profession, who barely prevents himself from falling into the "abyss" of utter poverty. Although he, like the Schlegels, pursues beauty, the narrator tells us that "his mind and body had been alike underfed, because he was poor" (Forster 2000, 38-39). The Schlegels meet him at a Beethoven concert, where Helen accidentally takes his umbrella when she leaves. While Margaret and Leonard are walking and talking as they leave the concert and go to the Schlegels' house to collect the umbrella, Leonard reflects on the anxieties that emerge from living so near to the brink of poverty and which continuously distract him in his pursuit of beauty. Thus, even when he succeeds in learning something, in taking a step forward in his pursuit of culture, the "steady beat" of the anxieties of his life persists. In this specific case it is the umbrella, but there is "always something that distracted him in the pursuit of beauty" (34).

Forster, then, engages with the material limitations of the Schlegels' "good life", in the pursuit of both beauty and meaningful relationships. The limitation that Leonard's financial situation places on his ability to trust is first seen immediately after Helen takes his umbrella. Margaret offers to bring it round to his home but, fearing a con trick, Leonard refuses to give his address. His refusal gives Margaret "a glimpse into squalor. To trust people is a luxury in which only the wealthy can indulge; the poor cannot afford it" (30). This limiting of access to the Schlegel's good life is further sharpened when Leonard Bast goes home. The narrator first notes that the "very poor" are "unthinkable, and only to be approached by the statistician or the poet" (2000, 38). As David Lodge comments in his reading of Forster's novel, this description has the effect that "the 'very poor' are simultaneously elevated into the realm of tragedy and reduced to the level of dull social statistics" (Lodge 2000, xviii). Nevertheless, Leonard Bast becomes the site in *Howards End* for interrogating the relationship between beauty and poverty.

Once home, Leonard reads Ruskin, and the narration of the scene is worth considering closely:

> And the voice in the gondola rolled on, piping melodiously of Effort and Self-Sacrifice, full of high purpose, full of beauty, full even of sympathy and the love of men, yet somehow eluding all that was actual and insistent in Leonard's life. For it was the voice of one who had never been dirty or hungry, and had not guessed successfully what dirt and hunger are. (42)

The narrator follows Leonard, shifting between his reading, and commenting on Ruskin, with the effect that the critique of Ruskin presented here is done so with Leonard in close proximity. The narrator comments that Leonard listens to the voice in "reverence", yet what he hears does not take hold because it does not relate to his actual life. The narrator, consequently, critiques Ruskin's art as dissociated from the reality of the poor. Ruskin deals with abstract, ideal visions of beauty— "Effort", "Self-Sacrifice"—but these things are not able to fit into Leonard's life. Ruskin has invested in describing and imagining a certain beauty, but remains ignorant of "dirt and hunger". The critique is continued at the close of the same chapter:

> Ruskin had visited Torcello by this time, and was ordering his gondoliers to take him to Murano. It occurred to him, as he glided over the whispering lagoons, that the power of Nature could not be shortened by the folly, nor her beauty altogether saddened by the misery, of such as Leonard. (47)

Again, the shift in the narrator's perspective from Leonard Bast's experience of reading and his wife, Jacky, arriving home, to commenting on Ruskin, keeps Leonard as a presence in the description of Ruskin. He is maintained as both a reading subject and a subject for discussion, thus preventing Ruskin's view from assuming primacy. Even as Ruskin tries to avoid the reality of poverty, the narrative technique ensures that Leonard haunts Ruskin in that very attempt. There is also a critical distance here between the narrator and Ruskin's view: "It occurred to him", to Ruskin, that the beauty of Nature is not "altogether saddened" by poverty. The narrator implies that Ruskin is "gliding over", as it were, the realities of poverty by focussing on Nature. For Ruskin, the power and beauty of Nature are not decreased by "such as Leonard". If, however, nature is seen as not being diminished by poverty, then "such as Leonard" are rendered irrelevant and ignorable as far as beauty is concerned. Additionally, the use of narrative voice in this description of Ruskin brings into focus Leonard's inability to critique Ruskin himself. He is longing for beauty, attempting to gain access to it, is aware of his poverty as an obstacle, but is not at the point of being able to formulate his own critique of Ruskin's philosophy. The narrative technique here thus renders what would otherwise remain obscure, including Leonard Bast in a conversation that would try to exclude him.

Forster, regardless of the overall position of *Howards End* on the exclusivity of culture—seen primarily in the devastating results of the Schlegels' attempts to help him—is not, then, unaware of the limitations of this view. Smith, we could say, continues this, and the relationship between beauty and the misery of life will be important. Another aspect of Smith's engagement with the question posited by Leonard Bast, however, is the introduction into her novel of the dispossessed: the Haitians who, in Levi's words, are "oppressed, suppressed and every other kind of pressed" (Smith 2005, 355). For Choo, the Hyppolite painting (which Carlene bequeaths to Kiki) seems to have little to do with beauty: he is primarily concerned with how much money the painting would have brought had Kipps (who he thinks owns it) paid a fair price. A very instrumental view of art, Smith is careful to balance it and show that Choo does not neglect beauty entirely. He recognises the skills of the artist, and recommends Haitian music to Levi, providing a glimpse of beauty being valued in a less utilitarian manner. Smith does not, then, seem to suggest that Choo is unable to see beauty. Rather, the pressures of being extremely poor are able to restrict the value of beauty to how it may be employed in alleviating those pressures.

The most obvious correspondence in *On Beauty* with Leonard, however, is Carl Thomas. Carl, like Leonard, is a member of the lower class. He is a twenty-year-old black man from Roxbury and, like Leonard, he pursues beauty. As he puts it to Levi, he gets his culture where he can

CHAPTER FOUR: THE BEAUTY OF THE MORTAL HUMAN 213

(76). It is for this reason that he is at the performance of Mozart's *Requiem* where there is the accidental pilfering of his property—a Discman, instead of an umbrella. The main difference between Leonard and Carl begins to surface when Carl is introduced to the Belsey family: Carl creates beauty. Levi introduces him as a "street poet", but Carl clarifies that he does Spoken Word: "I don't know if I be calling myself a street poet" (76). Though he is very gifted, Carl evidences an awareness of cultural hierarchies in which Spoken Word is not valued as highly as written poetry. This awareness of hierarchy is inadvertently given voice by Zora. The conversation shifts to Claire Malcolm, so Zora asks him,

> 'Do you know Claire Malcolm?'
> 'Nope... can't say I do,' replied Carl, releasing another one of his winning smiles, just nerves probably, but each time he did, you warmed to him further.
> 'She's like a *poet* poet,' explained Zora.
> 'Oh... A *poet* poet.' Carl's smile disappeared. (77)

This phrase, "*poet* poet", becomes exemplary of the elitism in art that Carl is very conscious of and resistant to. Carl's immediate response—the vanishing smile, the speedy escape from the conversation—shows his sensitivity to the phrase's implications: Claire, the white professor of English at Wellington and Howard's lover, is a real poet while Carl, a black man from the ghetto, is not.

Carl brings up this phrase twice in the novel, each time when he faces this elitism. The first time is when he gets turned away from the Belsey party. Howard refuses him entrance even though he names Levi as a friend.

> 'Look,' said Howard rudely, 'I don't mean to be rude, but Levi shouldn't really have been inviting his... friends—this is really quite a small affair-'
> 'Right. For *poet* poets.'
> 'Excuse me?'
> 'Shit, I don't know why I even came here—forget it,' said Carl. He was off immediately down the drive and out the gate, a proud, quick, bouncy walk. (105–106)

The pause that Howard places before "friends" loads the word with both contempt and doubt. Contempt for the kind of friends that Levi is making; doubt as to whether he actually is Levi's friend or if this is an attempted con trick. Howard's suspicion leads Carl to comment that the party is only for "*poet* poets". The phrase becomes a shorthand for class difference and exclusion. The second time that he uses it, this fact comes out quite forcefully. He has been speaking to Zora after their accidental meeting at the gym when he asks her to invite Levi to listen to him at the Bus Stop, a venue where spoken word poetry is performed. Carl's mention that he will be in Wellington causes Zora to ask, "Don't you live in Boston?" (140). Carl reacts as if Zora had suggested that he was breaking a segregation law:

'Yeah, and? It ain't far—we're allowed to come into Wellington, you know. Don't need a pass. *Man*. Wellington's OK—that part of it is, Kennedy Square. It ain't all students—there's brothers too. Anyway... Just tell your bro if he wants to hear some rhymes he should come. It might not be *poetry* poetry,' said Carl, walking away before Zora had a chance to answer, 'but it's what I do.' (140)

Carl is very aware of elitism. Although he wasn't actually insulted by Zora's comment, the sardonic manner in which he employs this phrase shows that his reaction against elitism is essentially a refusal of the designation of his work as inferior.

As it turns out, Carl is indeed justified in rejecting that designation. When the promised performance occurs, its brilliance leads the Wellington students to describe him as "Keats with a knapsack" (230). Carl's rhyming is complex, precise, witty and articulate. His talent is undeniable, amazing everybody in the room. It is not only the rhymes themselves, but their rhythm, the contrast between the chorus and the verses, the cleverness of the lyrics. The way in which the different parts function together is seamless and presents a subtle, skilful work. Carl's use of the phrase "*poet* poets" here comes to an end as he meets Zora after coming off stage. He has been vindicated. "He'd won at the Bus Stop. He'd *killed* at the Bus Stop. All was good with the world" (233). He gives Zora "an enormous sweaty kiss full on her mouth" and makes clear his vindication from the designation of his work as inferior: "'See that?' he said. '*That* was poetry'" (232).

The untutored brilliance of Carl's is in stark contrast to Leonard Bast in *Howard's End*. Leonard yearns for a literary life, but fails to achieve it. At the end of their second meeting with Leonard, Margaret is talking to Henry Wilcox about him. Henry asks if Leonard is "one of that writer sort", eliciting a telling reply: "No—oh no! I mean he may be, but it would be loathsome stuff. His brain is filled with the husks of books, culture—horrible; we want him to wash out his brain and go to the real thing" (Forster 2000, 124). If Leonard were to attempt to write, either poetry or prose, it would be "loathsome stuff". The sisters have hope for Leonard, but he is a pale shadow of Carl's brilliance. Adams is right, then, in noting that Smith "attempts to jettison Forster's seemingly unsavory focus on the exclusionary nature of aesthetic appreciation" (2011, 391). Adams proceeds to contend that *On Beauty*, because it does not distinguish between beauty in general and art as a cultural product, is unable to reject Forster's argument that "the discrimination needed to fully appreciate a work of art is not possessed by all" (and thereby maintains art as exclusionary) (392). I will return to this later.

Smith continues her engagement with this aspect of Forster through the second character in *On Beauty* who correlates with Leonard Bast: Howard Belsey, who, we could say, represents the fulfilment of Leonard Bast's financial ambitions. Howard, a Brit whose father was a butcher, has successfully lifted himself out of his lower class origins (Smith 2005, 18). He has fulfilled Leonard's aspirations, becoming a middle class professor of art history. Yet Zadie Smith casts Howard as rejecting beauty, rather than pursuing it, disdaining the idea of genius (brought to the fore through changing Beethoven to Mozart), rather than admiring it. The reason, I want to suggest, is that Howard is a fulfilment of Leonard Bast in a very strict sense: he only fulfils the aspirations to climb higher on the social ladder and to acquire learning. Where Leonard was at risk of missing the "real thing", Howard has completely missed it, indeed, repudiated it. If books serve as a signpost to a real experience of beauty (as they do for the Schlegels), then for Howard there are only signposts with no destination. The beauty presented in books and art in general is, for Howard, constructed, a farce. In a sense, all that he has are the "husks of books", and he claims that there never was any real beauty, only these husks. More than this, these constructions of beauty are masks of power and exclusion. Zadie Smith thus effects an inversion of sorts. The poor 'Leonard Bast' is in her novel the one who has hit on the "real thing". He produces inspiring works of Spoken Word. When he joins Claire Malcolm's poetry class he begins to learn the forms of the art that he was already intuitively using, shifting into conscious crafting and confirming that his work is *poetry* poetry. His creativity and approach to his art is the inverse of Leonard Bast's. Leonard is attempting to move from books to the "real thing" while Carl is moving from an intuitive use of the "real thing" into the formal construction of an art. The middle class professor, meanwhile, becomes the one who lives in the husks of books and culture, denying that there ever was a real thing.

Through her engagement with the figure of Leonard Bast, and by changing the inheritance in the story and the signification of houses, Smith explores the question of the connection between beauty and poverty. That Howard's rejection of beauty is also an echo of Leonard taken to an extreme, links this to him, bringing it into the purview of his recognitions. This is given an additional layer in that Howard's arguments are a representation of a position not entirely uncommon in modern universities, and against which Elain Scarry argues in *On Beauty and Being Just*. Scarry's importance for the novel, then, becomes pervasive, inflecting this question of the elitism of art and the financial limitations of beauty. Many of Scarry's arguments—on the value of the university, the experience of error in the field of beauty, the connection between beauty and justice, the vulnerability of the observer of a beautiful person—are woven into Smith's novel. However, where critics have tended to observe only the close allegiance of the narrative to the philosophical argument (see, for example Wall [2008] and Adams [2011]), Smith also contests some of Scarry's claims, particularly the vulnerability of the beautiful.

Beauty has become a subject that, Sarah Nuttall (2006) notes, "receives relatively little, often guarded, attention from scholars" (8). Fields that once employed the language of beauty have since become devoid of any reference to it. Joe Winston (2006), for example, notes several UK publications that argue for the "educational and cultural value of the arts" but do so "with no reference at all to beauty" (286). After this long silence on questions of beauty, however, there is a steadily increasing amount of work being produced on the topic, of which Scarry's is one of the more prominent. This being said, beauty is not a new concern for Smith. Although it is not as central, the question of beauty is also raised in *White Teeth* (2001)—for example with regard to the characters Millat and Irie. Beauty is something that has interested Smith from the beginning. In conjunction with the more general resurgence of interest in questions of beauty, is an increasing awareness of the importance of considering the significance of the aesthetic within postcolonial thought and criticism (Bahri 2003, 2). It is particularly intriguing, then, that Smith engages with a thinker, who has produced what Nuttall characterises as "one of the more recent and controversial books on the subject of beauty" (2006, 14).

Scarry's argument is divided into two parts, "On Beauty and Being Wrong" and "On Beauty and Being Fair". The title of the first section is used by Smith as the title of a section of the novel. From this same section she also draws the quote that makes up the epigraph to part two of her novel. In it, Scarry unfolds her argument for the alliance between beauty and truth. Though she discusses several features of the experience of beauty (two of which we will return to below since they are significant for Smith's novel), it is essentially two features that create this link: the experience of conviction and the experience of error. The experience of conviction is the subjective certainty, akin to a moment of recognition, that this particular object is indeed beautiful—what Scarry terms beauty's "clear discernibility" (1999, 31). Importantly, this experience of certainty is a pleasurable one, thus creating a desire, and indeed a quest, for the "state of certainty" (31).

While introducing us (and Scarry suggests it may indeed be our first introduction) to this state of certainty, beauty does not "satiate our desire" for it. This is because beauty also introduces us to "our own capacity for making errors" (31). The experience of being wrong about our judgments of what is beautiful (whether negatively or positively) is, Scarry argues, intrinsic to the experience of perceiving beauty in the world. While knowing and desiring the state of certainty, we are, then, simultaneously made aware of our ability to be wrong. It is this combination of experiences that thus initiates a quest to attain certainty. Scarry writes,

> [Beauty] ignites the desire for truth by giving us, with an electric brightness shared by almost no other uninvited, freely arriving perceptual event, the experience of conviction and the experience, as well, of error [....] It comes to us, with no work of our own; then leaves us prepared to undergo a giant labor. (52–53)

Having considered the relation of beauty to truth, Scarry considers in part two its relation to justice. She details two types of ethico-political objections to beauty. The first is that since beauty occupies our attention, we are distracted from social ills and eventually become completely indifferent to them. The second is that to make something the object of our regard is damaging to that object. Scarry begins by arguing that not only do the objections contradict each other (one assumes the gaze is good, the other that it is bad), but the second objection is generally incoherent. Scarry's positive case for beauty is made in response to the first objection. She argues that rather than causing indifference, there are in fact two features of beauty that assist us in the pursuit of justice. The first is the feature of symmetry, playing on the double meaning of "fair" as both beautiful and just. The generally recognised beauty of symmetry acts as a call for equal treatment between people; Fairness is a call for "a symmetry of everyone's relation to one another" (93). The second is what Scarry calls "radical decentring" (109). The experience of beauty is one in which we gladly abdicate our imagined position of being the centre of our world to the beautiful object. This decentring is, of course, not unique to the experience of beauty. What is unique in this experience as it relates to the beautiful thing, however, is that it is pleasurable, and is thus sought after (114). The pleasurable experience of being adjacent thus aids justice as it increases our willingness to be adjacent elsewhere. And when we feel adjacent or decentred is when the situation is likely most egalitarian or fair.

Scarry's defence of beauty in arguing for its intrinsic connection to the pursuit of both truth and justice has naturally been received differently across the spectrum of intellectual positions. While there seems to be a general agreement on the morally and politically motivated banishment of beauty, the justification of its return is viewed as slightly more dubious. On the more positive side, Joe Winston argues that to foster a love for beauty is to foster a love for virtue. To this end, he takes his cue from Iris Murdoch. For him, the usefulness of Scarry's study on beauty is that she has "expanded [Murdoch's] parameters to include, specifically, how beauty can promote social justice" (2006, 286). Winston makes particular use of Scarry's argument concerning the pressure towards lateral distribution.

The more interesting receptions of Scarry's work, however, are those that attempt to dislocate the question of beauty from that of ethics or politics completely. A fascinating and persuasive critique of Scarry is that by Alexander Nehamas (2000), who engages with the arguments of what he views as two different extremes on the spectrum of beauty's return: the work of Scarry and the work of Dave Hickey. His rejection of ethics and politics as the means for justifying beauty is crucial; beauty is, for Nehamas, ultimately unjustifiable. He comments that

> until we can explain how beauty and injustice can characterise a single society, how a single individual can be both devoted to beauty and capable of evil, no abstract philosophical argument of the sort Scarry offers to connect beauty and justice can possibly succeed. (397)

The fundamental flaw for Nehamas, in both Scarry and Hickey's work despite their radical differences, is that the two thinkers are allied in this attempt to link beauty and justice (401). For Nehamas this is futile. Beauty, for him, should be celebrated precisely because it is unjustifiable. If beauty is not "a determinate feature of things" but rather the mark of an object's inexhaustibility—that we do not or cannot know it completely—then beauty becomes an adventure, a risk. Ultimately, for Nehamas, beauty is the "enemy of certainty". In his argument, then, it is misleading to consider the question of the connection between beauty and evil. I am not convinced, however, that this connection can be so easily dismissed. Nehamas notes that there has often been a connection between beauty and evil, that beauty "often characterizes objects that serve oppression or falsehood, and even makes them better at it" (402). Winston, in addition, notes the use beauty was put to in promoting Nazi ideology. The examples could be multiplied. It seems to me that the fact that "beauty can be harnessed into the service of evil" (2006, 291), necessitates an investigation into its relation to both oppression and justice.

It is within a specifically postcolonial response to the question of beauty that the importance of the relationship between beauty and oppression or discrimination becomes vital. Sarah Nuttall notes that the understanding of beauty as it relates to "Africa and its diasporas" has historically been one that supports racism and Eurocentrism. She argues that there are fundamentally four modes of the "inscription" of Africa. She summarises them as follows: "of Africa and Africans as the figure of the *ugly*; of beauty within the registers of anthropology, especially the '*ethnographic*'; of African aesthetics within the global *market*; and of African beauty within the registers of *frivolity*" (2006, 28, emphasis in original). In the light of this it is, perhaps, not surprising to locate within the field of postcolonial studies a strong rejection of Scarry's work as, in fact, promoting discrimination and oppression. It is simultaneously, however, a good example of the functioning of recognition in the experience of beauty—something that will be particularly important for Howard.

Rita Barnard's (2006) critique of Scarry views geographical location as of vital importance when considering the question of beauty. Not only does location shape what is viewed as beautiful or ugly, but it further shapes the understanding of beauty that one has (104). Elaine Scarry's understanding of beauty is, for Barnard, one that it is only possible to hold in the scenic location where Scarry writes, and where there is very little cultural contestation (108–109). It is in Zakes Mda's *The Heart of Redness* that Barnard locates a different, and, for her, less problematic understanding of beauty; one which has been shaped by being located in "contact zones" of colonialism (109). In contrast, Scarry's understanding is, for Barnard, exclusionary. In Howard's terms, it would serve as an example of the "rarefied language of exclusion" that is aesthetics (Smith 2005, 155). In Barnard's words, Scarry's work is "parochial elitism", "high minded musings" that avoid anything "that may bring up the spectre of class—or culture—specific discrimination" (2006, 105). Barnard's article presents a fairly multifarious critique of Scarry's work, putting forward a number of difficulties that she finds in it. The main thrust of the argument, however, and the reason why Scarry's work is for Barnard exclusionary, is that Scarry does not consider with any clarity or depth the reality of ugliness and the closely related question of the "mutability of taste" (106).

Dolly Parton's idea of what is glamorous serves for Barnard as an example of what Scarry's work discriminates against. For Barnard, *On*

Beauty and Being Just "makes little room for the likes of Dolly Parton" whose idea of glamour was deeply influenced by her childhood perception of a prostitute (104). Parton's taste would, in Barnard's reading, "fall under the rubric of 'error[s] of overcrediting' or an 'imperfect version' of the impulse toward imitation" (105). The bad seed in the argument from which this discriminatory fruit grows seems to be Scarry's notion of beauty as "clearly discernable". It is this that "seems designed to de-emphasise" the "mutability of taste", and it is this de-emphasis that consequently results in Scarry dealing with the questions of "(aesthetic) discrimination" and cultural difference in what Barnard finds a very unsatisfactory manner (106).

There are several problems, however, with Barnard's reading. The whole thrust of her argument misreads what Scarry is attempting to do. A good point at which to begin is Barnard's understanding of what Scarry means by "clearly discernable". For Barnard, this is a phrase that represents an understanding of beauty as being clear to everyone. We see this when she comments, "the 'beauty' of the place is [not necessarily] a matter of consensus or 'clear discernibility'" (114). "Clear discernibility" and "consensus" here are interchangeable, and it is with this understanding of the phrase that she reads Scarry's work as not having any space for "the likes of Parton"—and consequently relegating Parton's experience to "error[s] of overcrediting" (104–105).

We can, however, trace in Barnard's own article, indeed in her description of Parton's experience of beauty, the functioning of what Scarry means by clear discernibility. Barnard writes:

> [Parton] recalls that on a visit to town [...] she noticed the local hooker standing on the street corner, all dolled up for trade. 'Now, *that* is beautiful,' Parton thought to herself, resolving to discard her own dull rags as soon as possible and to emulate the colourful *nymphe du pave*. (104, emphasis in original)

The young Dolly Parton is here having a moment of recognition. The beauty of the prostitute, as shown by the emphasis on "that", was for the young Parton suddenly, starkly clear to her. Scarry comments that beauty "provides by its compelling 'clear discernibility' an introduction [...] to the state of certainty" (Scarry 1999, 31). This "state of certainty" can be seen in Parton's experience. "Clear discernibility" is not a matter of consensus. Barnard's comment that Parton's experience would be considered an "error of overcrediting" is similarly (and consequently) a misreading. Scarry is clear that what is viewed as (certainly) beautiful is susceptible to change. Thus she speaks of the experience of error, that goes together with that of clear discernibility. When Scarry talks of errors of overcrediting, she is not stating, as Barnard seems to think, that what some people think of as beautiful other people judge as being such an error. Rather, if Parton were to have an experience in which she no longer sees the prostitute's outfit as beautiful, in which she renounces as lacking beauty that to which she previously attributed it, then she would have had an experience of the error of overcrediting. The two genres of error for Scarry do not, then, place different opinions of beauty into a hierarchy of some being cases of overcrediting and others of under-crediting. It is simply a case of describing the subjective experience of error in the realm of beauty.

Barnard's central objection, against the apparent elitism of Scarry's understanding of beauty, resonates, however, with Smith's dialogue with Forster on this point, and we will have reason to return to it. In terms of the more general problem of beauty having been associated with evil and oppression, it is worth noting that Scarry's argument is not that beauty, by itself, is a sufficient cause of justice. Rather, Scarry argues that the *experience* of beauty is a natural ally of justice, initiating—not presenting the conclusion to—the quest for increased justice and fairness. Examples of this alliance being twisted, of beauty being used to evil ends, would be what Scarry terms a "misguided version" of it. Her comment on this, while in relation to a different point, applies equally well: "To disparage beauty for the sake not of one of its attributes but simply for a misguided version of one of its otherwise beneficent attributes is a common error made about beauty" (1999, 10). It is the beneficent attributes, which lend themselves to the pursuit of justice, on which Scarry focuses. Nevertheless, Barnard is right in noting a certain de-emphasis of the question of ugliness, and it is on this point that Smith's engagement with Scarry develops a useful nuancing of her argument.

There are two features of the experience of beauty that I noted in passing, and which are particularly relevant for *On Beauty*. The first is that "beauty prompts a copy of itself" (Scarry 1999, 4). Beholding something beautiful gives birth to the desire to replicate that beauty, to ensure that there is more of it in the world. The simplest manifestation of this is the act of staring; the impulse towards replication does not necessarily result in the production of something beautiful in turn, though it can do so. The beautiful object that inspired the replication, further, remains present in the newly begotten one. Smith's novel can, as Tynan (2008) has observed, be read as an enactment of Scarry's argument, which "*authorizes* the act of reformulation with which *On Beauty* incorporates it and other sources within itself" (79). While the presence of the "generative object" is not necessarily immediately obvious in the new one, in this case it is possible to trace the presence of the previous works.

A further desire associated with beauty is the willingness or eagerness to move, to change location, in order to retain the "beautiful thing" in the field of vision. This movement and subsequent retention is often brought about by things that are distinct from the beautiful object. They are "precious things" that serve as openings or ladders that lead onto beauty (Scarry 1999, 8). These openings or ladders, however, are susceptible to being destroyed. The precious thing that Scarry draws attention to is the university, implicated, as we have seen, in the elitism that would exclude Carl. It is from this point of Scarry's argument that Smith draws one of her epigraphs: "To misstate, or even merely understate, the relation of the universities to beauty is one kind of error that can be made. A university is amongst the precious things that can be destroyed" (8). In Scarry's argument, the university is vitally important as a means for perpetuating beauty in the world. Smith's use of this quote as an epigraph, however, dislocates it from the context of Scarry's work, endowing it with ambiguity—especially for a reader unfamiliar with Scarry. The university, the ambiguity suggests, does not simply offer an opening onto beauty which may be vulnerable to destruction, it is in its entirety 'a precious thing' which may be destroyed. This epigraph presides over the section of the novel titled "The Anatomy Lesson", referring to Rembrandt's painting *The Anatomy Lesson of Dr Nicolaes Tulp* (called, in the novel, *Dr Nicolaes Tulp Demonstrating the Anatomy of the Arm*). The painting is a representation of a lecture in which a group of observers are shown the inner workings of the arm. In Howard's words, the painting is a "clarion call of an Enlightenment not yet arrived, with its rational apostles gathered around a dead man, their faces uncannily lit by the holy light of science" (Smith

2005, 144). We are thus led to reflect, by both the epigraph and the title of this section of the narrative, on both the beginnings of the university, its potential destruction, and (through the framing of the picture) its relation to beauty.

Scarry, using a comet as an example of the importance of education for seeing beauty, notes, "One submits oneself to other minds (teachers) in order to increase the chance that one will be looking in the right direction when a comet makes its sweep through a certain patch of sky" (1999, 7). The importance of the university for fulfilling this function, however, is interrogated by Smith. Carl, sensitive to elitism, insists that "all you're paying for" at a university is "to talk to other people about that shit [here, Carl means the question of genius raised by Mozart]" (Smith 2005, 137), though his repeated insistence seems to indicate an awareness that it is more complex than this. The charge of universities as exclusionary which underwrites Carl's antagonism is not, however, done away with, and the question remains of whether it is actually something worth saving. In addition to this, Scarry writes that "sometimes [the university's] institutional gravity and awkwardness can seem tonally out of register with beauty" (1999, 8). This falling out of touch with beauty, a blurring of a correct understanding of the university's relation to beauty, can destroy it as a precious thing—and this is indeed what seems to be happening in Smith's novel, particularly in Howard's classes.

In "The Anatomy Lesson", the narrator shows us the experiences of Katie Armstrong as she prepares for Howard's class, which is a detailed account of a slowly growing recognition of the beauty of aging that results from everyday life. Katie only appears in the novel in the scenes of her preparation and the seminar itself, with the result, as Kathleen Wall notes, that "her relationship to the Rembrandt paintings she is examining for Howard's class is exemplary" (2008, 767). For her preparations she engages with two of Rembrandt's pictures, *Jacob Wrestling with an Angel* and what the narrator calls *Seated Nude* but which is, the author informs us in the "Author's Note", *Woman on a Mound*. In her reading of these pictures (a reading deeply informed by Schama's *Rembrandt's Eyes*) Katie is powerfully moved, particularly by the etching. It is not that Katie thinks *Jacob Wrestling with an Angel* is not beautiful—she finds it "impressive, beautiful, awe-inspiring" (Smith 2005, 251)—it is simply that it does not connect with her experience; *Woman on a Mound* does so in a profound way.

Katie's initial experience is one of shock, a response not far from that of repulsion found in the "famous commentaries". Upon further reflection, however, her experience of the painting changes:

> Is she really so grotesque? [....] Katie began to notice all the exterior, human information, not explicitly in the frame but implied by what we see there. Katie is moved by the crenulated marks of absent stockings on her legs, the muscles in her arms suggestive of manual labour. That loose belly that has known many babies, that still fresh face that has lured men in the past and may yet lure more. Katie—a stringbean, physically—can even see her own body contained in this body, as if Rembrandt were saying to her, and to all women: 'For you are of the earth, as my nude is, and you will come to this point too, and be blessed if you feel as little shame, as much joy, as she!' This is what a woman *is*: unadorned, after children and work and age, and experience—*these are the marks of living*. (251–252, emphasis in original)

Katie's engagement with the painting is an engagement, simultaneously, with life. All of the features of the woman that at first caused shock or repulsion are in fact "the marks of living", and it is her emotional response to them that catalyses her recognition of them as beautiful. Katie sees what is often described as Rembrandt's departure from the classical nude (which usually maintains a symmetry not found in the actual human body) as making a powerful point about the beauty of living, and how what is held as the ideal of physical beauty does not actually exist at the end of a fully lived life. She finds a profound insight into what it means to be a woman, that "all women" one day, inevitably, reach this same point and they are "blessed" if they are as content as she is.

Katie's reading here concurs with that found in Schama's *Rembrandt's Eyes*. Smith makes the comment in her acknowledgements that Schama's book "helped [her] to see paintings properly for the first time". As a reading it therefore has a degree of intertextual authority, in addition to that conferred by Katie's anomalous appearance. Intriguingly, however, as far as Schama is concerned, Katie and Howard (whose reading I will turn to in a moment) are both incorrect in declaring the etching a departure from the classical nude. In support, Schama points to the fact that

Rembrandt had to satisfy his patrons. It was also reproduced shortly after Rembrandt made it, signifying the likelihood that although it seems unusual to us, the etching was within the norms of the time (Schama 2000, 393). Where Katie is more in agreement with Schama than Howard is in noting what Schama observes as the central point of the etching: the woman's nakedness (as opposed to her nudity). That is, the revealing of the woman as a woman, together with the "embarrassment and awkwardness" that accompanies this exposure (393); not as an idealised object freely available for our gaze. When we look at *Woman on a Mound* we see a real woman rather than an idealised Athena or Diana (393–396). This understanding of the etching is integrated into Katie's response to it. The "marks of living" that she (and not Schama) notes would be included in the depiction of a real woman who is naked. In addition to this alliance of Katie with Schama, though, the narrator inflects the reader's reception of Katie's recognition in her favour.

The reader is directly addressed twice during Katie's preparations, drawing them into a more immediate relation with her. Maintaining the focalization through Katie, and thus this empathy for her position, the narrator goes on to present us with Howard's starkly different reading of the etching in his class. Howard begins by stating that they are trying to interrogate "the mytheme of artist as autonomous individual with privileged insight into the human" (Smith 2005, 252). When Howard receives no response from his class, he continues:

> To reframe: is what we see here really a rebellion, a turning away? We're told that this constitutes a rejection of the classical nude. OK. But. Is this nude not a confirmation of the ideality of the vulgar? As it is already inscribed in the idea of a specifically gendered class debasement? (252)

For Howard the etching is but a reinforcement of "the vulgar". By departing from the (assumed) norm of the nude, Howard does not see, as Katie does, a critique of the ideal of beauty. Where Katie found an unashamed, joyful woman, a woman beautiful in a way quite different from the ideal, Howard sees another example of the exclusion brought about by aesthetics. Additionally, the etching is not simply a confirmation that anyone can be vulgar: in aesthetics it is ultimately the provenance of lower class women.

Howard is, then "tonally out of register with beauty" in the extreme (Scarry 1999, 8), and the narrator continues to make use of our empathy for Katie's position to reinforce this. Despite her eagerness and determination to engage with the class, Katie fails to follow the discussion that takes place. Even though her view on the paintings is never uttered during the class, in a technique echoing what we saw in Forster's critique of Ruskin, the narrator does not allow Howard to dominate the narrative. He dominates in the lecture and the discussion goes along the route that he desires, ironically (considering Howard's declared intentions) silencing and excluding Katie. Yet the fact that the scene is focalised through Katie, together with the alignment of her reading with Schama's, maintains her priority and aligns the narrative in her favour. In addition, Katie's questioning that we saw in her preparation ("is she really so grotesque?") is a sincere enquiry. Thus, throughout this section of the narrative, Howard's, to use his own phrase, "rarefied language" is effectively juxtaposed against Katie's reading of Rembrandt, and the narrator exploits her omniscience to distance Howard from the reader.

This also, however, indicates the difficulty with Adams' argument, noted earlier, that Smith does not counter Forster's claim for the exclusivity of art. As an example, Adams presents Kiki, who "is open to experiences and sensitive to what she sees" but lacks Howard's expert knowledge. As a result, although Kiki's view is "clearly validated by the text", this "does not render her sensibility superior to that of her husband's" (2011, 392). The problem for this argument is that Katie, an undergraduate student who certainly does not surpass Howard in technical knowledge, is nevertheless able to access Rembrandt's work in a way that is, at this point in the narrative, completely beyond him. While Katie's view is (intertextually) informed by the work of Simon Schama, within the world of the novel aesthetic appreciation is more readily accessible than Adams would suggest. This is confirmed in the various responses to Mozart's *Requiem*. Zora engages with the performance in great technical detail, following an academic commentary while listening to it, yet she can barely remember it a month later. It is Carl that is most affected, and who with a little bit of further research into its composition—specifically the completion of the "Lacrimosa" by Süssmayr after Mozart's death—comes to the conclusion that "you can be so close to genius that it like lifts you up [...] I was tripping when I read that shit" (Smith 2005, 137). Not only does this show Carl's aesthetic appreciation, but this is also in stark contrast to Howard's view of genius as essentially exclusive ("the mytheme of artist as autonomous individual with privileged insight into the human" [252]).[53] For Carl, genius makes it possible for anyone—not only those who "[fit] in with their idea of who can and who can't make music like this" (137)—to create art. *On Beauty* is, then, comprehensive in its response to the exclusivity of *Howards End*, showing a greater appreciation of both music and paintings through the relatively uneducated Carl and Katie.

Howard, however, expressly denies the beauty and genius of Rembrandt's work. Katie, on the other hand, loves Rembrandt and, echoing Carl's view of the university, "used to dream about one day attending a college class about Rembrandt with other intelligent people who loved Rembrandt and weren't ashamed to express this love" (250). As a result, Katie's experience of the university is not one of opening up new possibilities of seeing beauty. This disconnection does not, however, result in discarding the university. Carl benefits from gaining access to its resources; likewise, Katie herself is exposed to more paintings and is required to engage with them. There seems, then, to be a tension in the novel between the university as a space of new possibilities as well as of limitation: the university is seen to be important, but at risk of failing as an opening onto beauty. Indeed, the university in Smith's novel presents a tragic difficulty, similar to that observed in the previous novels, in separating its ethically valuable aspects from its ethically detrimental ones, and exemplifying, in Scarry's terms, a precious thing at risk of being destroyed.

Katie's reflections have a significance beyond the question of the university, though, becoming one of the central moments for the novel where individual beauty is concerned. Scarry's reflections on the beauty of persons are situated in her response to the critique that gazing at the beautiful object harms it. Her argument is quite simple: "the vulnerability of the beholder is equal to or greater than the vulnerability of the beheld" (Scarry 1999, 75). While Smith agrees with Scarry on the vulnerability of the beholder, she is also interested to explore the vulnerability of the beautiful person in a way that Scarry does not. In "The Anatomy Lesson",

---

[53] For a good overview of the development of the modern idea of genius see Bate (1997), Schama (2000), Abrams (1971), and Tonelli (1973).

Claire Malcolm gives Jack French a poem titled "On Beauty", linking it to Smith's exploration of this topic (Smith 2005, 153)[54]. It is a pantoum. Claire explains: "It's basically interlinked quatrains, usually rhyming a-b-a-b, and the second and fourth line of each stanza go on to be [...] the first and third lines of the *next* stanza"; Claire's is a "broken pantoum" (152). Critics have understood the poem in contradictory ways. For Wall, it is an ironic counterpoint to the novel's title, illustrating the separation between form and content that is the cause of Howard's aesthetic difficulties (1994, 766–767), while for Lopez (2010) it is exemplary of the failure of speech to articulate beauty (353). Both, however, find the meaning of the poem elusive, and liken this elusiveness to the difficulty of defining beauty.

Greater attention to the details of the poem, though, dispels some of the ambiguity. The benefit of a pantoum is that repeating entire lines of the poem allows a focused detailing of its topic. Key lines, through repetition in slightly different linguistic contexts, are layered with further meaning. The repeated lines also link the stanzas into a whole—particularly in this poem where the final stanza links back to the first one, closing the circle as it were. That it is a broken pantoum (line three of stanza four does not repeat line four of stanza three and the rhyming scheme is irregular) is significant considering the subject matter: the poem tells us of the vulnerability of the beautiful, the hurt that they suffer, and the beauty of the poem is, like the beautiful, broken. Wall notes that the lines do not enjamb (that is, run on), and that this obfuscates the poem's meaning. It is precisely this breaking of form that, rather than causing "form [...] to have become the repression of content, not its achievement" (Wall 2008, 767), instead causes it to match and complement the content. That this also serves to increase the poem's beauty is not without significance.

The speaker of the poem begins, and ends, by telling us that "No, we could not itemize the list". The "list" is of "sins" that the beautiful "can't forgive us" and defies being broken down into individual parts or specific transgressions. It is not that the sins are too numerous to be made into an itemised list, but that they are too heinous and interconnected to be simply written down. The speaker states that "Of sins they can't forgive

---

[54] In an interview with *The New Zealand Herald*, Smith notes that Nick Laird wrote the poem in response to Scarry's *On Beauty and Being Just*. As an independent piece of writing then, the poem is concerned with Scarry's argument on the beauty of persons (Herrick 2005).

us/speech is beautifully useless". Speech fails when trying to detail the hurts inflicted upon the beautiful. Yet this failure of speech only makes things worse. The speaker repeats the failure of speech, adding to its significance: "Speech is beautifully useless./They *are* the damned./The beautiful know this". The beautiful are alone with their wounds, and, consequently, are filled with the knowledge that they "*are* the damned". This is given a further layer of meaning in its final two repetitions. The third stanza begins, "*They* are the damned/and so their sadness is perfect". The emphasis that is produced by the italics shifts from "are" to "they". The speaker seems to be drawing attention to the fact that it is specifically the beautiful that are the damned. "And so", due to the beauty of those who are damned, "their sadness is perfect". It is this beautification of the sadness of the damned that the speaker seems to close with as the greatest wound: "and so their sadness is perfect./The beautiful don't lack the wound./Hard, it is decorated with their face./No, we could not itemize the list". The speaker has come full circle. Having begun with the wound of the beautiful, he ends with this wound being "decorated with their face". The wound is itself beautiful, as is the broken pantoum, and this, the final repetition of the opening line seems to suggest, is part of the reason why the list ultimately defies being merely a series of items (Smith 2005, 153).

Rather than concerning the limitation of words to express beauty, the poem seems to address the pain of the beautiful. This vulnerability of being beautiful, the "list of sins", is expanded when Victoria breaks off her affair with Howard, declaring, "'This,' she said and touched her face, her breasts, her hips, 'that's what you know. But you don't know *me*. And you were the one who wanted *this*—that's all anybody ever...' She touched the same three places. And so that's what I...' (390). Victoria here expresses her vulnerability as a beautiful person. It is not so much that the admiring gaze directly hurts her, as that it misses who she is. It is her beautiful body, her face, breasts and hips, that people want. The person that is Victoria Kipps is subsequently lost in the preoccupation with her physical beauty. In an echo of Levinas's concern with the face-to-face relation and the danger of the image,[55] Smith suggests that part of the vulnerability of the beautiful is that the individuality of the beautiful person risks being bypassed. Developing Ghosh's insight that the space between individuals can always be bridged with violence, here we see that any interest in a

---

[55] See Levinas (1987).

beautiful person could also come to a stop on their body alone, their image.

Smith does, however, explore Scarry's vulnerable beholder as well as the benefits of being beautiful. Scarry, concerning the vulnerability of the beholder, writes,

> for it is simply the case—isn't it? —that each of us has, upon suddenly seeing someone beautiful, tripped on the sidewalk, broken out in a sweat of new plumage, dropped packages (as though offering a gift or sacrifice)—all while the bus we were waiting for pulls up and pulls away. (1999, 76)

An important element of the vulnerability is this distractedness. The beauty of the other person so draws our attention that everything else is forgotten, and thus begins to go wrong: we trip, we drop our bags, we miss the bus. We can see this in Zora and Carl's conversation as they walk from the gym. Zora struggles to pay attention to Carls words, so distracted is she by his beauty (Smith 2005, 137). Carl's beauty is an important factor in determining the way in which he is received. The first time he is introduced, the Belseys cannot ignore "the fact that he was stupidly good-looking" (74). His good looks cause everyone to warm to him, with increased exposure resulting in increased friendliness. It is his beauty that motivates Kiki to attempt to "patch the thing up" after Zora's blunder about *poetry* poetry at the concert. At which the narrator notes that "it's remarkable what a face like Carl's makes you want to do in order to see it smile again" (77–78).

Carl's good looks, then, seem to have positive effects on strangers by making them more hospitable to him. This is soon complicated, though, in Carl's later encounters with the Belseys. A significant factor is not just that Carl is beautiful, but that a young black man from the ghetto is beautiful. Due to his position in society, Carl's beauty is often viewed with suspicion. Thus, when Howard meets him in the doorway, he thinks Carl is "pretty, *too* pretty like a conman" (105). Because Carl is male and black, his looks do nothing to make Howard more welcoming. Similarly, while Zora is talking to him after the gym, she fears "that all these questions were a kind of verbal grooming that would later lead—by routes she didn't pause to imagine—to her family home and her mother's jewellery and the safe in the basement" (139). The friendliness that Carl is exhibiting makes her suspicious of what precisely it is that he wants. Beauty, as Barnard notes, is never just simply received. While Smith does present Carl's beauty as being "clearly discernable" to many around him, there is some degree in which the response to this beauty is shaped by the perceiver's cultural location. Barnard writes that "human beings do many things with the objects they consider beautiful: they judge them, they sell them, they wear them" (2006, 105–106). Smith here seems to agree, nuancing the representation of beauty in the novel.

The most critical extension of this more multifaceted understanding, however, is accomplished through Kiki. Through her, Smith challenges the conventional ideal of beauty that Victoria and Carl exemplify. Kiki is, at this stage of her life, large and over-weight, though her face is very beautiful. Yet, through several moments in the narrative—all of which occur in "The Anatomy Lesson"—Kiki is portrayed as possessing a beauty that is to be admired and acknowledged. The first such moment is the most oblique. Carlene tells Kiki about the Hyppolite painting which is of the "voodoo goddess, Erzulie" who represents "love, beauty, purity, the ideal female and the moon... and she's the *mystere* of jealousy, vengeance and discord, *and*, on the other hand, of love, perpetual help, goodwill, health, beauty and fortune" (Smith 2005, 175, emphasis in original). This is the painting that becomes Kiki's by Carlene's will, and of which, as the item of inheritance, Kiki is the spiritual heir. In addition to this, Fischer (2005) notes that it is from Erzulie that Kiki gets her name, linking her even more strongly to these ideals: "Erzulie Dantor, the Black Virgin of Carlene's painting, cries 'ke-ke-ke-ke-ke'" (31).[56]

Though important, it is not only this extra-textual reference that presents Kiki as a challenge to the usual ideal of beauty. When Claire is at the Bus Stop with Zora she reflects extensively on the Belseys and her affair with Howard. Before thinking about Kiki, she laments that women of today are "objects of desire instead of [...] desiring subjects", and the destructive effects this has: women starving and cutting themselves (226). This is an effect of beauty that Scarry does not consider. Scarry argues that

---

[56] See King (2009) for an interesting discussion suggesting that Carlene is the key representative of Erzulie. Such a reading would add to the significance of the inheritance symbolised by the painting: Kiki, we could add to King's argument, becomes the heir of this signification.

it is only in terms of "pairs of lovers" that one wants to be as beautiful as the one admired, and if not beautiful oneself, then to present something that is (Scarry 1999, 77). In terms of beauty that is in the "public sphere" (77), however, she states that "we look at things without wishing to be ourselves beautiful" (78). Claire's reflections on the girls in her class, together with Zora feeling "her own bad design" in Carl's presence (though this could, perhaps be read as an aspirational "pair of lovers") (Smith 2005, 134), contests Scarry's claim. The vulnerability of the perceiver of beauty is more than just distractedness. While there may be no desire to be beautiful for the sake of the stranger that is being perceived, yet there is a desire to be as beautiful as the stranger.

For Claire it is "in exactly this sense" that Kiki stands out. Not only was she extremely beautiful in her youth, but "more than this she radiated an essential female nature Claire had already imagined in her poetry—natural, honest, powerful, unmediated, full of something like genuine desire. A goddess of the everyday (227). Reiterating, through the description of "goddess", the link with Erzulie, Kiki presents an alternative, though not an opposition (considering her previous beauty), to purely physical beauty. That Kiki is a "goddess of the *everyday*" forges a further connection, between her and Katie's reflections on Rembrandt's *Woman on a Mound* (presented in the novel shortly after this moment). The woman in Rembrandt's painting, like Kiki, has a "still fresh face that has lured men in the past and may yet lure more", and it is the everyday "marks of living" that she bears without shame (251–252). That Rembrandt, contrary to Howard, does present "insight into the human" is confirmed when Kiki, having tea with Carlene—the same tea when she sees the Hyppolite for the first time—is complimented on her beauty (252). Kiki's response is revealing:

> You know... I see Zora worrying all the time about her looks, and I want to say to her, honey, any woman who counts on her face is a *fool*. She doesn't want to hear that from me. It's how it is, though. We *all* end up in the same place in the end. That's the *truth*. (173, emphasis in original)

While Kiki's use of the word "truth" here is colloquial for expressing a strongly held opinion, rather than positing metaphysical claims, Kiki's inter- and intra-textual links draws it out of its immediate context:

the truth of the matter is that beauty is fleeting; there is no variation in the final end of physical beauty. This is not to deny the beauty that Carl and Victoria have. Rather, Kiki and Rembrandt's etching broaden what is beautiful to include the marks of everyday life: that which in the novel's terms of the "classic nude" would be considered "grotesque" (251).

Despite this challenge to conventional definitions of beauty that Kiki presents, she is nevertheless still vulnerable and hurt as a result of her looks, particularly Howard's suggestion that the change in her appearance was the cause of his infidelity. Kiki is painfully aware of the dramatic physical difference between her and Claire, telling Howard: "You married a big black bitch and you run off with a fucking leprechaun?" (206). It is not in response to any argument from Howard that she brings up Claire's appearance; it is an intricate part of her pain that Howard betrayed her with someone so different to her. Thus, while Kiki serves to critique conventional definitions of beauty and is more secure with her appearance than the girls in Claire's class, she is nevertheless also vulnerable to the pain that beauty can inflict.

III

Howard's pivotal position in the novel in relation to each of these engagements with questions of beauty—the elitism and importance of the university, the conventional ideal of beauty, and the role of art in meaningfully articulating truths about the human—makes his recognitions particularly significant. He is not the only one to have moments of recognition. Indeed, the plot of the novel slowly builds up to a knot of multiple recognitions that form its climax: when Jerome recognises that Victoria had an affair with his father, it is revealed that Kipps also had an affair with his student Chantelle, and Kiki discovers Levi has stolen the Hyppolite painting, and subsequently finds the note from Carlene bequeathing it to her (417–431). It is a climax where, to transpose the narrator's description of Jerome's recognition, each character travels "down a formerly concealed path to a dark destination: the truth" (417); it is a sequence of events that clears the deceit and duplicity which had developed amongst the characters, and paves the way for Howard's final recognition, when his position on beauty and art crumbles.

This moment of realization for Howard is the result of a series of recognitions that coalesce in the final scene. The first recognition that sets this in motion is during his preparation for his "shopping" lecture (142), in which the students assess whether they want to take the course. Set in the section "Anatomy Lesson", the lecture is on the painting after which the section is named: Rembrandt's *The Anatomy Lesson of Dr Nicolaes Tulp*. In his lecture, Howard will present the picture as a "clarion call of an Enlightenment not yet arrived" in which its "apostles", appropriating religious imagery, request "admiration for the fearless humanity of the project, the rigorous scientific pursuance of the dictum *Nosce te Ipsium*, 'Know thyself'" (144). It is the first in a lecture series that will question "the redemptive humanity of what is commonly called 'Art'" (155). Delivering the lecture for the sixth time, Howard knows the picture so well "he could no longer see it at all". Yet, as he prepares the PowerPoint for the lecture, this suddenly changes: "But today Howard felt himself caught in the painting's orbit. He could see himself laid out on that very table, his skin white and finished with the world, his arm cut open for students to examine" (144). Each of Howard's recognitions is marked by three features, all present here. In each of them, Howard is "caught" by the art, against his will; they all share the same predicate: mortality, here his vision of himself on the dissection table; and lastly, each recognition has as it background the deterioration of his relationship with Kiki. Moments before Howard is "caught in the painting's orbit", he is remembering the previous night and Kiki's silent tears as he joined her in bed. The narrator transitions, almost without interruption, from Howard's recollection of that emotionally trying night to this captivity within the painting's "orbit", closely linking this emotional vulnerability—as was also seen in the previous novels considered in this book—to the recognition, enabling it to occur.

This emerges more clearly in the subsequent recognition, where the predicate of Howard's own mortality expands to include the mortality of his family—and in particular Kiki. I noted earlier that Smith changed the Beethoven concert in *Howards End* to a performance of Mozart's *Requiem*. Mozart, as one of the more iconic artistic geniuses, brings into sharper focus Howard's concern with the idea of the "artist as autonomous individual with privileged insight into the human" (252), and, as we saw, allows Carl to challenge the exclusivity of art. Whereas Howard slept through Mozart's *Requiem* before the exposure of his lies and the disintegration of his relationship with Kiki, his second recognition occurs when listening to another piece by Mozart. The Belsey family is attending the funeral of Carlene Kipps, due to Kiki's friendship with her. Howard's usual modus operandi at funerals is to spend the time doodling and reflecting on the unpleasant relationships between the individuals at the funeral, which are, for the space of a couple of hours, rendered non-existent (287). This funeral, however, turns out very differently. It begins with Howard trying to ignore the presence of the coffin, to which end he resorts to looking up "into the simple concameration of the roof, hoping for escape or relief or distraction" (286). What he finds instead is an outpouring of music:

> It poured down on his head from above, from a balcony. There eight young men [...] were lending their lungs to an ideal of the human voice larger than any one of them.
> Howard, who had long ago given up on this ideal, now found himself—in a manner both sudden and horrible—mortally affected by it. He did not even get the opportunity to check the booklet in his hand; never discovered that this was Mozart's *Ave Verum*, and this choir, Cambridge singers; no time to remind himself that he hated Mozart, nor to laugh at the expensive pretence of bussing down Kingsmen to sing at a Willesden funeral. It was too late for all that. The song had him. (286–287)

This music, without Howard knowing it, is a perfect example of all that he is against. The music is by Mozart, an archetypal original genius; the vocals are in Latin. These singers singing this piece of music is, one could say, the pinnacle of privilege and high art. Yet these facts do not condition his response to the music as they usually would. It is irrelevant who they are and what they are singing; irrelevant that Howard presumably does not understand Latin; irrelevant for the simple reason that "the song had him". What is conditioning Howard's response to the music is the beauty of the music itself. The combination of the subtle, beautiful movements of music— "the faint, hopeful leap of the first three notes, the declining dolour of the following three"—coupled with the "coffin passing so close to Howard's elbow" (287)—brings Howard to a powerful recognition of the immanence and inevitability of death. He begins to sob. And though he was "certain he was making embarrassing noises", he was completely "powerless to stop them. His thoughts fled from him and rushed down their dark holes. Zora's gravestone. Levi's. Jerome's. Everybody's. His own. Kiki's. Kiki's. Kiki's. Kiki's" (287). Howard flees.

In this moment, which again evokes the link between Kiki and Erzulie through the echo of her cry "ke-ke-ke-ke-ke" (Fischer 2005, 31), the beauty of the music brings Howard to recognise the immanence and inescapability of death, not now only of his own, but of his family. It is, for Howard, terrifying. The riveting of Howard's attention onto the coffin, and the insight that this, coupled with the music, brings into the inescapability of death causes him to break down. Scarry argues that the recognition of error is "announced by a striking sensory event, a loud sound, an awful smell" (Scarry 1999, 13). In this case, it is sharp emotional pain. Importantly though, this is only half of the experience of error. Howard does not at this moment acknowledge the beauty of Mozart's music; but it is the beauty of the music, together with his estrangement from Kiki, that catalyses a realization of the inevitability of death.

This recognition of the immanence of death leads to the final realization, in the novel's closing scene, of the value of art in capturing the beauty of the everyday, mortal life of the human. That something has changed in Howard is evident from the fact that, as he is driving to his lecture, he is listening to the "Lacrimosa"—the last movement from Mozart's *Requiem* generally considered to be composed by him (Wolff 1994, 29), but in the novel an example of the wider accessibility of art and beauty. Enjoying the piece by the artist he used to hate, he arrives late. It is Howard's last chance for tenure, and his affair with Victoria has emerged into general knowledge with the result that he and Kiki are now separated. Having run the stretch from his car to the university, his is halfway through his apologies to the audience for his inexperience with PowerPoint when "Howard visualized with perfect clarity the yellow folder that remained where he had left it, on the back seat of his car, five blocks from here". He had arrived without his notes. With nothing else to do, Howard begins the presentation. As the lights dim, Howard spots Kiki, "sixth row, far right, looking up with interest at the image behind him, which was beginning to refine itself in the coming darkness". The shifts of narrative voice between the responses of members of the audience and Howard's experience shapes the presentation of Howard's gradual recognition of the beauty of the painting and its insight into human life. The scene unfolds in almost total silence, and the narrator tells us that "the man from

Pomona began to nod appreciatively. Howard pressed the red button. He could hear Jack French saying to his eldest son, in his characteristically loud whisper: *You see, Ralph, the order is meaningful*" (Smith 2005, 442). The narrator has already shown us, however, that Howard is not doing anything meaningful. He is continuing to press the button because that is all he can do. There may have been a purpose behind the order of the paintings in that Howard wanted to lecture on them in a specific sequence, but here, rather than attempting to lecture, Howard is becoming increasingly absorbed in the paintings and in Kiki.

Once the slideshow has come to it end, the audience becomes perplexed. The only thing Howard manages to say is "*Hendrickje Bathing, 1654*". His audience is still hopeful for a lecture: "they looked at her and then at Howard and then at the woman once more, awaiting elucidation". The narrative voice shifts again, however, showing that Howard is absorbed in the painting and not even thinking about the lecture. The language that the narrator gives to Howard's experience is quite distinct from anything he has used in the past, expressing engagement with the painting: "The woman, for her part, looked away, coyly, into the water. She seemed to be considering whether to wade deeper. The surface of the water was dark, reflective—a cautious bather could not be certain of what lurked beneath" (442). Rather than trying to expose the hidden workings of power as he usually does, he is completely taken in by the representation of Hendrickje. What she may be thinking and feeling, her coyness, her caution, come alive for him and engages him in the situation he is currently in.

This growing experience of the painting is immediately mirrored and amplified in Howard's turning to look at his wife, with the verb "look" becoming prominent in its repetition (Lanone 2007, 193): "Howard looked at Kiki. In her face, his life. Kiki looked up suddenly at Howard—not, he thought, unkindly. Howard said nothing. Another silent minute passed" (Smith 2005, 442-443). The audience is further perplexed as Howard fails to fulfil their expectations. Instead of beginning to lecture, Howard zooms in on both the picture and his wife. They are the final sentences of the novel and worth quoting at length:

> Howard made the picture larger on the wall, as Smith had explained to him how to do. The woman's fleshiness filled the wall.

He looked out into the audience once more and saw Kiki only. He smiled at her. She smiled. She looked away, but she smiled. Howard looked back at the woman on the wall, Rembrandt's love, Hendrickje. Though her hands were imprecise blurs, paint heaped on paint and roiled with the brush, the rest of her skin had been expertly rendered in all its variety—chalky whites and lively pinks, the underlying blue of her veins and the ever present human hint of yellow, intimation of what is to come. (443)

Howard only sees two things: Kiki and Hendrickje. As he focuses in on the one, he also focuses in on the other. He sees Kiki, "his life", and, Hendrickje, "Rembrandt's love". The growing correlation between the two becomes a growing sense of beauty, and Howard smiles. Kiki smiles in response, and with the pleasure of this smile Howard turns to the painting. For the first time he seems to enjoy the details of it: the "chalky whites and lively pinks, the underlying blue of her veins". Even the "imprecise blurs" are noted. This paralleling of Kiki and Hendrickje, and Howard's epiphany of Kiki's beauty and importance for his life, for his sense of home, has been well documented by critics.[57] Importantly, the earlier recognitions of the inevitability of death are here incorporated into the beauty of the work: "the ever present human hint of yellow, intimation of what is to come" (443). The fragility of human life, the ephemeral, becomes through Rembrandt's painting and Kiki's importance for him, a thing of beauty. At the funeral, the beauty of the music causes the fragility of life to forcefully intrude into his awareness and results in terror. Here, Howard's circumstances force him to engage with the painting as a representation of life, and with the emotional resonance of Kiki's presence, recognises the beauty of the fleeting human life and the role of art in revealing it.

Howard's final recognition, then, overturns his earlier position on aesthetics and the illusion of artistic beauty and insight. It is precisely through the midwifery of art that he attains his realization of error in the field of beauty. This is a powerful conclusion to an intricately woven novel. Connecting multiple arguments on beauty—the exclusivity of aesthetic appreciation, the role (and risk) of the university in appreciating beauty, the vulnerability of the beautiful and the beholder—they converge in this

---

[57] See Adams (2011, 389-390), Lanone (2007, 193-194), Lopez (2010, 364), and Wall (2008, 774).

final moment in the unspoken acknowledgement of the artist as providing insight into the human condition. Many of the critical moments take place in the "The Anatomy Lesson", linking the dictum "know thyself", mentioned by Howard, to the work as a whole and the role of art more specifically. And Howard indeed comes to this self-knowledge. As such, while Smith does not advance our discussion of the ethics of remembering violence and of religion,[58] she does present, through a series of recognitions, a nuanced engagement with the beauty of the human, in particular making a realization of the inevitability of death a beautiful experience that can be desired.

---

[58] The main implication in the novel is, as Magdalena Mączyńska (2013) notes, that the religiously fanatic (such as Kipps) are "handicapped" in their appreciation of Art and beauty, while "flexible, open-mided characters, on the other hand, take pleasure in classical music (Jerome, Kiki), religious artworks (Kiki, Carlene, Levi) and pop (Levi, Carl)" (135).

Conclusion
Elizabeth Costello

In 1997, J.M. Coetzee delivered, at Princeton University, the prestigious Tanner Lectures on Human Values. While meeting the expectation of engaging with a serious ethical issue, Coetzee's lectures did so through presenting two short stories, rather than the more usual philosophical essay. In the stories/lectures, Elizabeth Costello, a renowned and aging Australian author (this dates from before Coetzee's immigration to Australia) is invited to the prestigious (fictional) Appleton College in the United States to deliver two lectures on any topic of her choice. She chooses to lecture on animal suffering, and the majority of the narrative tells her lecture and subsequent seminar on this topic. As Derek Attridge points out, this was not the first—or the last—time that Coetzee would deliver a lecture in story format (2004a, 194–195). Every time that he did so, he told of the experiences of Elizabeth Costello giving a lecture on the chosen topic. These lectures/stories were later collected, edited and added to, finally becoming *Elizabeth Costello: Eight Lessons* (2004). The act of presenting a story as a lecture forcefully opens the question of the relationship between philosophy and literature that I discussed in the introduction. I want now to bring this study to close through a brief discussion of these two lectures and, later, *Elizabeth Costello*, not only for their act of restating literature as a method of philosophical investigation, but also because of the resonance of the topic—the lives of animals and the questioning of the category of the human—with what has been observed throughout this book, transforming Costello into a closing synecdoche for this study.

The move of presenting a story instead of a traditional lecture has, as one would expect, been variously received. Peter Singer (1999), a leading philosopher in animal studies, formulates his response to Coetzee as a short story as well, although with less literary finesse: the main character, Peter, is preparing a response to "that South African novelist, J.M. Coetzee, who's giving a special lecture about philosophy and animals" (85). Peter, we learn, is frustrated because he prefers "to keep truth and fiction clearly separate" (86), and doesn't know how to respond since "Coetzee's fictional device enables him to distance himself from [Costello's arguments]" (91). The story closes with his daughter advising that he writes a story in turn. The very close mirroring of reality and fiction in Singer's story has the result of conveying a clear sense of annoyance: Peter's frustration, we assume, is also Singer's. Costello's arguments, which Singer understands as presenting a case for radical egalitarianism between humans and animals, are, for him, weak, but Coetzee includes a character, Norma, who points out that they are weak, pre-empting any critical response from the audience, or subsequent readers. That there might be some distance, however, between the fictional and the real Peter, as he suggests there might be between Coetzee and Costello, is seen in the fact that Peter Singer has co-edited a collection on the fiction of Coetzee and its relationship to ethics: *J.M. Coetzee and Ethics: Philosophical Perspectives on Literature* (Leist and Singer 2010b). Any great discrepancy between the two Peters is likely a mirage, though, considering that Singer's own contribution to the volume (co-authored with Karen Dawn) is concerned with proving, through interviews, non-fiction essays and more recent fiction, that Elizabeth Costello's views are indeed those of her creator (Dawn and Singer 2010).[59]

In this essay, Singer and Dawn are responding, in part, to Cora Diamond's (2003) argument that "at [the story's] centre" is "the life of this speaking and wounded and clothed animal", Elizabeth Costello, who "is one of the 'lives of animals' that the story is about" (4). There is no doubt that *The Lives of Animals* is about more than the argumentative content of Costello's lectures—indeed Singer and Dawn concede as much (2010, 110)—yet Diamond presses this further, presenting the philosophical responses as a case of "deflection", characteristic of philosophical discourse, which, in this case, results in the wounded body, "our own bodies", be-

---

[59] In the introduction to the collection, Singer and Leist (2010a) are ambiguous about the possible interactions between philosophy and literature, suggesting that it is postmodernist philosophers who find literature of most value, while for analytical philosophers it is superfluous in terms of actual philosophising: "Philosophers who still favour the ideas of the Enlightenment see literature as a supplement to philosophy and the sciences, something to be made use of educationally and politically for an improved way of life" (5). Apart from the problematic reduction of philosophy to either postmodern or analytical (with pragmatism thrown in on the postmodern side for good measure), this also neglects the complex negotiation of the legacy of the Enlightenment characteristic of, for example, Foucault (see Foucault [1984]), and which has been a theme throughout this study.

coming "mere facts—facts which may or may not be thought of as morally relevant in this or that respect, depending on the particular moral issue being addressed" (2003, 13). She comments that "what is meant not to be done is [...] pulling out ideas and arguments as if they had been simply clothed in fictional form as a way of putting them before us" (9). The fact that Coetzee is presenting these stories in the context of the Tanner Lectures, however, suggests that the content of Elizabeth's lectures is indeed significant (regardless of their proximity to their creator's own view). I will consider what else Costello is doing later. I want to begin, though, by following Stephen Mulhall (2009), who says that

> just as Costello does her philosophers the credit of taking it that, when they are writing about an animal, they are writing, in the first place, about an animal, so we should do her the credit of taking it that, when she is writing about philosophy and its arguments, she is writing, in the first place, about philosophy and its arguments. (21–22)[60]

My interest in Costello's arguments here is not in the case she presents for a particular animal ethics as such. Instead, as my claim of Costello's synecdochic relationship to this book implies, it is the connections between Costello's ethical position and the critique of the idea of the human that interest me. To recall: Throughout this book, I have been developing an increasingly textured picture of the idea of the human that is found in the works I have considered. Across all of the authors discussed, the idea of a shared humanity is seen to be prominent. In Ghosh and Phillips's engagement with the question of humanism, what emerges is the importance of an ethical subject who differs saliently from the classical humanist subject of the Enlightenment. The bridging of difference through the recognition of similarities is seen as both possible and important; it is not, however, easy. The characters are seen to be irrevocably shaped by the interplay of differences. Deeti and Neel in *Sea of Poppies* understand themselves according to caste distinctions; Emily's self-conception in

---

[60] Mulhall's study is, similarly to Diamond's, concerned to show the role of literature in exploring the difficult reality that eludes philosophy. It is notable, though, that is lacks any discussion of the extensive work of Nussbaum that preceded him in this enterprise

Cambridge is constructed in opposition to her understanding of slaves. In each case, the differences between people are not easily overcome. This historically and discursively located subject was further seen to be an embodied one. Across all of the works considered, emotions play a fundamental role in causing recognitions and their corresponding ethical changes. In nearly each case, the most deeply ingrained cultural and racial distinctions are breached through moments of vivid emotional intensity: moments of crisis in Phillips, emotional resonance in Ghosh, the awakening of love in Adichie, and the fear of mortal loss in Smith.

This decentring of the Enlightenment subject is, in one sense, taken furthest in Phillips. While Ghosh depicts the fundamental pervertibility of the space between selves, and queries the boundaries of the human in the traditional human/animal opposition, in Phillips we are introduced to a deeply dislocated subject for the first time: Emily's unreliability reveals her ethical vulnerability. Although the ubiquity of the impurity of ethics (tragic ethical conflict) in all the novels corresponds to an understanding of the world where ethical vulnerability is possible, in *Cambridge* Emily is greatly affected by it. In a situation not entirely of her own making, she is nevertheless required to make decisions for which she is responsible. This is a crucial challenge to the traditional understanding of the ethical subject as possessing full—that is, fully free and aware—responsibility. This takes the critique of the Enlightenment subject to its fullest only in one sense, however, because while Phillips presents a radically different sense of subjectivity, the rejection of a clear human/animal hierarchy and the emotional embodiment of the subject as a knowing self are equally important for the critique of humanism within what is often termed posthumanism.

This is important to note, since it is not the case that reinstating the category of the human, as the authors in this book do, is a return to a full-blooded humanism. As Cary Wolfe (2010), one of the more prominent philosophers engaged with this question, comments,

> posthumanism in my sense isn't posthuman at all—in the sense of being 'after' our embodiment has been transcended—but is only posthumanist, in the sense that it opposes the fantasies of disembodiment and autonomy, inherited from humanism itself. (xv)

Wolfe is responding to an idea of the posthuman that results from increased integration of technology into the human organism—what is generally now termed transhumanism—where "'the human' is achieved by escaping or repressing not just its animal origins in nature, the biological, and the evolutionary, but more generally by transcending the bonds of materiality and embodiment altogether" (xv). The ideal in this case would be downloading one's consciousness into a computer. Instead of being posthuman, as Wolfe comments elsewhere, "visions of the posthuman such as those associated with transhumanism would appear to be rather regressively humanist, in that they attempt to make good on the age-old attempt to transcend the finitude of embodiment itself" (Wolfe 2011, 450). The emphasis on the circumscribed agency and embodiment of the characters through the functioning of their emotions in catalysing their recognitions is, then, as I outlined in the introduction, a forceful undermining of the Enlightenment ethical subject.

In questioning of the distinction between human and animal a further element of this embodiment emerges. Ghosh's *The Hungry Tide* negotiates the tragic conflict of values that transpires when the traditional designation of animals as outside the realm of ethics is overturned. This decentring of the ethical self, the overturning of the illusion of full autonomy, is, however, only part of the critique of humanism. Drawing on the late work of Derrida, Wolfe argues for two levels of the decentring of the subject. The second level we have just seen in the circumscribing of autonomy and self-awareness—though for Derrida this is achieved particularly in language, to which we always arrive late, as it were. The more fundamental "finitude" that deposes the classical subject of humanism is the sheer materiality of existence: "physical vulnerability, embodiment, and eventually mortality" (Wolfe 2009, 570). It is this aspect that Cora Diamond focuses on in her reading of *The Lives of Animals*.

Responding to Nagel's argument about the difficulty of imagining the lives of animals, Costello discusses the imagining of death. She describes a vivid realization of mortality: "the knowledge we have is not abstract [...] but embodied. For a moment we *are* that knowledge. We live the impossible: we live beyond our death, look back on it, yet look back as only a dead self can" (Coetzee 1999, p.32, emphasis in orignal). This vivid, embodied confrontation with the reality of physical vulnerability, with death, is not sustainable. Costello continues that "[for] an instant, *before my whole structure of knowledge collapses in panic*, I am dead and alive at the same time" (32, emphasis mine). It is this confrontation with death, however, that gives us an embodied connection to animals. As Cora Diamond comments: "The awareness we each have of being a living body, being 'alive to the world,' carries with it exposure to the bodily sense of vulnerability to death, sheer animal vulnerability, the vulnerability we share with them" (2003, 22). Costello concludes her point: "if we are capable of thinking our own death, why on earth should we not be capable of thinking our way into the life of a bat?" (Coetzee 1999, 32–33). It is this common substrate of finitude that, beyond philosophical reasoning, for Costello and Diamond, presents us with a morally forceful connection to the suffering animal. In Smith's novel, we saw a careful exploration of this confrontation with death. The panic that results from realizing the reality of one's mortality is precisely what caused Howard to flee the funeral of Carlene Kipps. We saw, however, that Smith presents beauty and aesthetics, in the form of art in particular, as being able to mediate this recognition of animal vulnerability in a pleasurable way. Howard's experience of the painting in the closing scene of the novel makes this knowledge of death more bearable, suggesting the ability of art to draw individuals into the recognition of this finitude—and thus, by extension, making such an encounter with the suffering animal more possible.

Wendy Doniger's (1999) response to Coetzee's stories/lectures draws this discussion into the orbit of religion. When Costello's debating partner in the seminar/second lecture, Thomas o'Hearne, a philosopher, challenges Costello by claiming that "[the] notion that we have an obligation to animals [....] is very recent, very Western, and even Anglo-Saxon" (1999, 60), she replies by noting the long history of pets and children's love for animals. For Doniger, Costello "challenges him too weakly" (93). Drawing on centuries of religious reflection in the Hindu, Buddhist and Jain traditions, Doniger proceeds to detail the long, substantial engagement with the question of human-animal relations. What is interesting—and echoes Adichie's exploration of a different legacy of Christianity in Nigeria—is that it is not Christianity per se that leads to the eating of animals. Doniger shows how, while the Christian understanding of humanity—as opposed to animals—being created in the image of God can authorise violence against animals (and this is Costello's argument, through her example of Aquinas [1999, 22–23]), "most mythologies assume that animals, *rather than humans*, are the image of god—which may be a reason *to eat them*" (100, emphasis in original). Religion, then, rather than causing the exploitation of animals in any straightforward manner, provides rich resources for thinking and engaging with the question of what our relationship to animals means. This includes myths, as Doniger describes them, "of natural transformation, in which [humans] become quintessentially natural and eat what animals eat (food that may in fact include other animals)" (101).

This ethical ambiguity of religion has been evident throughout the study of the four authors. The complicity of Christianity with colonialism, in part through the reckoning of certain human populations as more animalistic and thus acceptable to kill (for example in *The Hungry Tide* and *Cambridge*), is balanced by Ghosh's exploration, in both of his novels considered, of the possibility of syncretic and hybrid religion as a mode of discourse that is resistant to humanistic thought. This, we might say, is taken further in Adichie. Exploring the negotiation of religious difference, and the possibilities of inculturation, *Purple Hibiscus* presents Catholicism as a viable ethical framework, while both of Adichie's novels critique the essentializing of the religious. The complexity of the legacy that is negotiated in a work such as Adichie's, however, is evoked by Phillips's own engagement with the theme of religion. In his novels it is seen as an inextricable element of the discourse of civilization to which both Cambridge and Emily subscribe, and which served as an epistemic alibi for colonialism. It is a difficult legacy to negotiate, as Eugene, Kambili and Nash show. Zadie Smith's novel is more oblique, by contrast, favouring tolerant faith through the vicissitudes of the more radical characters.

The one ethical theme that has been considered in this book but at first glance appears absent from *The Lives of Animals*, is that of the remembrance of violence. There was, with the exception of Smith, a continual engagement with the ethics of remembrance across all the novels. It was observed that in Ghosh the primary concern was with challenging historiography. Excavating stories that fall beyond History's purview, concerned as it is with narratives of progress, Ghosh humanised these stories, deploying the historical situations as singular moments that require a singular emotional response. The ethics of the remembrance of past violence was brought to the forefront in Adichie's work, particularly the tension between the need for accuracy and the needs of creative licence and for the commemoration of historical trauma to be affectively *felt*. This, as with the question of humanism, was developed in a more complex way in the work of Phillips. Navigating this ethical tension, he deftly folded it back into Ghosh's concern with recuperating lost or suppressed stories, through his narrative technique and the multiplicity of narrative voices and types.

The apparent absence of this concern in Costello's lectures is, however, misleading. The most controversial point of her lecture, in fact, draws on the paradigmatic example of remembering historical violence, which has recurred in my discussions: the holocaust. For Costello, the continual slaughter of animals, at the level of billions a year, is comparable to the determined killing of Jews by the Nazis: "Let me say it openly: we are surrounded by an enterprise of degradation, cruelty, and killing which rivals anything that the Third Reich was capable of, indeed dwarfs it" (Coetzee 1999, 21). The argument here is summed up succinctly in a letter sent to Costello by Abraham Stern, a poet who refuses to eat with her because of the analogy: "the Jews died like cattle, therefore cattle die like Jews, you say" (49). His articulation of the violation caused by this analogy is critical:

> You misunderstand the nature of likenesses [...] Man is made in the image of God but God does not have the likeness of man. If the Jews were treated like cattle, it does not follow that cattle are treated like Jews. *The inversion insults the memory of the dead. It also trades on the horrors of the camps in a cheap way.* (49–50, emphasis mine)

In a strong echo of Olanna's rejection of Odenigbo's appropriation of her cousin's death to support his Muslim stereotype in *Half of a Yellow Sun*, Abraham Stern states that Costello is cheapening the memory of the dead to make her point. She is, for him, in violation of the ethical demand to remember the victims of violence in an accurate and sympathetic way. That, as Dawn and Singer point out, it is likely that Coetzee holds to this analogy himself (2010, 116)—what Singer in his response terms a "radical egalitarianism about humans and animals" (1999, 86)—is, for our purposes, beside the point. What is salient is the raising of this question of the memory of violence in Costello's lectures.

All three ethical themes, then, can be observed in *The Lives of Animals*. Coetzee's lectures/stories not only raise the question of literature as a way of engaging philosophical questions, but do so in a way that resonates with the novels considered throughout this study, placing *The Lives of Animals* in a relationship of synecdoche to the arguments developed throughout this book. I want to complete this synecdochic picture by turning, lastly, to Attridge's reading of *Elizabeth Costello* and demonstrating the final aspect of my study—recognition—within Coetzee's completed novel. In the novels that I have considered, I have shown that the characters' recognitions and related emotional responses are integral to the unfolding of what I have called their ethical sense, and that the ethics thus explored is often marked by the ethical impurity that, in the introduction, I argued should be understood as tragic. It is a framework that draws together the work a number of theorists and philosophers, but most notably Martha Nussbaum's reading of Aristotelian ethics and David Scott's work on modernity. Lastly, I added to it the additional aspect of recognition, drawing on Terence Cave's landmark study. Reworking recognition as an ethical lynchpin in the novel—thus arguing for an ethical understanding as distinct from the more prominent political one put forward by Charles Taylor—*anagnorisis* enables a flexible approach to ethics in the novel. Since recognition is always the recognition *of* something, *anagnorisis* comes to designate a feature of narrative that is both structural and thematic, with the recognition's predicate open to variation. It is precisely this flexibility of the term that is productive as it provides a common approach to the novels while simultaneously allowing sensitivity to the particular ethical concerns that each one engages with.

This, as was made clear, is distinct from the apporach to ethics in literature developed by Derek Attridge, and this difference can also be observed in his reading of *Elizabeth Costello*. I have shown the exposure to the suffering animal that Diamond locates in the *The Lives of Animals*— both in Costello herself, and animals more generally through Costello's own suffering. This sense of exposure is akin to Attridge's experience of literature in the event—literature experienced in its moment of unfolding. For Attridge, as for Diamond, the arguments present in Costello's lectures are important but not the complete picture: "The mistake would be to think that in [taking the arguments seriously] one had responded to the full ethical force of the fictions themselves" (2004a, 197). The lessons (to broaden the discussion to all the sections of *Elizabeth Costello*) are, for Attridge, essentially "events":

They are [...] events staged within the event of the work; they invite the reader's participation not just in the intellectual exercise of positions expounded and defended but in the human experience, and the human cost, of exposing conivctions, beliefs, doubts, and fears in a public arena. (198)

The reader is confronted with the text as with a person, and engages with the present unfolding—"the arguments [...] should more strictly be called *arguings*" (198, emphasis in original)—of positions and the vulnerability of Costello's wounding.

The final lesson in *Elizabeth Costello*, "At the Gate", makes explicit what is underlying each lesson and, indeed, some responses (such as Singer and Dawn's) to it: "the issue of belief": "Does Coetzee, does the reader, believe in what Elizabeth Costello [...] [has] to say about the treatment of animals, the fictional representation of evil, the oral novel, the value of the humanities?". Costello finds herself at the gate of a world, that, with its descriptions of light and the presence of tribunals, "we (and she) assume is some kind of heavenly reward" (204). Before she can pass through the gate, however, she has to satisfy a tribunal by making a statement of belief (Coetzee 2004, 194). (It is suggestive that the gatekeeper explains himself by saying "We all believe. *We are not cattle.* For each of us there is something we believe" [194, emphasis mine]. Costello's equation of humans to cattle during her Appleton lectures is here subtly undermined, complicating too close a connection between Costello and her creator). A statement of belief proves problematic for her, however.

First she states that as a writer she should not have beliefs: "In my work a belief is a resistance, an obstacle" (Coetzee 2004, 200), suggesting, as Attridge notes, a separation in belief between Coetzee and Costello. Nevertheless, this statement of belief fails to satisfy the tribunal, and she tries again. This time, she presents a detailed description of frogs in a river in rural Victoria. Attridge glosses the description, noting its consistency with the first one: "she is presenting either a tautology ("the realist novelist believes in the real world") or an instance of extreme arbitrariness" (2004a, 205). And for Attridge, this is where the story ends. We are never informed if her new statement of belief is acceptable to her judges, with the result that "it leaves us strongly aware that what has mattered, for Elizabeth Costello and for the reader, is the event—literary and ethical at the same time—of storytelling, of testing, of self-questioning, and not the outcome" (2004a, 205).

While Attridge is correct in noting that there is no overt conclusion to the novel, there is a final moment of recognition that does give an outcome to Costello's reflections. After her final statement before the tribunal, she speaks to the gatekeeper, asking if he thinks she stands a chance of passing through.

> He shrugs. 'We all stand a chance.' [....]
> 'But as a writer,' she persists—'what chance do I stand as a writer, with the special problems of a writer, the special fidelities?'
> *Fidelities.* Now that she has brought it out, she recognizes it as the word on which all hinges.
> He shrugs again. 'Who can say,' he says. 'It is a matter for the boards.' (Coetzee 2004, 224)

We have here, in Costello's final recognition, the critical term for her beliefs: fidelity. As a novelist (Attridge makes the important point that this question of belief is distinct from Costello's beliefs as a person) her main duty and calling is to be faithful in her representation of the voices and realities which call out to her. There is no final stamp of appproval, but this closing *anagnorisis* does conclude Costello's own reflections on her work as a writer with a single, organizing term.

The figure of Elizabeth Costello, both in the arguments she makes and in the fuller narrative of her story, shows the intertwining of the three ethical concerns discussed throughout this study, as well as the functioning of recognition for the unfolding of a novel's ethical sense. It has become clear that the ethical engagement of each novel has been strongly informed by postcolonial concerns, revealing the continued importance of the postcolonial for world literature. The approach to ethical criticism developed through this study, with the critical lens of *anagnorisis* and a corresponding focus on the particular, emotionally charged details of character's lives, the tragic shape of ethics, and the connecting of the particular and the universal, enables a flexible, nuanced approach to the continued study of ethics in world literature.

Bibliography

Abrams, Meyer Howard. 1971. *The Mirror and the Lamp: Romantic Theory and the Critical Tradition*. London: Oxford University Press.

Achebe, Chinua. 1960. *No Longer at Ease*. London, Melbourne, Toronto: Heinemann.

———. 2009a. *The Education of a British-Protected Child*. London: Penguin Books.

———. 2009b. *Things Fall Apart: Authoritative Text, Context and Criticism*. Edited by Francis Abiola Irele. New York, London: W W Norton & Company.

Adams, Ann Marie. 2011. "A Passage to Forster: Zadie Smith's Attempt to 'Only Connect' to *Howards End*." *Critique: Studies in Contemporary Fiction* 52 (4): 377–99. doi:10.1080/00111610903380220.

Adichie, Chimamanda Ngozi. 2005. *Purple Hibiscus*. London: Harper Perennial.

———. 2007a. *Half of a Yellow Sun*. London: Harper Perennial.

———. 2007b. "In the Shadow of Biafra." In *Half of a Yellow Sun*, Appendix 9–12. London: Harper Perennial.

———. 2009a. "A Private Experience." In *The Thing Around Your Neck*, 43–56. London: Fourth Estate.

———. 2009b. "The Headstrong Historian." In *The Thing Around Your Neck*, 198–218. London: Fourth Estate.

Afigbo, A E. 1980. "Christian Missions and Secular Authorities in South-Eastern Nigeria from Colonial Times." In *The History of Christianity in West Africa*, edited by O U Kalu, 187–99. London and New York: Longman.

Ahmed, Sara. 1998. *Differences That Matter: Feminist Theory and Postmodernism*. Cambridge: Cambridge University Press.

Akpome, Aghogho. 2013. "Focalisation and Polyvocality in Chimamanda Ngozi Adichie's Half of a Yellow Sun." *English Studies in Africa* 56 (2): 25–35. doi:10.1080/00138398.2013.856556.

Albrecht, Monika. 2013. "Comparative Literature and Postcolonial Studies Revisited. Reflections in Light of Recent Transitions in the Fields of Postcolonial Studies." *Comparative Critical Studies* 10 (1): 47–65. doi:10.3366/ccs.2013.0076.

Alter, Robert. 2005. "Howards End." *The New Republic*, October.

Anand, Divya. 2008. "Words on Water: Nature and Agency in Amitav Ghosh's *The Hungry Tide*." *Concentric: Literary and Cultural Studies* 34 (1): 21–44. http://gateway.proquest.com/openurl?ctx_ver=Z39.88-2003&xri:pqil:res_ver=0.2&res_id=xri:ilcs&rft_id=xri:ilcs:rec:mla:R04076619.

Anjaria, Ulka. 2008. "On Beauty and Being Postcolonial: Aesthetics and Form in Zadie Smith." In *Zadie Smith: Critical Essays*, edited by Tracey Lorraine Walters, 31–55. Oxford and New York: Peter Lang.

Appiah, Kwame Anthony. 1992. *In My Father's House: Africa in the Philosophy of Culture*. New York, Oxford: Oxford University Press.

Attridge, Derek. 2004a. *J.M. Coetzee and the Ethics of Reading: Literature in the Event*. Chicago: University of Chicago Press.

———. 2004b. *The Singularity of Literature*. New York: Routledge.

Bahri, Deepika. 2003. *Native Intelligence: Aesthetics, Politics, and Postcolonial Literature*. London and Minneapolis, MN: University of Minnesota Press.

Barnard, Rita. 2006. "The Place of Beauty: Reflections on Elaine Scarry and Zakes Mda." In *Ugly Beautiful: African and Diaspora Aesthetics*, edited by Sarah Nuttall, 102–21. Durham, NC and London: Duke University Press.

Bate, Jonathan. 1997. *The Genius of Shakespeare*. London: Picador.

Bewes, Timothy. 2006. "Shame, Ventriloquy, and the Problem of the Cliché in Caryl Phillips." *Cultural Critique* 63: 33–60.

———. 2011. *The Event of Postcolonial Shame*. Princeton, NJ: Princeton University Press.

Boddy, Kasia. 2009. "*In The Falling Snow* by Caryl Phillips: Review." *The Telegraph*. http://www.telegraph.co.uk/culture/books/fictionreviews/5722724/In-the-Falling-Snow-by-Caryl-Phillips-review.html.

Boehmer, Elleke. 2005. *Colonial and Postcolonial Literature*. Oxford: Oxford University Press.

———. 2009. "Achebe and His Influence in Some Contemporary African Writing." *Interventions* 11 (2): 141–53. doi:10.1080/13698010903052982.

———. 2014. "The World and the Postcolonial." *European Review* 22 (2): 299–308. doi:10.1017/S106279871400012X.

Booth, Wayne Clayson. 1988. *The Company We Keep: An Ethics of Fiction*. Berkeley, CA and London: University of California Press.

Bose, Brinda, ed. 2003. *Amitav Ghosh: Critical Perspectives*. Delhi: Pencraft International.

Boutros, Fatim. 2012. "Bidirectional Revision: The Connection between Past and Present in Caryl Phillips's *Crossing the River*." In *Caryl Phillips: Writing in the Key of Life*, edited by Bénédicte Ledent and Daria Tunca, 175–90. Amsterdam and New York: Rodopi.

British Council. 2016a. "Kazuo Ishiguro: Biography." *British Council Literature*. https://literature.britishcouncil.org/writer/kazuo-ishiguro.

———. 2016b. "Zadie Smith: Biography." *British Council Literature*. https://literature.britishcouncil.org/writer/zadie-smith.

Burns, Lorna. 2015. "Postcolonial Singularity and a World Literature Yet-to-Come." *Journal of the Theoretical Humanities* 20 (4): 243–59. doi:10.1080/0969725X.2015.1096650.

Casanova, Pascale. 2004. *The World Republic of Letters*. Edited by M B DeBevoise. Convergences. Cambridge, MA and London: Harvard University Press.

———. 2005. "Literature as a World." *New Left Review* 31: 71–90.

Catholic Online. 2010a. "Anathema." *Catholic Encyclopedia Digital Version*. July 30. http://www.catholic.org/encyclopedia/view.php?id=710.

———. 2010b. "Excommunication." *Catholic Encyclopedia Digital Version*. August 1. http://www.catholic.org/encyclopedia/view.php?id=4487.

Cave, Terence. 1988. *Recognitions: A Study in Poetics*. Oxford: Clarendon Press.

Chakrabarty, Dipesh. 2000. *Provincializing Europe: Postcolonial Thought and Historical Difference*. Princeton, NJ and Oxford: Princeton University Press.

Chatterjee, Partha. 1993. *Nationalist Thought and the Colonial World: A Derivative Discourse?* Minneapolis, MN: University of Minnesota Press.

Chennells, Anthony. 2009. "Inculturated Catholicisms in Chimamanda Adichie's *Purple Hibiscus*." *English Academy Review* 26 (1): 15–26. doi:10.1080/10131752.2012.695495.

Coetzee, J M. 1999. *The Lives of Animals*. Edited by Amy Gutmann. Princeton, NJ: Princeton University Press.

———. 2004. *Elizabeth Costello: Eight Lessons*. London: Vintage Books.

Cohn, Dorrit. 1983. *Transparent Minds: Narrative Modes for Presenting Consciousness in Fiction*. Princeton, NJ: Princeton University Press.

Cooper, Brenda. 2008. *A New Generation of African Writers: Migration, Material Culture & Language*. Oxford: James Currey.

Dalley, Hamish. 2014. *The Postcolonial Historical Novel: Realism, Allegory, and the Representation of Contested Pasts*. Basingstoke: Palgrave Macmillan.

Damrosch, David. 2003. *What Is World Literature?* Princeton, NJ.: Princeton University Press.

Damrosch, David, and Gayatri Chakravorty Spivak. 2011. "Comparative Literature/World Literature: A Discussion With Gayatri Chakravorty Spivak and David Damrosch." *Comparative Literature Studies* 48 (4): 455–85.

Das, Saswat S. 2006. "Home and Homelessness in The Hungry Tide: A Discourse Unmade." *Indian Literature* 50 (5): 179–85.

Davies, Tony. 2008. *Humanism*. London and New York: Routledge.

Davison, Carol Margaret Davison. 2009. "Crisscrossing the River: An Interview with Caryl Phillips." In *Conversations with Caryl Phillips*, edited by Renee T Schatteman, 19–26. Jackson: University Press of Mississippi.

Dawn, Karen, and Peter Singer. 2010. "Converging Coonvictions: Coetzee and His Characters on Animals." In *J.M. Coetzee and Ethics: Philosophical Perspectives on Literature*, edited by Anton Leist and Peter Singer, 109–18. New York: Columbia University Press.

Deresiewicz, William. 2005. "On Everything." *The Nation*, October.

Derrida, Jacques. 2002. "Force of Law." In *Acts of Religion*, edited by Gil Anidjar, 228–98. London and New York: Routledge.

Diamond, Cora. 2003. "The Difficulty of Reality and the Difficulty of Philosophy." *Partial Answers: Journal of Literature and the History of Ideas* 1 (2): 1–26. doi:10.1353/pan.0.0090.

Doniger, Wendy. 1999. "Wendy Doniger." In *The Lives of Animals*, edited by Amy Gutmann, 93–106. Princeton, NJ: Princeton University Press.

Durrant, Sam. 2004. *Postcolonial Narrative and the Work of Mourning: J.M. Coetzee, Wilson Harris, and Toni Morrison*. Albany, NY: State University of New York Press.

Eckel, Leslie Elizabeth. 2014. "Oceanic Mirrors: Atlantic Literature and the Global Chaosmos." *Atlantic Studies* 11 (1): 128–44. doi:10.1080/14788810.2014.869007.

Eckstein, Lars. 2006. *Re-Membering the Black Atlantic: On the Poetics and Politics of Literary Memory*. Amsterdam: Rodopi.

Ekelund, Bo G. 2005. "Misrecognizing History: Complictious Genres in Kazuo Ishiguro's *The Remains of the Day*." *The International Fiction Review* 32: 70–90.

Ekwensi, Cyprian. 1980. *Divided We Stand: A Novel of the Nigerian Civil War*. Enugu, Nigeria: Fourth Dimension Publishers.

Emecheta, Buchi. 1982. *Destination Biafra*. London; New York: Allison and Busby.

Faber & Faber. 2014. "Kazuo Ishiguro." http://www.faber.co.uk/tutors/kazuo-ishiguro/.

Fischer, Susan Alice. 2005. "The Shelter of Each Other." *The Women's Review of Books* 23 (2): 30–31.

———. 2007. "'A Glance from God': Zadie Smith's *On Beauty* and Zora Neale Hurston." *Changing English* 14 (3): 285–97. doi:10.1080/13586840701714424.

———. 2008. "'Gimme Shelter': Zadie Smith's *On Beauty*." In *Zadie Smith: Critical Essays*, edited by Tracey Lorraine Walters 107–121. Oxford and New York: Peter Lang.

Forster, E.M. 2000. *Howards End*. London: Penguin Books.

Foucault, Michel. 1972. *Archaeology of Knowledge*. London and New York: Tavistock Publications.

———. 1984. "What Is Enlightenment?" In *The Foucault Reader*, edited by Paul Rabinow, 1st ed., 32–50. New York: Pantheon Books.

Gallagher, Michael Paul. 2003. *Clashing Symbols: An Introduction to Faith and Culture*. London: Darton, Longman & Todd.

Gandhi, Leela. 1999. *Postcolonial Theory: A Critical Introduction*. Delhi: Oxford University Press.

Gardner, Helen. 1971. *Religion and Literature*. London: Faber.

Ghosh, Amitav. 2001. *The Glass Palace*. London: Harper Collins.

———. 2005a. *The Hungry Tide*. London: Harper Collins.

———. 2005b. *The Shadow Lines*. Boston and New York: Houghton Mifflin.

———. 2008. *Sea of Poppies*. London: John Murray.

———. 2015. *Flood of Fire*. London: John Murray.

Giles, Jana María. 2014. "Can the Sublime Be Postcolonial? Aesthetics, Politics, and Environment in Amitav Ghosh's *The Hungry Tide*." *The Cambridge Journal of Postcolonial Literary Inquiry* 1 (2): 223–42. doi:10.1017/pli.2014.18.

Goyal, Yogita. 2003. "Theorizing Africa in Black Diaspora Studies: Caryl Phillips's *Crossing the River*." *Diaspora: A Journal of Transnational Studies* 12 (1): 5–38.

Gray, J.A. 2006. "Beauty Is As Beauty Does." *First Things* 11: 48–53.

Gunesekera, Romesh. 1998. *Reef*. London: Granta.

Hall, Stuart. 1996. "When Was the 'Post-Colonial?': Thinking at the Limit." In *The Post-Colonial Question: Common Skies, Divided Horizons*, edited by Iain Chambers and Lidia Curti, 242–60. London and New York: Routledge.

Hallward, Peter. 2001. *Absolutely Postcolonial: Writing between the Singular and the Specific*. Manchester and New York: Manchester University Press.

Han, Stephanie. 2013. "Amitav Ghosh's *Sea of Poppies*: Speaking Weird English." *The Explicator* 71 (4): 298–301. doi:10.1080/00144940.2013.842150.

Hawley, John C. 2005. *Amitav Ghosh: An Introduction*. Delhi: Foundation Books.

———. 2008. "Biafra as Heritage and Symbol: Adichie, Mbachu, and Iweala." *Research in African Literatures* 39 (2): 15–26.

Heim, David. 2006. "Language Games." *Christian Century*, May.

Herrick, Linda. 2005. "Zadie Smith Talks about *On Beauty*." *The New Zealand Herald*, October 1. http://www.nzherald.co.nz/lifestyle/news/article.cfm?c_id=6&objectid=10348195.

Hodges, Hugh. 2009. "Writing Biafra: Adichie, Emecheta and the Dilemmas of Biafran War Fiction." *Postcolonial Text* 5 (1): 1–13.

Hoydis, Julia. 2011. *"Tackling the Morality of History": Ethics and Storytelling in the Works of Amitav Ghosh*. Heidelberg: Winter.

Huggan, Graham. 2001. *The Postcolonial Exotic: Marketing the Margins*. London: Routledge.

―――. 2011. "The Trouble with World Literature." In *A Companion to Comparative Literature*, edited by Ali Behdad and Dominic Thomas, 490–506. Hoboken, NJ: Wiley-Blackwell.

Huggan, Graham, and Helen Tiffin. 2007. "Green Postcolonialism." *Interventions* 9 (1): 1–11. doi:10.1080/13698010601173783.

―――. 2010. *Postcolonial Ecocriticism: Literature, Animals, Environment*. London and New York: Routledge.

Hulme, Peter. 1990. "The Spontaneous Hand of Nature." In *The Enlightenment and Its Shadows*, edited by Peter Hulme and L J Jordanova, 18–34. London: : Routledge.

―――. 1992. *Colonial Encounters: Europe and the Native Caribbean 1492–1797*. London: Routledge.

Ifemesia, C C. 1980. "The 'Civilising' Mission of 1841: Aspects of an Episode in Anglo-Nigerian Relations." In *The History of Christianity in West Africa*, edited by O U Kalu, 81–102. London; New York: Longman.

Ike, Chukwuemeka. 1976. *Sunset at Dawn: A Novel About Biafra*. London: Collins and Harvill Press.

Ishiguro, Kazuo. 2005. *The Remains of the Day*. London: Faber.

Isichei, Elizabeth. 1995. *A History of Christianity in Africa: From Antiquity to the Present*. London: SPCK.

Iyayi, Festus. 1986. *Heroes*. Harlow: Longman.

Jaggi, Maya. 1994. "Crossing the River: Caryl Phillips Talks to Maya Jaggi." *Wasafiri* 10 (20): 25–29.

Johansen, Emily. 2008. "Imagining the Global and the Rural: Rural Cosmopolitanism in Sharon Butala's *The Garden of Eden* and Amitav Ghosh's *The Hungry Tide*." *Postcolonial Text* 4 (3): 1–18. issn: 17059 100

Kalu, O. U., ed. 1980. *The History of Christianity in West Africa*. London and New York: Longman.

Kearney, Richard. 1999. "Narrative and the Ethics of Remembrance." In *Questioning Ethics: Contemporary Debates in Philosophy*, edited by Richard Kearney and Mark Dooley, 18–31. London and New York: Routledge.

———. 2002a. "Levinas and the Ethics of Imagining." In *Between Ethics and Aesthetics: Crossing the Boundaries*, edited by Dorota Glowacka and Stephen Boos, 85–96. Albany, NY: State University of New York Press.

———. 2002b. *On Stories*. London: Routledge.

———. 2004. "Jacques Derrida: Terror, Religion, and the New Politics." In *Debates in Continental Philosophy: Conversations with Contemporary Thinkers*, edited by Richard Kearney., 3–14. New York: Fordham University Press.

Kemp, Peter. 2005. "*On Beauty* by Zadie Smith." *The Sunday Times*, September 4. http://www.thesundaytimes.co.uk/sto/culture/books/article146426.ece.

King, Nicole. 2009. "Creolisation and *On Beauty*: Form, Character and the Goddess Erzulie." *Women: A Cultural Review* 20 (3): 262–76. doi:10.1080/09574040903285719.

Krishnan, Madhu. 2012. "Abjection and the Fetish: Reconsidering the Construction of the Postcolonial Exotic in Chimamanda Ngozi Adichie's *Half of a Yellow Sun*." *Journal of Postcolonial Writing* 48 (1): 26–38. doi:10.1080/17449855.2011.577640.

Lanone, Catherine. 2007. "Mediating Multi-Cultural Muddle: E.M. Forster Meets Zadie Smith." *Études Anglaises* 60: 185–97.

Ledent, Bénédicte. 2002. *Caryl Phillips*. Manchester: Manchester University Press.

Leist, Anton, and Peter Singer. 2010a. "Introduction." In *J.M. Coetzee and Ethics: Philosophical Perspectives on Literature*, edited by Anton Leist and Peter Singer, 1–15. New York: Columbia University Press.

———. , eds. 2010b. *J. M. Coetzee and Ethics: Philosophical Perspectives on Literature*. New York: Columbia University Press.

Leverton, Tara. 2014. "Gender Dysphoria and Gendered Diaspora: Love, Sex and Empire in Amitav Ghosh's *Sea of Poppies*." *English Studies in Africa* 57 (2): 33–44. doi:10.1080/00138398.2014.963282.

Levinas, Emmanuel. 1987. "Reality and Its Shadow." In *Collected Philosophical Papers*, edited and translated by Alphonso Lingis, 1–13. Dordrecht, Boston and Lancaster: Martinus Nijhoff Publishers.

———. 1998. *Otherwise Than Being Or Beyond Essence*. Translated by Alphonso Lingis. Pittsburgh, PA: Duquesne University Press.

———. 2003. *On Escape*. Stanford, CA: Stanford University Press.

Lewis, Barry. 2000. *Kazuo Ishiguro*. Manchester and New York: Manchester University Press.

Li, Victor. 2009. "Necroidealism, or the Subaltern's Sacrificial Death." *Interventions* 11 (3): 275–92. doi:10.1080/13698010903255478.

Lodge, David. 2000. "Introduction." In *Howards End*, by E.M. Forster, vii–xxx. London: Penguin Books.

Lopez, Gemma. 2010. "After Theory: Academia and the Death of Aesthetic Relish in Zadie Smith's *On Beauty* (2005)." *Critique: Studies in Contemporary Fiction* 51 (4): 350–65. doi:10.1080/00111610903380030.

Low, Gail. 1998. "'A Chorus of Common Memory': Slavery and Redemption in Caryl Phillips's *Cambridge* and *Crossing the River*." *Research in African Literatures* 29 (4): 122–40.

Luo, S.-P. 2013. "The Way of Words: Vernacular Cosmopolitanism in Amitav Ghosh's *Sea of Poppies*." *The Journal of Commonwealth Literature* 48 (3): 377–92. doi:10.1177/0021989413476292.

Macaulay, Thomas, and G M Young. 1935. *Speeches by Lord Macaulay, with His Minute on Indian Education*. London: Oxford University Press.

Mączyńska, Magdalena. 2013. "'That God Chip in the Brain': Religion in the Fiction of Zadie Smith." In *Reading Zadie Smith*, edited by Philip Tew, 127–39. London: Bloomsbury Academic.

Manathodath, Jacob. 1990. *Culture, Dialogue, and the Church: A Study on the Inculturation of the Local Churches according to the Teaching of Pope Paul VI*. New Delhi: Intercultural Publications.

Martin, Mark. 2005. "High Art as a Strait Jacket." *The New Leader*.

Marx, John. 2008. "Failed State Fiction." *Contemporary Literature* 49 (4): 597–633.

Mason, Wyatt. 2005. "White Knees: Zadie Smith's Novel Problem." *Harper's Magazine*, October.

Mondal, Anshuman A. 2007. *Amitav Ghosh*. Manchester and New York: Manchester University Press.

Moretti, Franco. 2000. "Conjectures on World Literature." *New Left Review* 1: 54–68. doi:10.1371/journal.pone.0078871.

———. 2005. *Graphs, Maps, Trees: Abstract Models for a Literary History*. London: London: Verso.

Morgan, Ann. 2015. *Reading the World: Confessions of a Literary Explorer*. London: Harvill Secker.

Morton, Stephen. 2003. *Gayatri Chakravorty Spivak*. Routledge Critical Thinkers. London and New York: Routledge.

Mukherjee, Upamanyu Pablo. 2010. *Postcolonial Environments: Nature, Culture and the Contemporary Indian Novel in English*. Basingstoke: Palgrave Macmillan.

Mulhall, Stephen. 2009. *The Wounded Animal: J. M. Coetzee and the Difficulty of Reality in Literature and Philosophy*. Princeton, NJ and Oxford : Princeton University Press.

Mundow, Anna. 2006. "Her Stories of War Are Also Her Stories of Family." *Boston Globe*. October 8.

Nehamas, Alexander. 2000. "The Return of the Beautiful: Morality, Pleasure, and the Value of Uncertainty." *Journal of Aesthetics and Art Criticism* 58 (4): 393–403.

Newton, Adam Zachary. 1995. *Narrative Ethics*. Cambridge, MA and London: Harvard University Press.

Ngwira, Emmanuel Mzomera. 2012. "'He Writes About the World That Remained Silent': Witnessing Authorship in Chimamanda Ngozi Adichie's *Half of a Yellow Sun*." *English Studies in Africa* 55 (2): 43–53. doi:10.1080/00138398.2012.731289.

Norridge, Zoë. 2012. "Sex as Synecdoche: Intimate Languages of Violence in Chamanda Ngozi Adichie's *Half of a Yellow Sun* and Aminatta Forna's *The Memory of Love*." *Research in African Literatures* 43 (2): 18–39.

Nussbaum, Martha. 1986. *The Fragility of Goodness: Luck and Ethics in Greek Tragedy and Philosophy*. Cambridge: Cambridge University Press.

———. 1990. *Love's Knowledge: Essays on Philosophy and Literature*. New York, Oxford: Oxford University Press.

———. 2001. *Upheavals of Thought: The Intelligence of Emotions*. Cambridge: Cambridge University Press.

Nuttall, Sarah. 2001. "Reading, Recognition and the Postcolonial." *Interventions* 3 (3): 391–404. doi:10.1080/713769062.

———. 2006. "Introduction: Rethinking Beauty." In *Ugly Beautiful: African and Diaspora Aesthetics*, edited by Sarah Nuttall, 6–29. Durham, NC and London: Duke University Press.

Nwapa, Flora. 1975. *Never Again*. Enugu: Nwamife Publishers Limited.

O'Brien, Susie. 1996. "Serving a New World Order: Postcolonial Politics in Kazuo Ishiguro's *The Remains of the Day*." *Modern Fiction Studies* 42 (4): 787–806.

O'Callaghan, Evelyn. 1993. "Historical Fiction and Fictional History: Caryl Phillips's *Cambridge*." *The Journal of Commonwealth Literature* 28 (34): 34–47. doi:10.1484/J.RPH.5.100799.

Okpi, Kalu. 1982. *Biafra Testament*. Basingstoke: Macmillan Education.

Osinubi, Taiwo Adentunji. 2009. "Literacies of Violence After Things Fall Apart." *Interventions* 11 (2): 157–60. doi:10.1080/13698010903053006.

Paproth, Matthew. 2008. "The Flipping Coin: The Modernist and Postmodernist Zadie Smith." In *Zadie Smith: Critical Essays*, edited by Tracey Lorraine Walters, 9–29. New York and Oxford: Peter Lang.

Parrinder, Edward Geoffrey. 1969. *Religion in Africa*. Harmondsworth: Penguin.

Phelan, James. 1996. *Narrative as Rhetoric: Technique, Audiences, Ethics, Ideology.* Columbus. OH: Ohio State University Press.

———. 2005. *Living to Tell about It: A Rhetoric and Ethics of Character Narration.* Ithaca, NY and London: Cornell University Press.

Phillips, Caryl. 1985. *The Final Passage.* London: Faber.

———. 1986. *A State of Independence.* London: Faber.

———. 1989. *Higher Ground: A Novel in Three Parts.* London: Viking.

———. 1993. *Cambridge.* New York: Vintage International.

———. 1997. *The Nature of Blood.* London: Faber.

———. 2006. *Crossing the River.* London: Vintage.

Pichler, Susanne. 2011. "Memory in Caryl Phillips's Novel *Crossing the River* (1993)." *Acta Scientiarum: Language and Culture* 33 (1): 1–12.

Porter, David. 2011. "The Crisis of Comparison and the World Literature Debates." *Profession*, 1 (November). Modern Language Association: 244–58. doi:10.1632/prof.2011.2011.1.244.

Pratt, Mary Louise. 2008. *Imperial Eyes: Travel Writing and Transculturation.* London: Routledge.

Robins, Jill. 1999. *Altered Reading: Levinas and Literature.* Chicago and London: University of Chicago Press.

Rollasson, Christopher. 2011. "'In Our Translated World': Transcultural Communication in Amitav Ghosh's *The Hungry Tide*." *Yatra Christopher Rollasson.* http://yatrarollason.info/files/GhoshHungryTide.pdf.

Said, Edward W. 1993. *Culture and Imperialism.* London: Vintage Books.

Scarry, Elaine. 1999. *On Beauty and Being Just.* Princeton, NJ: Princeton University Press.

Schama, Simon. 2000. *Rembrandt's Eyes.* London: Penguin.

Schine, Cathleen. 2009. "Adventures in the Opium Trade." *New York Review of Books.* Januray 15

Scott, David. 2004. *Conscripts of Modernity: The Tragedy of Colonial Enlightenment.* Durham, NC and London: Duke University Press.

Shaffer, Brian W. 1998. *Understanding Kazuo Ishiguro.* Columbia, SC: University of South Carolina Press.

Shohat, Ella. 1992. "Notes on the 'Post-Colonial.'" *Social Text* 31/32: 99–113.

Sim, Wai-chew. 2006. *Globalization and Dislocation in the Novels of Kazuo Ishiguro.* New York: The Edwin Mellen Press.

Singer, Peter. 1999. "Peter Singer." In *The Lives of Animals*, edited by Amy Gutmann, 85–91. Princeton, NJ: Princeton University Press.

Slaughter, Joseph. 2007. *Human Rights Inc.: The World Novel, Narrative Form, and International Law*. New York: Fordham University Press.

Smith, Zadie. 2001. *White Teeth*. London: Penguin Books.

———. 2005. *On Beauty: A Novel*. London: Hamish Hamilton.

Spivak, Gayatri Chakravorty. 1999. *A Critique of Postcolonial Reason: Toward a History of the Vanishing Present*. Cambridge, MA and London: Harvard University Press.

Stobie, Cheryl. 2010. "Dethroning the Infallible Father: Religion, Patriarchy and Politics in Chimamanda Ngozi Adichie's *Purple Hibiscus*." *Literature and Theology* 24 (4): 421–35. doi:10.1093/litthe/frq051.

Sutherland, John. 1998. "Why Hasn't Mr Stevens Heard of the Suez Crisis?" In *Where Was Rebecca Shot? Curiosities, Puzzles and Conundrums in Modern Fiction*, 185–89. Frome and London: Weidenfeld & Nicolson.

Swift, Graham. 2009. "Caryl Phillips Interviewed by Graham Swift." In *Conversations with Caryl Phillips*, edited by Renée T Schattemna, 11–18. Jackson. MS: University Press of Mississippi.

Taylor, Charles. 1988. "Critical Notice of Martha C. Nussbaum, *The Fragility of Goodness: Luck and Ethics in Greek Tragedy and Philosophy* (Book Review)." *Canadian Journal of Philosophy* 18 (4): 805–14.

———. 1994. "The Politics of Recognition." In *Multiculturalism: Examining the Politics of Recognition*, edited by Amy Gutmann, 25–73. Princeton, NJ: Princeton University Press.

Taylor, Christopher. 2009. "Dislocation, Dislocation, Dislocation: Caryl Phillips's New Novel Covers Three Generations of Emigrant Distress." *The Guardian*. May 30 http://www.guardian.co.uk/books/2009/may/30/caryl-phillips-in-the-falling-snow.

Thompson, Heather. 2008. "Captain of the Ibis." *Times Literary Supplement*. June 30 2008

Thurston, Herbert. 1911. "Missal." In *The Catholic Encyclopedia*. New York: Robert Appleton Company. http://www.newadvent.org/cathen/10354c.htm.

Tomsky, Terri. 2009. "Amitav Ghosh's Anxious Witnessing and the Ethics of Action in *The Hungry Tide*." *The Journal of Commonwealth Literature* 44 (53): 53–65. doi:10.1177/0021989408101651.

Tonelli, G. 1973. "Genius from the Renaissance to 1770." In *Dictionary of the History of Ideas*, 293–97. New York: Charles Scribner's Sons.

Tunca, Daria. 2005. "Interview." *The Chimamanda Ngozi Adichie Website*. January 27. http://www.l3.ulg.ac.be/adichie/cnainterview.html.

———. 2012. "Appropriating Achebe: Chimamanda Ngozi Adichie's *Purple Hibiscus* and 'The Headstrong Historian.'" In *Adaptation and Cultural Appropriation: Literature, Film and the Arts*, edited by Pascal Nicklas and Oliver Lindner, 230–50. Berlin: De Gruyter.

———. 2013. "The Confessions of a 'Buddhist Catholic': Religion in the Works of Chimamanda Ngozi Adichie." *Research in African Literatures* 44 (3): 50–71. doi:10.2979/reseafrilite.44.3.50.

———. 2014. *Stylistic Approaches to Nigerian Fiction*. Basingstoke: Palgrave Macmillan.

Tynan, Maeve. 2008. "'Only Connect': Intertextuality and Identity in Zadie Smith's *On Beauty*." In *Zadie Smith: Critical Essays*, edited by Tracey Lorraine Walters, 73–89. Oxford and New York: Peter Lang.

Ubah, C N. 1988. "Religious Change Among the Igbo during the Colonial Period." *Journal of Religion in Africa* 18 (1): 71–91.

VanZanten, Susan. 2015. "'The Headstrong Historian': Writing with *Things Fall Apart*." *Research in African Literatures* 46 (2): 85–103. http://www.jstor.org/stable/10.2979/reseafrilite.46.2.85.

Vatican Council I. 1990. "Vatican I: 1869–1870." In *Decrees of the Ecumenical Councils: Volume Two. Trent to Vatican II*, edited by Norman P. Tanner, 800–816. London and Washington, DC: Sheed & Ward and Georgetown University Press.

Vatican Council II. 1990. "Vatican Council II: 1962–1965." In *Decrees of the Ecumenical Councils: Volume Two. Trent to Vatican II*, edited by Norman P. Tanner, 817–1135. London and Washington, DC: Sheed & Ward and Georgetown University Press.

Vijay Kumar, T. 2007. "'Postcolonial' Describes You as a Negative." *Interventions* 9 (1): 99–105. doi:10.1080/13698010601174203.

Viswanathan, Gauri. 1989. *Masks of Conquest: Literary Study and British Rule in India*. New York: Columbia University Press.

Walder, Dennis. 2011. *Postcolonial Nostalgias: Writing, Representation and Memory*. New York and London: Routledge.

Wall, Kathleen. 1994. "*The Remains of the Day* and its Challenges to Theories of Unreliable Narration." *The Journal of Narrative Technique* 24 (1): 18–42.

———. 2008. "Ethics, Knowledge, and the Need for Beauty: Zadie Smith's *On Beauty* and Ian McEwan's *Saturday*." *University of Toronto Quarterly* 77 (2): 757–88. doi:10.3138/UTQ.77.2.757.

Walter, Natasha. 2003. "The Sadness of Strangers: England Disappoints Both Immigrant and Native in Caryl Phillips's *Distant Shore*." *The Guardian*. http://www.guardian.co.uk/books/2003/mar/15/featuresreviews.guardianreview15.

Ward, Abigail. 2007. "An Outsretched Hand: Connection and Affiliation in *Crossing the River*." *Moving Worlds: A Journal of Transcultural Writings* 7 (1): 20–32.

———. 2011. *Caryl Phillips, David Dabydeen, and Fred D'Aguiar: Representations of Slavery*. Manchester: Manchester University Press.

Winston, Joe. 2006. "Beauty, Goodness and Education: The Arts Beyond Utility." *Journal of Moral Education* 35 (3): 285–300.

Wolfe, Cary. 2009. "Human, All Too Human: 'Animal Studies' and the Humanities." *PMLA* 124 (2): 564–75.

———. 2010. *What Is Posthumanism?* Posthumanities. Minneapolis, MN: University of Minnesota Press.

———. 2011. "Beastly Culture." *American Literary History* 23 (2): 449–62. doi:10.1093/alh/ajr010.

Wolff, Christoph. 1994. *Mozart's Requiem: Historical and Analytical Studies, Documents, Score*. Berkeley, CA: University of California Press. https://books.google.com/books?id=ZjFqJy1bE-sC&pgis=1.

Yehoshua, Abraham B. 2005. "The Moral Connections of Literary Texts." In *Ethics, Literature, Theory: An Introductory Reader*, edited by Stephen K George, 11–20. Oxford and New York: Rowman & Littlefield Publishers.

Young, Robert. 2001. *Postcolonialism: An Historic Introduction*. Malden, MA and Oxford: Blackwell.

———. 2008. *The Idea of English Ethnicity*. Malden, MA and Oxford: Blackwell.

———. 2014. "World Literature and Postcolonialism." In *The Routledge Companion to World Literature*, edited by Theo d'Haen, David Damrosch, and Djelal Kadir, 213–22. London and New York: Routledge.

Index

Achebe, Chinua 3, 87, 88, 94–96, 99, 182
  No Longer at Ease 94
  Things Fall Apart 3, 87, 94–96, 182
Adichie, Chimamanda Ngozi 45, 46, 47, 50, 83, 85–131, 134, 135, 137, 140, 163, 169, 170, 180, 194, 195, 202, 203, 244, 246, 247
  "A Private Experience" 122, 123
  Half of a Yellow Sun 21, 46, 85–87, 92, 95, 96, 104, 110, 111–129, 130, 135, 137, 248
  Purple Hibiscus 46, 85, 86, 91, 96–111, 113, 117, 121, 129, 169, 172, 195, 247
  "The Headstrong Historian" 87–91, 93, 94, 96
Appiah, Kwame Anthony 7, 8, 9, 82, 126
Attridge, Derek 11–14, 25, 26, 241, 249–251
Boehmer, Elleke 2, 3, 6, 8, 87, 94, 95
Booth, Wayne C. 1, 7, 12, 21
Cave, Terence 22–24, 52, 56, 58, 115, 120, 124, 249
Christianity 49, 85, 86, 87–91, 93–97, 100, 121, 129, 160, 161, 171, 180, 246, 247
  and inculturation 93–96

Catholicism 85, 86, 88, 94, 96–107, 109, 110, 129, 131, 247
  spread into Africa 88–91
Coetzee, J.M. 11–13, 26, 45, 47, 122, 241–251
  Elizabeth Costello 249–251
  The Lives of Animals 122, 241–249
Cooper, Brenda 95, 98, 102, 110, 112–115, 121, 124, 125
Damrosch, David 2, 4, 5, 27, 28, 38
Derrida, Jacques 9, 14, 201, 245
Diamond, Cora 242, 245, 246
Eckstein, Lars 133, 135–140, 146, 157, 173, 174, 185, 198, 199, 202
Ethics 1–27, 42–47, 82, 83, 85, 242
  Aristotelian 15–18, 249
  Environmental 77–81, 241–247
  Of singularity and otherness 4, 5, 9–13
  Levinasian and Derridean 9, 11, 25–27, 74, 81
  Of Remembrance 45, 46, 112, 113, 123–129, 137–139, 247, 248
Forster, E.M. 204–212, 215, 222, 227
  Howards End 204–212, 228, 235

Foucault, Michel 19, 156–158, 242

Ghosh, Amitav 13, 20, 45, 46, 47, 49–83, 85, 130, 131, 134, 140, 160, 163, 170, 173, 194–196, 202, 203, 230, 243–245, 247
  Flood of Fire 49, 50
  Sea of Poppies 49–64, 67, 74, 81, 82, 160, 169, 243
  The Glass Palace 51
  The Hungry Tide 13, 20, 21, 46, 49–53, 62, 64–83, 86, 110, 146, 245, 247
  The Shadow Lines 51

Hawley, John C. 50, 73, 74, 112, 114, 128

History 46, 50, 51, 136–138, 175, 247
  and memory 138, 175
  recovery 50, 51, 82

Hoydis, Julia 49, 50, 52, 53, 62–64, 68, 69, 73, 74, 77, 83

Huggan, Graham 3, 28, 52, 73, 77–81

Hulme, Peter 2, 6, 29, 145, 146, 158

Humanism 19, 39, 45, 49, 50, 52, 53, 73–76, 81, 82, 131, 203, 241
  and animals 79, 80, 244–246
  and Posthumanism 45, 52, 244, 245

Ishiguro, Kazuo 6, 11, 27–45, 171, 195
  The Remains of the Day 6, 11, 14, 27–45, 195

Islam 87, 91–93

Kearney, Richard 9, 26, 113, 123, 126, 137, 138, 201, 202

Ledent, Bénédicte 133, 139, 142–144, 147, 154–156, 159, 162, 172, 176, 184, 186, 187, 190–194, 197, 202

Levinas, Emmanuel 9, 10, 14, 25, 26, 45, 74, 75, 201, 230

Low, Gail 141, 144, 148, 153, 163, 175–178, 181, 183–185, 187, 190–194

Mondal, Anshuman 49–51, 53, 67, 77–79

Moretti, Franco 27, 28

Mukherjee, Upamanyu Pablo 51, 52, 64, 65, 68, 70–72, 74

Newton, Adam Zachary 9–12, 14, 15, 25, 32–38, 44, 173, 185

Nussbaum, Martha 15–20, 24, 25, 44, 169, 243, 249
  The Fragility of Goodness 15–18
  Upheavals of Thought 17, 169

Parrinder, Edward Geoffrey 88, 91, 92

Phelan, James 7, 14, 15, 32–38, 44, 170, 171

Phillips, Caryl 45–47, 131, 133–203, 243, 244, 247, 248
  A State of Independence 133
  Cambridge 134–175, 177, 178, 190, 194–196, 198–200, 236, 244, 247
  Crossing the River 21, 133, 134, 135, 141, 173–194, 196, 198, 200

Higher Ground 133, 141
The Final Passage 133
The Nature of Blood 134

Recognition (Anagnorisis) 22–25, 52, 56, 58, 115, 120, 124, 249

Scarry, Elaine 204, 205, 216–224, 227–229, 231, 232, 237

Scott, David 9, 18, 19, 45, 163, 249

Singer, Peter 241, 242, 248, 250

Smith, Zadie 45–47, 202–240, 244, 246, 247
On Beauty 203–240
White Teeth 217

Spivak, Gayatri Chakravorty 4, 5, 38, 45

Taylor, Charles 16–18, 22, 133, 249

The Enlightenment 7–9, 18–20, 24, 25, 45, 46, 60, 64, 85, 152, 154, 163, 195, 204, 223, 235, 242–245
and (post)colonialism 8, 9, 18–20, 45, 163, 249

The exotic 3

The Postcolonial 1–9, 45, 46

Tragedy 15–22

Tunca, Daria 86, 87, 94, 101, 108, 121, 124, 125

Vatican Council 93, 100, 101, 104

Violence 45, 46, 67, 112, 113, 123–129, 137–139, 247, 248

Wolfe, Cary 244, 245

Young, Robert 3, 4, 6, 27, 32, 45

ibidem-Verlag

Melchiorstr. 15

D-70439 Stuttgart

info@ibidem-verlag.de

www.ibidem-verlag.de
www.ibidem.eu
www.edition-noema.de
www.autorenbetreuung.de